# ON THE LIMITS OF POETRY

# ON THE

# LIMITS OF POETRY

*Selected Essays: 1928-1948*

## ALLEN TATE

> *Therefore is the mind too strait*
> *to contain itself.*
> . . . ST. AUGUSTINE

*Essay Index Reprint Series*

 BOOKS FOR LIBRARIES PRESS
FREEPORT, NEW YORK

*to* HUNTINGTON CAIRNS

# CONTENTS

# III

# IV

# V

# PREFACE

AT THE kind suggestion of Mr. Alan Swallow, who has not entirely removed my doubts that it should be done, I have put this book together from three earlier books written over a period of twenty years. Most of the articles were written in the uneasy time between the wars; whether the new age which is just beginning will be less harassed, or more, it is too early to predict. Its "problems" will seem at any rate to be different. Neo-Humanism, for example, is not likely to revive again, and I have omitted from this collection a long essay on this topic which had a little notoriety in 1930. Many of the pieces are controversial (or were); the controversies of twenty or even five years ago turn into private history, of little interest to any public. The earliest writing in the book is a part of the essay on Emily Dickinson, written in 1928 and incorporated in a longer discussion which was first published in 1932. Only two of the pieces were written without an eye to periodical publication. The book can therefore be expected to have as little unity as my previous critical volumes: if my interests of the moment happened to coincide with an editor's, an essay or a review was the result.

The temptation to revise one's early views in the light of what one would like to regard as more mature knowledge must always, I think, be resisted. I have made here and there a few changes of word and phrase which I hope will clarify without altering either emphasis or sense. The great difficulty for the critical writer (besides the insuperable frustration of learning to write) is to learn how to write for an occasion without being submerged in it. There is the greater difficulty of deciding—and this is partly a matter of propriety —how much of one's imperfect insight and small knowledge to bring to bear upon the brief treatment of a subject. I have felt that sensibility ought to remain, in an informing position, in the background; that critical style ought to be as plain as the nose on one's face; that it ought not to compete in the detail of sensibility with the work which it is privileged to report on. Criticism, unless it is backed by formal aesthetics, is at best opinion; and aesthetics frequently does well enough, for its own purposes, without attending too closely to works of literature as they are commonly known. I have tried to remember, from the time I began to write essays, that I was writing, in the end, opinion, and neither aesthetics nor poetry in prose.

There are many subjects of which I should like to have tested my perception in essays, but I never got round to them, or I didn't know enough about them, or I was not asked by an editor to discuss them. Other subjects (like Existentialism or Kafka's guilt) arrive some morning like insulting letters which, if they are not answered the same day, do not need to be answered at all. Another source of regret is the toplofty tone of some of these essays and reviews. Minorities cringe or become snobs (if they are not disciplined by the *dignitas* of St. Bernard); snobbishness, of which the explanation is not the excuse, was the unredeemed course open to me. I am told that the "school" of critics of which I have been said somewhat perplexingly to be a member is no longer a minority. If this be true, I am not sure that it is good for me or for other members of the school, whoever they are; but I think it scarcely true.

If the title of this book recalls Lessing, the reader is warned

that he will find little of Lessing in it, beyond a few references
to the relation of poetry and painting. On reading my essays
over, I found that I was talking most of the time about what
poetry cannot be expected to do to save mankind from the
disasters in which poetry itself must be involved: that, I suppose, is a "limit" of poetry. Lessing says that poetry is not
painting or sculpture; I am saying in this book, with very
little systematic argument, that it is neither religion nor social
engineering.

**A.T.**

# PREFACE TO REACTIONARY ESSAYS ON POETRY AND IDEAS

*1936*

MODERN poets are having trouble with form, and must use "ideas" in a new fashion that seems willfully obscure to all readers but the most devoted. The public waits to be convinced that the poets behave as they do because they cannot help it.

How have poets used ideas in the past? How are they using them today? How shall we explain the difference between the poet's situation in the past and his present situation? Or, if explanation is beyond us, as it probably is, what terms shall we call in merely to record the changes that have brought about the modern situation? It is, I think, our task to find out what the poets have done, not what they ought to have done, and to guess what it was possible for them to do in their times. But even the right guess would be a truism: what a poet wrote was alone possible for him to write. It is nevertheless a duty of the modern critic to notice the implication of the impossible, if only to warn the reader of modern verse, who is exasperated, that poets cannot write now like poets in 1579, or 1890.

Poetry in some sense has a great deal to do with our experience. Historians exhibit its general features as evidence to support still more general theories of history and society.

But modern literary critics are reversing the procedure of the historian. They are using social theories to prove something about poetry. It is a heresy that has, of course, appeared before, yet never more formidably than now. We are trying to make an art respectable by showing that after all it is only a branch of politics: we are justifying poetry by "proving" that it is something else, just as, I believe, we have justified religion with the discovery that it is science.

To order our political interests is to practice one of the greater arts. Both politics and the arts must derive their power from a common center of energy. It is not certain that the old theory of art for art's sake is more absurd than its analogy—politics for politics' sake, which as an abstraction becomes Economics that we pursue as truth-in-itself. It is agreed that our political confusion is alarming. It is not agreed that it will continue to be alarming until we are able to see our belief in the absolute of a scientific society as at least a phase, if not profoundly the cause, of our confusion. Both politics and poetry, having ceased to be arts, are cut off from their common center of energy. They try to nourish each other. It is a diminishing diet. The neo-communists are not likely to grow fatter on it than their capitalist brethren by giving it a new name. For a political poetry, or a poetical politics, of whatever denomination is a society of two members living on each other's washing. They devour each other in the end. It is the heresy of spiritual cannibalism.

This heresy is a legitimate field of modern criticism, but because it denies the traditional procedure of poets and is thus negative, it will concern the poet only in his faculty of critic, not in his job as craftsman. The poet's special question is: How shall the work be done? Why it was done and why the work is what it is, questions of first interest to readers of poetry, are of little interest to poets who are able to remain artists in a difficult age.

For poetry does not explain our experience. If we begin by thinking that it ought to "explain" the human predicament, we shall quickly see that it does not, and we shall end up thinking that therefore it has no meaning at all. That is what Mr. I. A. Richards' early theory comes to at last, and it is the first assumption of criticism today. But poetry is at once more modest and, in the great poets, more profound. It is the art of apprehending and concentrating our experience in the mysterious limitations of form.

Philosophy even in the strict sense may be the material of poetry, but poets are not chiefly philosophers. A poet whose main passion is to get his doctrine—or his personality or his local color—into his poems is trying to justify a medium in which he lacks confidence. There is a division of purpose, and the arrogance of facile "solutions" that thinks it can get along without experience. The poet had better write his poetry first; examine it; then decide what he thinks. The poetry may not reveal all that he thinks; it will reveal all he thinks that is any good—for poetry. Poetry is one test of ideas; it is ideas tested by experience, by the act of direct apprehension.

There are all kinds of poetry readers. The innocent reader and the reader till lately called the moralist, who is now the social reader, are different from the critical reader, and they are both incurably intellectual. Their heads buzz with generalizations that they expect the poet to confirm—so that they will not have to notice the poetry. It is a service that the modern poet, no less amiable than his forebears, is not ready to perform: there is no large scheme of imaginative reference in which he has confidence. He must, in short, attach some irony to his use of "ideas," which tend to wither; he may look for a new growth but with the reservation that it too may be subject to the natural decay.

The innocent reader lives in the past; he likes to see in poetry, if not the conscious ideas, then the sensibility of a previous age. Our future sensibility the social reader, wise as he is, has no way of predicting, because he ignores the one source of that kind of prophecy—the present—grasped in terms, not of abstractions, but of experience; so he demands that poets shall set forth the ideas that he, in his facility, has decided that the future will live by. The poet—and it is he who is the critical reader—is aware of the present, any present, now or past or future. For by experiencing the past along with the present he makes present the past, and masters it; and he is at the center of the experience out of which the future must come. The social reader ought to remember that the specialist worries the major works of Spenser as a hungry dog his bone, but that The Divine Comedy has been at the center of our minds for six hundred years. The greater poets give us knowledge, not of the new programs, but of ourselves.

# PREFACE TO
# REASON IN MADNESS
## *1941*


THE essays collected here were written either for an occasion or upon assignment from an editor. Only one, "Literature as Knowledge," has been written specially for this book. Every essayist—and I distinguish the essayist from the systematic literary critic—must be grateful to his editors, as I am grateful, for suggestions that led to the writing of all but three of these essays.

The reader will expect to see here only the consistency of a point of view. I hope that he will not be disappointed if he does not find it. Yet I believe that all the essays are on one theme: a deep illness of the modern mind. I place it in the mind because that is the level at which I am interested in it. At any rate the mind is the dark center from which one may see coming the darkness gathering outside us. The late W. B. Yeats had for it a beautiful phrase, "the mad abstract dark," and we are all in it together.

Few of the questions which have agitated what used to be called the "press" in the five years since the first of the papers was written, appear in this book. There are war and democracy, which are only casually mentioned. Certain features of the present war may be unique in the history of war, and if they are they may also be a symptom of our peculiar illness. What those features are this is not the place to say; yet our limitation of the whole human problem to the narrow scope of the political problem is obviously one of them. We are justified in saving democracy if democracy can save something else which will support it. That "something else," which we name with peril, so great is our distress, hovers round the periphery of these essays. Unless we consider it, everything we write will look, after a generation, when the historical irony becomes visible, like another tale of a tub.

Every writer writes within a convention which he picks up from someone else or invents for himself. The convention of this book is the attack. It asks of people who profess knowledge: What do you know? But that is only another way of asking oneself the same question. I do not hear it asked very frequently these days.

# THE PRESENT FUNCTION

# OF CRITICISM

## *1940*

*Nous avons une impuissance de prouver,*
*invincible à tout le dogmatisme. Nous avons une idée*
*de la vérité, invincible à tout le pyrrhonisme.*
. . . PASCAL

WE ARE not very much concerned when we confess that communication among certain points of view is all but impossible. Let us put three persons together who soon discover that they do not agree. No matter; they quickly find a procedure, a program, an objective. So they do agree that there is something to be *done,* although they may not be certain why they are doing it, and they may not be interested in the results, the meaning of which is not very important: before they can consider the meaning they have started a new program. This state of mind is positivism. It assumes that the communication of ideas towards the formulation of truths is irrelevant to action; the program is an end in itself. But if we are interested in truth I believe that our intellectual confusion is such that we can merely write that interest upon the record of our time.

This essay represents a "point of view" which seems to have little in common with other points of view that are tolerated, and even applauded, today. It cannot be communicated at the level of the procedure and the program; it cannot, in short, be communicated to persons whose assumptions about life come out of positivism. (For positivism is not only a scientific movement; it is a moral attitude.) It has moved to contempt

and rage persons whose intelligence I respect and admire.
The point of view here, then, is that historicism, scientism,
psychologism, biologism, in general the confident use of the
scientific vocabularies in the spiritual realm, has created or
at any rate is the expression of a spiritual disorder. That disorder may be briefly described as a dilemma.

On the one hand, we assume that all experience can be
ordered scientifically, an assumption that we are almost ready
to confess has intensified if it has not actually created our
distress; but on the other hand, this assumption has logically
reduced the spiritual realm to irresponsible emotion, to what
the positivists of our time see as irrelevant feeling; it is irrelevant because it cannot be reduced to the terms of positivist procedure. It is my contention here that the high forms
of literature offer us the only complete, and thus the most
responsible, versions of our experience. The point of view of
this essay, then, is influenced by the late, neglected T. E.
Hulme (and not this essay alone). It is the belief, philosophically tenable, in a radical discontinuity between the
physical and the spiritual realms.

In our time the historical approach to criticism, in so far
as it has attempted to be a scientific method, has undermined
the significance of the material which it proposes to inves-
tigate. On principle the sociological and historical scholar
must not permit himself to see in the arts meanings that his
method does not assume. To illustrate some of the wide implications of this method I will try to see it as more than a
method: it is the temper of our age. It has profoundly influenced our politics and our education.

What will happen to literature under the totalitarian society that is coming in the next few years—it may be, so far
as critical opinion is concerned, in the next few months? The
question has got to be faced by literary critics, who as men
of explicit ideas must to a great extent define for imaginative
literature the *milieu* in which it will flourish or decay. The
first ominous signs of this change are before us. The tradi-

tion of free ideas is as dead in the United States as it is in Germany. For at least a generation it has suffered a slow extinction, and it may receive the *coup de grâce* from the present war. The suppression of the critical spirit in this country will have sinister features that the official Nazi censorship, with all its ruthlessness, has not yet achieved, for the Nazis are, towards opinion, crude, objective, and responsible. Although it has only a harsh military responsibility, this censorship is definite, and it leaves the profession of letters in no doubt of its standing. Under this regime it has no standing at all. Increasingly since 1933 the critical intelligence under National Socialism has enjoyed the choice of extinction or frustration in exile.

Could the outlook be worse for the future of criticism? In the United States we face the censorship of the pressure group. We have a tradition of irresponsible interpretation of patriotic necessity. We are entering a period in which we shall pay dearly for having turned our public education over to the professional "educationists" and the sociologists. These men have taught the present generation that the least thing about man is his intelligence, if he have it at all; the greatest thing his adjustment to Society (not to a good society): a mechanical society in which we were to be conditioned for the realization of a *bourgeois* paradise of gadgets and of the consumption, not of the fruits of the earth, but of commodities. Happily this degraded version of the myth of reason has been discredited by the course of what the liberal mind calls "world events"; and man will at any rate be spared the indignity of achieving it. What else can he now achieve? If history had dramatic form we might be able to see ourselves going down to destruction, with a small standard flying in the all but mindless hollow of our heads; and we should have our dignity to the end.

But this vision is too bright, too optimistic; for the "democracy" of appetites, drives, and stimulus-and-response has already affected us. What we thought was to be a condition-

ing process in favor of a state planned by Teachers College
of Columbia University will be a conditioning equally useful for Plato's tyrant state. The actuality of tyranny we shall
enthusiastically greet as the development of democracy, for
the ringing of the democratic bell will make our political
glands flow as freely for dictatorship, as, hitherto, for monopoly capitalism.

This hypocrisy is going to have a great deal to do with
literary criticism because it is going to have a very definite
effect upon American thought and feeling, at every level.
There is no space here to track down the intellectual pedi-
gree of the attitude of the social scientist. As early as 1911
Hilaire Belloc published a neglected book called *The Servile
State,* in which he contended that the world revolution would
not come out of the Second International. Nobody paid any
attention to this prophecy; the Marxists ignored it for the
obvious reason, and the liberals took it to mean that the
world revolution would not happen at all. Belloc meant that
the revolution was inherent in our pseudo-democratic intellectual tradition, buttressed by monopoly capitalism, and that
the revolution would not proceed towards social justice, but
would achieve the slave state. The point of view that I am
sketching here looks upon the rise of the social sciences and
their influence in education, from Comtism to Deweyism,
as a powerful aid to the coming of the slave society. Under
the myth of reason all the vast accumulation of *data* on social
behavior, social control, social dynamics, was to have been
used in building a pseudo-mystical and pseudo-democratic
utopia on the Wellsian plan. In this vision of mindless perfection an elementary bit of historical insight was permitted
to lapse: Plato had this insight, with less knowledge of history than we have. It is simply that, if you get a society made
up of persons who have surrendered their humanity to the
predatory impulses, the quickest way to improve matters is
to call in a dictator; for when you lose the moral and religious
authority, the military authority stands ready to supervene.
Professor Dewey's social integration does not supervene.

Under the actuality of history our sociological knowledge is a ready-made weapon that is now being used in Europe for the control of the people, and it will doubtless soon be used here for the same purpose.

To put this point of view into another perspective it is only necessary to remember that the intellectual movement variously known as positivism, pragmatism, instrumentalism, is the expression of a middle-class culture—a culture that we have achieved in America with so little consciousness of any other culture that we often say that a class description of it is beside the point. Matthew Arnold—in spite of his vacillating hopes for the middle class—said that one of its leading traits was lack of intelligence, and that industrialism, the creation of the middle class, had "materialized the upper class, vulgarized the middle class, and brutalized the lower class."

This lack of intelligence in our middle class, this vulgarity of the utilitarian attitude, is translatable into other levels of our intellectual activity. It is, for example, but a step from the crude sociologism of the normal school to the cloistered historical scholarship of the graduate school. We are all aware, of course, of the contempt in which the scholars hold the "educationists": yet the historical scholars, once the carriers of the humane tradition, have now merely the genteel tradition; the independence of judgment, the belief in intelligence, the confidence in literature, that informed the humane tradition, have disappeared; under the genteel tradition the scholars exhibit timidity of judgment, disbelief in intelligence, and suspicion of the value of literature. These attitudes of scholarship are the attitudes of the *haute bourgeoisie* that support it in the great universities; it is now commonplace to observe that the uncreative money-culture of modern times tolerates the historical routine of the scholars. The routine is "safe," and it shares with the predatory social process at large a naturalistic basis. And this naturalism easily bridges the thin gap between the teachers' college and the graduate school, between the sociologist and the literary source-hunter, between the comptometrist of literary "re-actions" and the enumerator of influences.

The naturalism of the literary scholar is too obvious to need demonstration here; his substitution of "method" for intelligence takes its definite place in the positivistic move-ment which, from my point of view, has been clearing the way for the slave state; and the scholar must bear his part of the responsibility for the hypocrisy that will blind us to the reality of its existence, when it arrives.

The function of criticism should have been, in our time, as in all times, to maintain and to demonstrate the special, unique, and complete knowledge which the great forms of literature afford us. And I mean quite simply *knowledge*, not historical documentation and information. But our lit-erary critics have been obsessed by politics, and when they have been convinced of the social determinism of literature, they have been in principle indistinguishable from the aca-demic scholars, who have demonstrated that literature does not exist, that it is merely history, which must be studied as history is studied, through certain scientific analogies. The scholars have not maintained the tradition of literature as a form of knowledge; by looking at it as merely one among many forms of social and political expression, they will have no defense against the censors of the power state, or against the hidden censors of the pressure group. Have the scholars not been saying all along that literature is only politics? Well, then, let's suppress it, since the politics of poets and novelists is notoriously unsound. And the scholars will say, yes, let's suppress it—our attempt to convert literature into science has done better than that: it has already extinguished it.

## II

WHAT the scholars are saying, of course, is that the mean-ing of a work of literature is identical with their method of studying it—a method that dissolves the literature into its history. Are the scholars studying literature, or are they not?

That is the question. If they are not, why then do they continue to pretend that they are? This is the scholars' contribution to the intellectual hypocrisy of the positivistic movement. But when we come to the individual critics, the word hypocrisy will not do. When we think of the powerful semiscientific method of studying poetry associated with the name of I. A. Richards, we may say that there is a certain ambiguity of critical focus.

Mr. Richards has been many different kinds of critic, one kind being an extremely valuable kind; but the rôle I have in mind here is that of *The Principles of Literary Criticism*, a curious and ingenious *tour de force* of a variety very common today. The species is: literature is not really nonsense, it is in a special way a kind of science. This particular variety is: poetry is a kind of applied psychology. I am not disposing of Mr. Richards in two sentences; like everybody else of my generation I have learned a great deal from him, even from what I consider his errors and evasions; and if it is these that interest me now, it is because they get less attention than his occasional and profound insights into the art of reading poetry.

In *The Principles of Literary Criticism* there is the significant hocus-pocus of impulses, stimuli, and responses; there are even the elaborate charts of nerves and nerve-systems that purport to show how the "stimuli" of poems elicit "responses" in such a way as to "organize our impulses" towards action; there is, throughout, the pretense that the study of poetry is at last a laboratory science. How many innocent young men—myself among them—thought, in 1924, that laboratory jargon meant laboratory demonstration! But for a certain uneasiness evinced by Mr. Richards in the later chapters, one could fairly see this book as a typical instance of the elaborate cheat that the positivistic movement has perpetrated upon the human spirit. For the uneasy conscience of one Richards, a thousand critics and scholars have not hesitated to write literary history, literary biography, literary criticism, with facile confidence in whatever scientific analogies came to hand.

With the candor of a generous spirit Mr. Richards has repudiated his early scientism: the critical conscience that struggled in the early work against the limitations of a positivist education won out in the end. What did Mr. Richards give up? It is not necessary to be technical about it. He had found that the picture of the world passed on to us by the poetry of the pre-scientific ages was scientifically false. The *things* and *processes* pointed to by the poets, even the modern poets, since they too were backward in the sciences, could not be verified by any of the known scientific procedures. As a good positivist he saw the words of a poem as *referents*, and referents have got to refer to something—which the words of even the best poem failed to do. If Mr. Richards could have read Carnap and Morris in the early twenties, he would have said that poems may *designate* but they do not *denote*, because you can designate something that does not exist, like a purple cow. Poems designate things that do not exist, and are compacted of *pseudo-statements*, Mr. Richards's most famous invention in scientese; that is, false statements, or just plain lies.

Perhaps the best way to describe Mr. Richards's uneasiness is to say that, a year or two later, in his pamphlet-size book, *Science and Poetry*, he came up short against Matthew Arnold's belief that the future of poetry was immense, that, religion being gone, poetry would have to take its place. The curious interest of Arnold's argument cannot detain us. It is enough to remember that even in *The Principles of Literary Criticism* Mr. Richards was coming round to that view. Not that poetry would bring back religion, or become a new religion! It would perform the therapeutic offices of religion, the only part of it worth keeping. In short, poetry would "order" our minds; for although science was true, it had failed to bring intellectual order—it had even broken up the older order of pseudo-statement; and although poetry was false, it would order our minds, whatever this ordering might mean.

To order our minds with lies became, for a few years, Mr. Richards's program, until at last, in *Coleridge on Imagination* (1935), the Sisyphean effort to translate Coleridge into naturalistic terms broke down; and now, I believe, Mr. Richards takes the view that poetry, far from being a desperate remedy, is an independent form of knowledge, a kind of cognition, equal to the knowledge of the sciences at least, perhaps superior. The terms in which Mr. Richards frames this insight need not concern us here: [1] I have sketched his progress towards it in order to remind you that the repudiation of a literal positivism by its leading representative in modern criticism has not been imitated by his followers, or by other critics who, on a different road, have reached Mr. Richards's position of ten years ago. They are still there. Whether they are sociologists in criticism or practitioners of the routine of historical "correlation," they alike subscribe to a single critical doctrine. It is the Doctrine of Relevance.

## III

THE Doctrine of Relevance is very simple. It means that the subject-matter of a literary work must not be isolated in terms of form; it must be tested (on an analogy to scientific techniques) by observation of the world that it "represents." Are the scene, the action, the relations of the characters in a novel, in some verifiable sense true? It is an old question. It has given rise in our time to various related sorts of criticism that frequently produce great insights. (I think here of Mr. Edmund Wilson's naturalistic interpretation of James's *The Turn of the Screw*. Mr. Wilson's view is not the whole view, but we can readily see that we had been missing the whole view until he added his partial view.)

The criterion of relevance, as we saw with Mr. Richards, has a hard time of it with an art like poetry. Of all the arts,

[1] See pp. 41-48, 107-113 for more detailed discussions of this point.

poetry has a medium the most complex and the least reducible to any one set of correlations, be they historical, or
economic, or theological, or moral. From the point of view
of direct denotation of objects about all that we can say about
one of Keats's odes is what I heard a child say—"It is something about a bird."

But with the novel the case is different, because the novel
is very close to history—indeed, in all but the great novelists,
it is not clearly set off from history. I do not intend here to
get into Aristotle and to argue the difference between history
and fiction. It is plain that action and character, to say
nothing of place and time, point with less equivocation to
observed or perhaps easily observable phenomena than even
the simplest poetry ever does. The novel points with some
directness towards history—or I might say with Mr. David
Daiches, to the historical process.

I mention Mr. Daiches because his *The Novel and the
Modern World* seems to me to be one of the few good books
on contemporary fiction. Yet at bottom it is an example of
what I call the Doctrine of Relevance, and I believe that he
gains every advantage implicit in that doctrine, and suffers,
in the range and acuteness of his perceptions, probably none
of its limitations. I cannot do justice to Mr. Daiches's treatment of some of the best novelists of our time; my quotations
from his final essay—which is a summary view of his critical
position—will do him less than justice. His statement of his
method seems to me to be narrower than his critical practice:

> The critic who endeavors to see literature as a process
> rather than as a series of phenomena, and as a process
> which is bound up with an infinite series of ever wider
> processes, ought to realize that however wide his con-
> text, it is but a fraction of what it might be.

Admirable advice; but what concerns me in this passage is
the assumption that Mr. Daiches shares with the historical
scholar, that literature is to be understood chiefly as a part
of the historical process. He goes on to say:

The main object is to indicate relevance and to show how understanding depends on awareness of relevance. That appreciation depends on understanding and that a theory of value can come only after appreciation, hardly need noting.

I must confess that after a brilliant performance of two hundred ten pages I feel that Mr. Daiches has let us down a little here. I am aware that he enters a shrewd list of warnings and exceptions, but I am a little disappointed to learn that he sees himself as applying to the novel a criterion of historical relevance not very different from the criterion of the graduate school. It is likely that I misunderstand Mr. Daiches. He continues:

> The patterning of those events [in a novel], their relation to each other within the story, the attitude to them which emerges, the mood which surrounds them, the tone in which they are related, and the style of the writing are all equally relevant.

Yes: but relevant to what? And are they *equally* relevant? The equality of relevance points to historical documentation; or may we assume here that since the "main object is to indicate relevance," the critic must try to discover the relevance of history to the work? Or the work to history? What Mr. Daiches seems to me to be saying is that the function of criticism is to bring the work back to history, and to test its relevance to an ascertainable historical process. Does relevance, then, mean some kind of identity with an historical process? And since "understanding depends on awareness of relevance," is it understanding of history or of the novel; or is it of both at once? That I am not wholly wrong in my grasp of the terms relevance and process is borne out by this passage:

> He [the critic] can neither start with a complete view of civilization and work down to the individual work of art, nor can he start with the particular work of art and

work up to civilization as a whole; he must try both methods and give neither his complete trust.

Admirable advice again; but are there actually two methods here? Are they not both the historical method? When Mr. Daiches says that it is possible to start from the individual work of art and work *up* (interesting adverb, as interesting as the *down* to which you go in order to reach the work of art), he doubtless alludes to what he and many other critics today call the "formalist" method. Mr. Daiches nicely balances the claims of formalist and historian. The formalist is the critic who doesn't work up, but remains where he started, with the work of art—the "work in itself," as Mr. Daiches calls it, "an end which, though attainable, is yet unreal." Its unreality presumably consists in the critic's failure to be aware of the work's relevance to history. There may have been critics like Mr. Daiches's formalist monster, but I have never seen one, and I doubt that Mr. Daiches himself, on second thought, would believe he exists. (Or perhaps he was Aristotle, who said that the nature of tragedy is in its structure, not its reception by the audience.) I am not sure. As a critic of the novel Mr. Daiches is acutely aware of unhistorical meanings in literature, but as a critical theorist he seems to me to be beating his wings in the unilluminated tradition of positivism. That tradition has put the stigma of "formalism" upon the unhistorical meaning. Critics of our age nervously throw the balance in favor of the historical lump. Mr. Daiches's plea for it rests upon its superior inclusiveness; the historical scholar can make formal analyses against the background of history; he has it both ways, while the formalist has it only one, and that one "unreal." But here, again, Mr. Daiches' insight into the vast complexity of the critic's task prompts at least a rueful misgiving about the "wider context"; he admits the superiority of the historian, "though it may be replied that inclusiveness is no necessary proof of such superiority." At this point Mr. Daiches becomes a little confused.

I have the strong suspicion in reading Mr. Daiches (I have

it in reading the late Marxists and the sociological and historical scholars) that critics of the positivist school would not
study literature at all if it were not so handy in libraries; they
don't really like it; or they are at any rate ashamed of it—
because it is "unreal." The men of our time who have the
boldness and the logical rigor to stand by the implications of
their position are the new logical positivists at Chicago—
Carnap and Morris, whom I have already mentioned; they
are quite firm in their belief—with a little backsliding on the
part of Morris [2]—that poetry, and perhaps all imaginative
literature, is, in Mr. Arthur Mizener's phrase, only "amiable
insanity": it designates but it does not denote anything "real."

I respect this doctrine because it is barbarism unabashed
and unashamed. But of the positivists who still hanker after
literature with yearnings that come out of the humane tradition, what can be said? The ambiguity or—since we are in our
mental climate and no longer with persons—the hypocrisy of
our liberal intellectual tradition appears again; or let us say
the confusion. Is Mr. Daiches wrestling with a critical theory,
or is he only oscillating between the extremes of a dilemma?
From the strict, logical point of view he is entitled merely to
the positivist horn, as the general critical outlook of our age
is so entitled.

This ought to be the end of literature, if literature were
logical; it is not logical but tough; and after the dark ages of
our present enlightenment it will flourish again. This essay
has been written from a point of view which does not admit
the validity of the rival claims of formalism and history, of
art-for-art's-sake and society. Literature is the complete knowledge of man's experience, and by knowledge I mean that
unique and formed intelligence of the world of which man
alone is capable.

[2] Charles W. Morris, "Science, Art, and Technology," in *The Kenyon Review*, Autumn 1939. Mr. Morris argues that, although poetry is nonsense
semantically, it is the realm of "value."

# LITERATURE AS KNOWLEDGE

*Comment and Comparison*

*1941*

MATTHEW ARNOLD'S war on the Philistines was fought, as everybody knows; but nobody thinks that it was won. Arnold conducted it in what he considered to be the scientific spirit. The Philistines had a passion for "acting and instituting," but they did not know "what we ought to act and to institute." This sort of knowledge must be founded upon "the scientific passion for knowing." But it must not stop there. Culture, which is the study of perfection and the constant effort to achieve it, is superior to the scientific spirit because it includes and passes beyond it. Arnold was, in short, looking for a principle of unity, but it must be a unity of experience. There was before him the accumulating body of the inert, descriptive facts of science, and something had to be done about it.

Yet if it is true, as T. S. Eliot said many years ago, that were Arnold to come back he would have his work to do over again, he would at any rate have to do it very differently. His program, culture added to science and perhaps correcting it, has been our program for nearly a century, and it has not worked. For the facts of science are not inert facts waiting for the poet, as emblematic guardian of culture, to bring to life in the nicely co-operative enterprise of scientist and poet which the nineteenth century puts its faith in. In this view the poet is merely the scientist who achieves completeness. "It is a result of no little culture," Arnold says, "to attain to a clear perception that science and religion are two wholly different things." Religion had yielded to the "fact" of science, but poetry on a positive scientific base could take over the work of religion, and its future was "immense." The "fact" had undermined religion, but it could support poetry.

Although Arnold betrayed not a little uneasiness about this easy solution, it was his way of putting literature upon an equal footing with science. If Arnold failed, can we hope to succeed? Whether literature and science considered philosophically, as Coleridge would phrase it, are the same thing, or different but equal, or the one subordinate to the other, has become a private question. It does not concern the public at large. While Arnold's poet was extending the hand of fellowship to the scientist, the scientist did not return the greeting; for never for an instant did he see himself as the inert and useful partner in an enterprise of which he would not be permitted to define the entire scope. He was not, alas, confined to the inertia of fact; his procedure was dynamic all along; and it was animated by the confident spirit of positivism which has since captured the modern world.

Had he been what Arnold thought he was, how conveniently the partnership would have worked! For what was Arnold's scientist doing? He was giving us exact observation and description of the external world. The poet could give us that, and he could add to it exact observation and description of man's inner life, a realm that the positivist would never be so bold as to invade. But the poet's advantage was actually twofold. Not only did he have this inner field of experience denied to the scientist, he had a resource which was his peculiar and hereditary right—figurative language and the power of rhetoric.

If the inert fact alone could not move us, poetic diction could make it moving by heightening it; for poetry is "thought and art in one." This is an injustice to Arnold; he was a great critic of ideas, of currents of ideas, of the situation of the writer in his time; and from this point of view his theory of poetry is of secondary importance. But since I am now interested in the failure, ours as well as his, to understand the relation of poetry and science, it has been necessary to put his poetic theory in terms that will bring out its defects. On one side it is an eighteenth-century view of poetic language as the rhetorical vehicle of ideas; and it is connected with Arnold's famous definition of religion as "morality touched with emotion." Poetry is descriptive science or experience at that level, touched with emotion.

If Arnold had taste, he had very simple analytical powers, and we are never quite convinced by his fine quotations from the poets. Why is this so? Because he admires good things for bad reasons; or because at any rate his reasons invariably beg the question. In the famous passage on Dryden and Pope in "The Study of Poetry" these poets are not poetic because they are not *poetic*. (Arnold himself is responsible for the italics.) And he looks to us for immediate assent to a distinction between a "prose" classic and a "poetic" classic that has not been actually made. He cites his "touchstones" for the purpose of moving us, and the nice discrimination of feeling which awareness of the touchstones induces will permit us to judge other passages of verse in terms of feeling. The "high seriousness" is partly the elevated tone, a tone which is a quality of the poet's feeling about his subject: it is the poet's business to communicate it to the reader.

This attitude, this tone, centers in emotion. But its relation to what it is about, whether it is external to the subject or inherent in it, Arnold refuses to make clear. The high seriousness may be said to reflect the subject, which must have Aristotelian magnitude and completeness. Arnold had a shrewd sense of the disproportions of tone and subject which he developed into a principle in the Preface to the 1853 edition of his poems. He was suppressing the very fine "Empedocles on Aetna" because, he said, it has no action; it is all passive suffering; and passive suffering is not a proper subject for poetry. (A view that has been revived in our time by the late W. B. Yeats.) Action, then, is the subject of the greatest poetry. This conviction is so strong—who will question its rightness, *as far as it goes?*—that he actually puts into quotation marks words which are not quoted from anybody at all but which represent for him the consensus of the ancients on the importance of action: " 'All depends upon the subject; choose a fitting action, penetrate yourself with the feeling of its situations, this done, everything else will follow.' " But will everything else follow? Does a great style follow? To a gift for action Shakespeare "added a special one of his own; a gift, namely, of happy, abundant, and ingenious expression. . . ." I think we should attend closely here to the words "added" and "ingenious," for they reveal Arnold's view of the function of language. And suppose you have lyric poetry which may be, like Arnold's own fine lyrics, more meditative than dramatic, and more concerned with the futility of action than with action itself? It has never, I believe, been pointed out that the Preface of 1853 cuts all the props from under lyric poetry. The lyric at its best is "dramatic," but there is no evidence that Arnold thought it so; for the lyric, though it may be a moment of action, lacks magnitude and completeness; it may be the beginning, or the middle, or the end, but never all three. What, then, is the subject of the lyric? Is it all feeling, nothing but feeling? It is feeling about "ideas," not actions; and the feeling communicates "power and joy."

This gross summary of Arnold's poetics omits all the sensitive discriminations that he felt in reading the poets; it omits all but the framework of his thought. Yet the framework alone must concern us on this occasion. Arnold is still the great critical influence in the universities, and it is perhaps not an exaggeration of his influence to say that debased Arnold is the main stream of popular appreciation of poetry. It would be fairer to say that Arnold the critic was superior to his critical theory; yet at the distance of three generations we may look back upon his lack of a critical dialectic—he even had a certain contempt for it in other critics—as a calamity for that culture which it was his great desire to strengthen and pass on.

His critical theory was elementary, and if you compare him with Coleridge a generation earlier, he represents a loss. His position is nearer to the neo-classicism of Lessing, whom he praises in *Culture and Anarchy* for humanizing knowledge, a leveling-off of distinctions of which Lessing as a matter of fact was not guilty. He shares with Lessing the belief—but not its dialectical basis—that the language of poetry is of secondary importance to the subject, that it is less difficult than the medium of painting, and that, given the action, all else follows.

This remnant of neo-classicism in Arnold has been ably discerned by Mr. Cleanth Brooks in *Modern Poetry and the Tradition.* I go into it here not to deny that action is necessary to the long poem; for Arnold's view contains a fundamental truth. But it is not the whole truth; asserted in his terms, it may not be a truth at all. The important question goes further. It is: What is the relation of language to the "subject," to the dramatic and narrative subject as action, or to the lyrical subject as "idea"? The question may be pushed even further: Is it possible finally to distinguish the language from the subject? Are not subject and language one?

For Arnold the subject is what we commonly call the prose subject; that is to say, as much of the poetic subject as we can put into ordinary prose. The poet takes it up at the level at which the scientist—or Arnold's simulacrum of him—takes it: the level of observation and description. The poet now puts it into language that will bring the inert facts to life and move us. The language is strictly what Mr. Richards calls the "vehicle"—it does not embody the subject; it conveys it and remains external to it.

For what are action and subject? The positivists have their own notion of these terms; and their language of physical determinism suits that notion better than the poet's. The poet's language is useless.

## I I

IS IT not easy to see how such a poetics gives the case for poetry away to the scientist? Not to Arnold's straw scientist, who politely kept to his descriptive place and left to litera- ture man's evaluation of his experience; but to the scientist as he is: a remarkably ingenious and dynamic fellow whose simple fanaticism brooks no compromise with his special projects. Whatever these on occasion may be, he demands an exact one-to-one relevance of language to the objects and the events to which it refers. In this relevance lies the "mean- ing" of all terms and propositions in so far as they are used for the purpose of giving us valid knowledge. It is, of course, knowledge for action; and apart from this specific purpose, the problem of meaning is not even a real problem.

"Meaning" has been replaced by a concept of "operational validity"—that is to say, the "true" meaning of a term is not its definition; it is the number of statements containing it which can be referred to empirically observed events. Along with meaning and definition, universals also disappear; and with universals, cognition. A proposition does not represent an act of knowing by a knower—that is, a mind; it is, in a chemical metaphor, the expression of an interaction among certain elements of a "situation."

This advanced position in the philosophy of science has been set forth in the new *International Encyclopedia of Uni- fied Science*, which is being published serially at the Uni- versity of Chicago. Of great interest from the point of view of literary criticism are the brilliant studies of "semiosis," or the functioning of language as "signs." Mr. Charles W. Morris's "Foundations for the Theory of Signs," [1] is a model of exact exposition in a field of enormous complication. This field is popularly known as "semantics," but semantics in any exact sense is only one "dimension" of semiosis. In this brief glance at the aesthetic and critical implications of Mr. Morris's writings, his theory as a whole cannot be set forth.

[1] *International Encyclopedia of Unified Science*, Vol. I, No. 2.

Semiosis is the actual functioning of language in three dimensions which are located and described by means of the science of "semiotic." Semiotic, then, is the study of semiosis. The three dimensions in which all language, verbal, or mathematical, functions are: (1) the semantical, (2) the syntactical, and (3) the pragmatical; and the respective studies in these dimensions are semantics, syntactics, and pragmatics. It must be borne in mind that in semiosis the three dimensions are never separate; in semiotic they are distinguished abstractly for study. Semiotic looks towards the formation of rules which will govern the use of all language (signs), and it lays claim to an ultimate unification of all "knowledge."

That need not concern us here. Let us take a simple declarative sentence: "This county has an annual rainfall of fifty-one inches." From the semantical point of view the sentence designates certain conditions, or a situation: it is the "sign-vehicle" for that designation. If upon investigation we find that the situation actually exists, then it has not only been designated; it has also been *denoted*. From the syntactical point of view we are not concerned with what the sign-vehicle points to; for syntactics deals with the formal structure of the sentence, the relations of the words. From the pragmatical point of view the meaning of the sentence is the effect it has upon somebody who hears it or reads it. If I am about to buy a farm in this county, and learn that "this county has an annual rainfall of fifty-one inches," I may go elsewhere; at the moment I hear the sentence I may light a cigarette, or look the other way, or laugh or swear. All this behavior would be the functioning of the sign in the pragmatic dimension.

The complex possibilities of semiotic may not be evident in this crude summary. Mr. Morris says: "The sign vehicle itself is simply one object." It is an object that may function in other sign-vehicles; it may be designated, denoted, or reacted to; and the process is infinite. The identification of signs and their relations is equally complex. There are, for example, a characterizing sign, a symbolic sign, an indexical sign, and an iconic sign; and any of these, in certain contexts, may function as any other. I shall return to them presently.

The only philosophic criticism of this system that I have seen is Howard D. Roelofs's article in the symposium on the "New Encyclopedists," published in the *Kenyon Review* (Spring 1939). Mr. Roelofs is concerned with Mr. Morris's rejection of the problem of universals and of cognition. It ought to be plain from my brief exposition of the pragmatic dimension of semiosis that the significant factor is what I *do*, not what I *think* leading to what I do; and that thus the bias of the science of semiotic is pragmatic in the ordinary sense, and even behavioristic. For Mr. Morris says: "A 'concept' [i.e., a universal] may be regarded as a semantical rule determining the use of characterizing signs." Mr. Roelofs's comment is interesting:

> Morris has no trouble with this problem [i.e., the problem of universals]. It is simply a rule of our language that such a term as "man" can be used as often as the conditions stated in its definition are fulfilled. That makes the term a universal. If we then ask how it happens those conditions are in fact frequently fulfilled, we are informed, "It can only be said the world is such." And those who are tempted by this fact to believe that universals are somehow objective, functioning in nature, are silenced with a threat: to talk as if universals were entities in the world is "to utter pseudo-thing sentences of the quasi-semantical type." . . . the heart of the problem is dismissed with a phrase and a language rule offered as a solution.

The bearing of Mr. Roelofs's criticism will be plainer in a moment. Now Mr. Morris, in discussing the syntactical dimension, says: "Syntactics, as the study of the syntactical relations of signs to one another *in abstraction* from the relations of signs to objects or to interpreters [persons], is the best developed of all the branches of semiotic." Exactly; because syntactics comes out of traditional formal logic and grammar, and because it "deliberately neglects what has here been called the semantical and the pragmatical dimensions of semiosis."

The rôle of syntactics in the semiotic science remains somewhat obscure; it seems to consist in a number of "transformation rules"—that is, in formulas by which given expressions in words, numbers, or symbols can be changed into equivalent but formally different expressions. What power of the mind there may be which enables us in the first place to form these expressions nowhere appears. (I daresay this statement is of the quasi-semantical type.) But Mr. Morris tells us how we are to think of the rules of the three dimensions of semiotic:

> Syntactical rules determine the sign relations between sign vehicles; semantical rules correlate sign vehicles with other objects; pragmatical rules state the conditions in the interpreters under which the sign vehicle is a sign. Any rule when actually in use operates as a type of behavior, and in this sense there is a pragmatical component in all rules.

If we imagine with Mr. Roelofs a situation in which semiosis is functioning, we shall see pretty clearly the behavioristic tendency of the science of semiotic; and we shall also see in what sense "there is a pragmatical component in all rules." A simplified process of semiosis, or the actual functioning of signs, is very easy to state. There is first of all the sign, which we get in terms of a sign-vehicle. It looks two ways; first, it points to something, designates something; and, secondly, what is designated elicits a response from persons who are present. The thing pointed to is thus the *designatum;* the response is the *interpretant.* By implication there is an interpreter, a person, a mind; but Mr. Morris is consistently vague about him: he is not a technical factor, he is a superfluous entity, in semiosis. That is to say, not only is he not needed in order to explain the functioning of signs; he would embarrass the explanation. Mr. Roelofs makes this clear, as follows:

> The innocent reader will take the analysis of the use of signs to be the analysis of a cognitive process. The correctness of the analysis as far as it goes conceals the fact that cognition itself has been eliminated. Consider this illustration. A maid enters the room and says to the three persons present, "The doctor called." One person thereupon takes a pen and writes a line in a diary; the second goes to a telephone and makes a call; the third says, "Did he?" According to the analysis offered by Morris, the words uttered by the maid are the sign-vehicle. The actual call of the doctor is the denotatum.[2] The three persons are the interpreters, and their three different actions are the interpretants, the responses of the interpreters to the denotatum via the sign-vehicle. No one is likely to deny these factors are present. It should be noted that the interpretants, to the extent that they are a sequence of physical actions, can be perceived. It should also be noted that such sequences of action are not cognitions . . . they are "interpretants," but their being such depends upon the cognitions of the interpreters. These responses are not themselves knowledge. They do depend upon knowledge, and that is precisely what Morris leaves out. . . . Morris objects to the term "meaning." This is not surprising. His analysis leaves out meaning in the primary sense of meaning. This is not to say that meanings are "like marbles" [Morris's phrase]. Meanings, indeed, like knowledge in general, are a unique kind of thing. There is literally nothing like knowledge except knowledge itself.

I have quoted Mr. Roelofs at length because what he has to say about the problem of cognition bears directly upon

---

[2] *Denotata* are real things; *designata* may be pointed to, but they are not necessarily real. For example, the Phoenix' "spicy nest." The doctor's call is a *designatum* which is also a *denotatum*—it's "real."

the semiotic version of the aesthetic problem. He sums up his argument:

> The procedure culminates in eliminating not only universals, but cognition itself. Just as the answer to the problem of universals is that they do not exist [that is, they are only a semantical rule], the answer to the problem of knowledge is that there is no such thing. There are responses, but no cognition; there is a language, but not knowledge. Knowledge cannot be reduced to exclusively perceptual terms. Therefore it does not exist. This is not empiricism. *It is positivism.* [Italics mine.]

In this positivist technique for the analysis of language, the interpreting mind, the cognizing intelligence, is lost in the perceptual account of its external behavior. Mr. Morris says: "In general, from the point of view of behavior, signs are 'true' in so far as they correctly determine the expectations of the users, and so release more fully the behavior which is implicitly aroused in the expectation or interpretation."

In Mr. Morris's aesthetics there is an aesthetic sign. Does it implicitly—or explicitly—arouse expectations in terms of behavior? Does it correctly determine our expectations? Is the aesthetic sign "true" in that it is a determinant of our behavior? Mr. Morris is not unequivocal in his answers to these questions.

### III

NO—and yes, replies Mr. Morris, in two essays [3] the cunning and scholastic ingenuity of which make even the beautiful essay on the general theory of signs look amateurish. No, he says, because the aesthetic sign is a special sort of sign: it is *iconic.* It does not correctly determine our behavior. Yes, because it bears the formidable responsibility of showing us what we ought to try to get out of our behavior. The function

[3] "Esthetics and the Theory of Signs," in *The Journal of Unified Science,* VIII, 1-3, pp. 131-150; and "Science, Art, and Technology," *The Kenyon Review,* I, 4, pp. 409-423.

of the aesthetic sign is nothing less than the "vivid presentation" of *values*, a presentation that is not only vivid, but
*immediate*—without mediation—for direct apprehension. The
iconic sign, in other words, designates without denoting; or
if it does denote anything its *denotatum* is already in its own
"properties." "In certain kinds of insanity," writes Mr. Morris,
"the distinction between the designatum and the denotatum
vanishes; the troublesome world of existences is pushed aside,
and the frustrated *interests* [italics mine] get what satisfaction they can in the domain of signs. . . ." Likewise *designata*
and *denotata* become in aesthetics the same thing; but in this
logical shuffle, worthy of a thirteenth-century *doctor subtilis*,
the aesthetic sign is never confused "with the object it designates." It is that alone which saves it from the ignominy of
insanity.

The difficulties of this theory must already be apparent.
First, the difference between insanity and art is the hair's-
breadth line, in the interpreter's response to the sign, between substituting the sign for reality and maintaining the
distinction between sign and reality. The first question that
one must ask, then, is this: With what does the interpreter
make this distinction? If the distinction is not inherent in the
nature of the sign, does the interpreter not perform an act
of cognition? If the distinction is a mere interpretant, a behavioristic response, why do we not respond to a work of art
uniformly; and why is that uniform response in every case
not insane *unless we are capable of a primary act of knowledge*, of simply knowing the difference?

Secondly, if art is the realm of values—that is, if the peculiar nature of the aesthetic sign is that it shall convey values
—the values must be inherent in the aesthetic sign, and must
therefore compel in the interpreter the distinction between
value and insanity; so that there is no possibility that the
interpreter, who is incapable of cognition, will confuse the
mere sign with reality. For the nature of the sign must
determine the interpretant, or response.

There must therefore be a special "differentia" for the aesthetic sign that distinguishes it from all other signs whatever. "Lyric poetry," Mr. Morris says, "has a syntax and uses terms which designate things, but the syntax and the terms are so used that what stand out for the reader are values and evaluations." [4] Does not Mr. Morris confess his difficulty when he uses the vague metaphorical expression, "stand out," and the even more vague "so used"? Just what is this use? It is significant that in Mr. Morris's two articles on aesthetics, in which the word poetry frequently appears, there is no actual analysis of a passage or even of a line of verse; and not even a quotation from any poem in any language. He contents himself with assertions that the future of semiotic in the field of poetry is immense, and that only the work has to be done.

Now, if the contradiction that I have pointed out in general terms exists, we may see its origin if we examine further Mr. Morris's idea of the aesthetic sign. It is a special variety of the iconic sign. To illustrate this it will be sufficient to relate the iconic to the characterizing sign, and to distinguish the icon from the symbol.

> A characterizing sign [he says] characterizes that which it can denote. Such a sign may do this by exhibiting in itself the properties an object must have to be denoted by it, and in this case the characterizing sign is an *icon;* if this is not so, the characterizing sign may be called a *symbol.* A photograph, a star chart, a model, a chemical diagram, are icons, while the word "photograph," the names of the stars and of chemical elements are symbols.

The terminology is quite special. Icon is the Greek (εἰκών) for a sculptured figure. Ordinarily a symbol is what Mr. Morris claims for the icon: it exhibits in itself the qualities it stands for—like Christ on the Cross; or it represents by convention something other than itself, like $\pi r^2$ for the circum-

<hr>

[4] "Foundations for the Theory of Signs," p. 58.

ference of a circle. But here the terms are roughly equivalent, icon to image, symbol to concept; but only roughly, since in Mr. Morris's list of symbols "photograph" is not any particular photograph, while the name of a star must be the name of a particular star. There is a fundamental obscurity, that we shall have to pass over, in attributing to verbal language a thoroughly *iconic* property. In the list of icons, there are *a* photograph, *a* star chart, *a* model, *a* chemical diagram— all of them spatial and perceptual objects; but, while language is always used in a spatial setting, words appear in temporal sequence, and have only the spatial character of their occasion. We cannot *see* the properties of words in the words. We have simply got to know *what* the words convey. The phrase "a star chart" is not a star chart itself. Mr. Morris appears to have found in the term *icon,* at any rate so far as it pertains to aesthetics, merely a convenient evasion of the term *image;* for image would doubtless have held him to the old ontological aesthetics.

The essay, "Esthetics and the Theory of Signs," deals with the specific problem "of stating the differentia of the esthetic sign." Mr. Morris is constantly reminding us that iconic signs appear in all discourse, and that all discourse is by no means aesthetic discourse. Yet the special function of the iconic sign makes it possible for us to use it as the aesthetic sign; and that function is stated in a "semantical rule":

> The semantical rule for the use of an iconic sign is that it denotes any object which has the properties (in practice, a selection from the properties) which it itself has. Hence when an interpreter apprehends an iconic sign-vehicle he apprehends directly what is designated; here mediated and unmediated taking account of certain properties both occur; [5] put in still other terms, every iconic sign has its own sign-vehicle among its denotata.

[5] There seems to be evidence in this clause that Mr. Morris is not interested in syntactics.

This is a difficult conception; perhaps it can be illustrated
with a few lines of verse:

> That time of year thou mayst in me behold
> When yellow leaves, or none, or few do hang
> Upon those boughs which shake against the cold . . .

According to Mr. Morris, the sign-vehicle here would be the
leaves hanging on the boughs. This verbal sign-vehicle has
the "properties" of the natural objects which it designates;
and that which it denotes is in the designation itself. That is,
leaves-bough does not point to a definite situation or condition beyond itself: we get "directly what is designated" because it is of the nature of the iconic sign to contain its own
*denotatum*. (I have simplified this analysis by ignoring "That
time of year," which I believe would make it impossible to
apply Mr. Morris's terms coherently.)

The treatment of the iconic sign in semiotic is mysterious.
If any generalization about it is legitimate, we may surmise
that certain terms, which Mr. Morris calls "primary terms,"
are untranslatable; that is to say, they cannot be handled by
any principle of reduction; they have a certain completeness
and finality. They denote themselves; certain iconic signs
seem to be such terms. They are sign-vehicles for images, and
our apprehension of them is direct. For while the iconic sign
may denote something beyond itself, its specific character as
an iconic sign is that part of what it denotes is the sign itself.
"These facts," says Mr. Morris, "taken alone, do not delimit
the esthetic sign, for blueprints, photographs, and scientific
models are all iconic signs—but seldom works of art." He continues in a passage of great interest:

> If, however, the designatum of an iconic sign be a *value*
> [italics mine] (and of course not all iconic signs designate
> values), the situation is changed: there is now not merely
> the designation of value properties (for such designation
> takes place even in science), nor merely the functioning
> of iconic signs (for these as such need not be esthetic

signs), but there is the direct apprehension of value properties through the very presence of that which itself has the value it designates.

There are thus three steps in the "delimitation" of the aesthetic sign: First, it is an iconic sign; secondly, it is an iconic sign which designates a value; thirdly, it is an iconic sign which designates a value in the sign itself, so that our "apprehension" of that value is unmediated, that is, *direct*.

The difficulties created by this aesthetic doctrine are slippery and ambiguous. We may, for convenience, see them in two ways. The first set of problems lies in the term "apprehension"; the second, in the term "value."

The primary meaning of apprehension is a grasping or a taking hold of. What does Mr. Morris mean? If it means taking hold of by means of perception, we are asked to see ourselves *perceiving a value;* but a value cannot be an object of perception. If, however, apprehension means a direct, unmediated knowledge of a value, then there is an act of evaluation involved which implies the presence of a knowing mind. For the implied "semantical rule" for the aesthetic sign obviously forbids us to check the value wholly in terms of a situation external to the properties of the sign itself. We have got to *know* the value in itself; and only in an act of cognition can we know it. But if Mr. Morris means by apprehension the response, or mere "interpretant," of semiosis, it is difficult to see how a mere response can be semantically correct unless the sign-vehicle points to a situation outside itself in terms of which the response is relevant. If there is no such situation, is not the interpretant a piece of insanity?

I cannot see how there can be any direct apprehension unless there is an agency to do the apprehending; and the interpretant is not an agent, it is a response. "One additional point may be noted to confirm the sign status of the work of art: The artist often draws attention to the sign-vehicle in such a way as to prevent the interpreter from merely reacting to it as an object and not as a sign. . . ." Mr. Morris's phrases, "in such a way," "so used that," remain painfully evasive. What is that way? Now, if the preventive factor is inherent in the work of art, why did not the birds refrain from trying to eat the grapes in Zeuxis's picture? The citizens of Athens did not mistake the sign-vehicle for an object. Why? Because they *knew* the difference.

Mr. Morris's theory of value will further illuminate his difficulty. It is an "interest" theory of value for which he acknowledges an indebtedness to the pragmatic tradition of Mead and Dewey. Objects, according to this ancient theory, have value in relation to interests. "Values," says Mr. Morris, "are consummatory properties of objects or situations which answer to the consummation of interested acts." If I satisfy my hunger by eating a banana, the banana has value in relation to the specific interest, hunger. Does it follow that we have similar aesthetic interests, which we similarly satisfy? No specific aesthetic interest appears in semiosis. The aesthetic satisfaction proceeds from the frustration of "real" interests, from the blockage of interests as they drive onward to real "consummations." The aesthetic sign is a value that has not been consummated. Art is the expression of what men desire but are not getting.

There are two passages in "Esthetics and the Theory of Signs" which reveal the fundamental ambiguity in Mr. Morris's conception of the aesthetic sign as a "value." We shall be struck, I believe, by the remarkable parallel between Mr. Morris's view of the aesthetic medium and the neoclassical view, which we saw in Matthew Arnold.

> Even though the complexity of the total icon is so very great that no denotatum (other than the esthetic sign vehicle itself) can in actuality be found, the work of art can still be considered a sign—for there can be designation without denotation.

But can the aesthetic sign—and this is the center of the problem—designate an interest "value" if it does not point to an interest? It seems to me that it cannot be a value in any "interest" theory of value whatever. And when the aesthetic sign is so complex that it does not lead to denotation, is not this complexity a semantical failure so great that Mr. Morris actually ought to take it to an institution for the insane?

The traditional prestige of the arts is formidable; so, rather than commit himself to his logic of the aesthetic sign as a designation of a value which cannot be located and which thus cannot be an interest-value, he offers us the ordinary procedure of positivism; that is to say, he shows us how we may reduce the aesthetic sign to a *denotatum* after all.

> Since a statement must say something about something, it must involve signs for locating what is referred to, and such signs are ultimately indexical signs [i.e., "pointing" signs]. An iconic sign in isolation cannot then be a statement, and a work of art, conceived as an iconic sign, cannot be true in the semantical sense of the term. Nevertheless, the statement that a work of art is "true" might under analysis turn out to be an elliptical form of syntactical, semantical, or pragmatical statements. Thus semantically it might be intended to affirm that the work in question actually is iconic of the value structure of a certain object or situation. . . .

The work of art is elliptical and iconic; that is, it is an image from which the semantical dimension is omitted, or in which it remains vague. By translating the icon, by expanding it and filling it in with a *denotatum*, we construct a situation external to the work of art: a situation which replaces it. In the usual terms of literary criticism, this situation is the "subject" which exists outside the language of the poem. For the language is merely "iconic of" this ordinary prose subject.

So a neo-classical theory of poetic language not only gave the case for poetry away to the scientist; it has become the foundation of the scientists' theory of poetry. When Mr. Richards remarked, in *Science and Poetry*, that we were now getting on a large scale "genuine knowledge" which would soon reduce poetry to the level of the "pseudo-statement," we could not see how right he was. Right—from the point of view of neo-classical theory. So long as the scientific procedure was observation, description, and classification, it was not very different from the procedure of common sense and its feeling for the reality of ordinary experience. As late as the first edition (1892) of *The Grammar of Science*, Karl Pearson said: "The aesthetic judgment pronounces for or against the interpretation of the creative imagination according as that interpretation embodies or contradicts the phenomena of life, which we ourselves have observed." But from the point of view of Unified Science, this principle of common-sense observation will no longer serve; it does not go far enough. And so we have a dilemma. Since the language of poetry can be shown to be not strictly relevant to objects and situations as these are presented by the positivist techniques, poetry becomes either nonsense or hortatory rhetoric.

The semiotic approach to aesthetics "has the merit of concreteness"; yet we have seen that Mr. Morris never quite gets around to a specific work of art. In "Science, Art, and Technology," he distinguishes three primary forms of discourse and relates them to the three dimensions of semiosis:

1. Scientific discourse: semantical dimension.
2. Aesthetic discourse: syntactical dimension.
3. Technological discourse: pragmatical dimension.

We have seen that the iconic sign is semantically weak; so the aesthetic sign, a variety of iconic sign, must function primarily at the syntactical level; that is, if we look at it "indexically" it "points" first of all to itself. Looking at the aesthetic sign from this point of view, we are forced to see that it wholly lacks cognitive content, and it is subject to the operation of "transformation rules." Does the "concreteness" of the semiotic approach to art consist in this? Again, is the syntactical dimension that in which direct apprehension of the aesthetic sign is possible? Once more it must be said that this direct apprehension seems impossible unless there is an agency of apprehension—a knowing mind; without this we get only an "interpretant," which is conceivable only at the pragmatic level; and if the interpretant is intelligible, it is so in terms of semantical relevance, or of the scientific form of discourse. For Mr. Morris himself confesses: ". . . in so far as the knowledge of value which art gives is the more than the having of value [i.e., is the *knowing* of value] there is no reason to suppose that this knowledge is *other than scientific in character.*"

It is significant here that Mr. Morris conceives the character of poetry in the relation of pragmatics and semantics. What is our response to poetry and how do we behave when we read it: what, in a word, does it lead to? There is a certain uneasy piety in the extravagant claim that poetry is the realm of values; and there is no way, I think, to get around the conclusion that, since the values are not attached to reality, they are irresponsible feelings. They are, in fact, rhetoric. And it is also significant that for Mr. Morris the study of rhetoric is a branch of pragmatics; it is even a kind of technological instrument. For, in the essay, "Science, Art, and Technology," poetry seems to acquire its main responsibility in the technological function of telling us what we *ought* to want and do. Here again neo-classical didacticism appears in terms of a rigorous instrumentalism.

Does the language of poetry mean what it says, or does it mean the "situation" that we get from it in a process of reduction? Although we have seen Mr. Morris's bias, we have also seen that he has not made up his mind: he would like to have it both ways. The origin of this dilemma is remote. But there is always "the sad ghost of Coleridge beckoning from the shades."

## I V

THE famous Chapter XIV of *Biographia Literaria* has been the background of the criticism of poetry for more than a hundred years. Its direct influence has been very great; its indirect influence, through Poe upon Baudelaire, and through the French symbolists down to contemporary English and American poets, has perhaps been even greater. This chapter is the most influential statement on poetry ever formulated by an English critic: its insights, when we have them, are ours, and ours too its contradictions. Yet the remarkable "definition" of poetry, which I shall now quote, is not, as we shall presently see, the chief source of the aesthetic dilemma that we inherit today. (That source is another passage.) Here is the definition:

> A poem is that species of composition, which is opposed to works of science, by proposing for its *immediate* object pleasure, not truth; and from all other species—(having this object in common with it)—it is distinguished by proposing to itself such delight from the *whole*, as is compatible with a distinct gratification from each component *part*.

Much of the annoyance and misunderstanding caused by this passage has not been Coleridge's fault; but is rather due to the failure of literary men to observe the accurate use of *species*. For Coleridge is giving us a strict Aristotelian definition of a *species* within a given *genus*. It is not a qualitative statement, and it does not answer the question: *What* is poetry? The *whatness* of poetry does not come within the definition; and I believe that nowhere else does Coleridge offer us an explicit qualitative distinction between poetry and other "species of composition" which may be "opposed" to it.

For what is Coleridge saying? (I have never seen a literal reading of the passage by any critic.) There is the generic division: composition. A poem is a species within the genus; but so is a work of science. How are the two species distinguished? By their immediate objects. It is curious that Coleridge phrases the passage as if a poem were a person "proposing" to himself a certain end, pleasure; so for *object* we have got to read *effect*. A poem, then, differs from a work of science in its immediate effect upon us; and that immediate effect is pleasure. But other species of composition may aim at the effect of pleasure. A poem differs from these in the relation of part to whole: the parts must give us a distinct pleasure, moment by moment, and they are not to be conceived as subordinate to the whole; they make up the whole.

If there is an objective relation of part to whole, Coleridge does not say what it is; nor does he distinguish that relation in terms of any specific poetic work. It is strictly a quantitative analogy taken, perhaps, from geometry. And the only purpose it serves is this: in the paragraph following the "definition" he goes on to say that "the philosophic critics of all ages coincide" in asserting that beautiful, isolated lines or distichs are not a poem, and that neither is "an unsustained composition" of uninteresting parts a "*legitimate* poem." What we have here, then, is a sound but ordinary critical insight; but because it is merely an extension of the pleasure principle implicit in the "definition," we are not prepared by it to distinguish objectively a poem from any other form of expression. The distinction lies in the effect, and it is a psychological effect. In investigating the differentia of poetry— as Mr. Morris would put it—we are eventually led away from the poem into what has been known since Coleridge's time as the psychology of poetry.

The difficulties of this theory Coleridge seems not to have been aware of; yet he illustrates them perfectly. In the second paragraph after the famous definition he writes this remarkable passage:

> The first chapter of Isaiah—(indeed a very large portion of the whole book)—is poetry in the most emphatic sense; yet it would be no less irrational than strange to assert, that pleasure, not truth, was the immediate object of the prophet. In short, whatever specific import we attach to the word, Poetry, there will be found involved in it, as a necessary consequence, that a poem of any length neither can be, nor ought to be, all poetry. Yet if an harmonious

whole is to be produced, the remaining parts must be preserved in keeping with the poetry; and this can no otherwise be effected than by such a studied selection and artificial arrangement, as will partake of one, though not a peculiar property of poetry. And this again can be no other than the property of exciting a more continuous and equal attention than the language of prose aims at, whether colloquial or written.

This is probably the most confused statement ever uttered by a great critic, and it has probably done more damage to critical thought than anything else said by any critic. Isaiah is poetry in "the most emphatic sense," although his immediate object (effect) is truth. It will be observed that, whereas in the definition our attention is drawn to a species of composition, a poem, we are here confronted with the personage, Isaiah, who does have the power of proposing an object; and Isaiah's immediate object is truth. But are we to suppose that the effect of the poem and the object of the prophet are to be apprehended in the same way? Is our experience of truth the same as our experience of pleasure? If there is a difference between truth and pleasure, and if an immediate effect of pleasure is the specific "property" of poetry (how a property can be an effect it is difficult to see), how can the first chapter of Isaiah be poetry at all? It cannot be, looked at in these terms; and as a matter of fact Coleridge rather slyly withdraws his compliment to Isaiah when he goes on to say that a "poem of any length neither can be, nor ought to be, all poetry." Isaiah is not all poetry; he is partly truth, or even mostly truth. And the element of truth, while it is strictly speaking insubordinate and unassimilable, can be used by means of an artificial arrangement—meter. There is no doubt that meter does on the whole what Coleridge attributes to it: it demands a "continuous and equal attention." Does he mean to say that the insubordinate element of truth—insubordinate to the immediate effect of pleasure—should be given such conspicuous emphasis? Or does he perhaps mean that the attention will be fixed upon the metrical pattern, so that the nonpoetic element will be less conspicuous?

Coleridge's theory of meter is not quite pertinent here: in the later and more elaborate discussion of meter in *Biographia Literaria* there is the general conclusion that meter is indispensable to poetry. In Chapter XIV, now being examined, he speaks of meter as "an artificial arrangement . . . not a peculiar property of poetry."

There is, then, in Coleridge's poetic theory a persistent dilemma. *He cannot make up his mind whether the specifically poetic element is an objective feature of the poem, or is distinguishable only as a subjective effect.* He cannot, in short, choose between metaphysics and psychology. His general emphasis is psychological, with metaphysical ambiguities.

The distinction between Fancy and Imagination is ultimately a psychological one: he discusses the problem in terms of separate faculties, and the objective poetical properties, presumably resulting from the use of these faculties, are never defined, but are given only occasional illustration. (I have in mind his magnificent analysis of "Venus and Adonis," the value of which lies less perhaps in the critical principles he supposes he is illustrating, than in the perfect taste with which he selects the good passages for admiration.) When Coleridge speaks of the "esemplastic power" of the Imagination, it is always a "faculty" of the mind, not an objective poetic order. When he says that a poem gives us "a more than usual state of emotion with more than usual order," we acknowledge the fact, without being able to discern in the merely comparative degree of the adjective the fundamental difference between the poetic and the philosophic powers which Coleridge frequently asserts, but which he nowhere objectively establishes. The psychological bias of his "system" is perfectly revealed in this summary passage of Chapter XIV:

My own conclusions on the nature of poetry, in the strict-
est use of the word, have been in part anticipated in some
of the remarks on the Fancy and Imagination in the early
part of this work. What is poetry?—is so nearly the same
question with, what is a poet?—that the answer to the
one is involved in the solution to the other. For it is a
distinction resulting from the poetic genius itself, which
sustains and modifies the images, thoughts, and emotions of the poet's own mind.

There can be little doubt that Coleridge's failure to get
out of the dilemma of Intellect-or-Feeling has been passed
on to us as a fatal legacy. If the first object of poetry is an
effect, and if that effect is pleasure, does it not necessarily
follow that truth and knowledge may be better set forth in
some other order altogether? It is true that Coleridge made
extravagant claims for a poetic order of truth, and it is upon
these claims that Mr. I. A. Richards has based his fine book,
*Coleridge on Imagination:* Mr. Richards's own testimony
is that the claims were not coherent. The coherent part of
Coleridge's theory is the fatal dilemma that I have described.
Truth is only the secondary consideration of the poet, and
from the point of view of positivism the knowledge, or truth,
that poetry gives us is immature and inadequate. What of
the primary consideration of the poet—pleasure?

Pleasure is the single qualitative feature of Coleridge's
famous definition; but it is not *in* the definition objectively.
And with the development of modern psychology it has
ceased to be qualitative, even subjectively. It is a *response*.
The fate of Coleridge's system, then, has been its gradual
extinction in the terminology of experimental psychology.
The poetry has been extinguished in the poet. The poetic
"effect" is a "response" to a "stimulus"; and in the early
works of Mr. Richards we get for the first time the questions,
rigorously applied: Is the poetic response relevant to the
real world? Is it relevant to action? Poetry has come under

the general idea of "operational validity." So we must turn briefly to Mr. Richards.

## V

IN *Science and Poetry* (1926) Mr. Richards condensed in untechnical language the position that he had set forth in detail earlier, in *The Principles of Literary Criticism.* The positivist side of Mr. Richards's thought at that time is plainly revealed in a passage like this:

> You contrive not to laugh [in church]; but there is no doubt about the activity of the impulses in their restricted form. The much more subtle and elaborate impulses which a poem excites are not different in principle. *They do not show themselves as a rule, they do not come out into the open, largely because they are so complex.* [Italics mine.] When they have adjusted themselves to one another and become organized into a coherent whole, the needs concerned may be satisfied. *In a fully developed man a state of readiness for action will take the place of action when the full appropriate situation for action is not present.*[6] [Mr. Richards's italics.]

The mere state of readiness for action is the poetic experience in terms of value and relevance. The readiness points to the "direct apprehension" of an interest-value in Mr. Morris's sense; but the failure of the action to come off, the lack of the "full appropriate situation for action," indicates the absence of a *denotatum.* We receive the designation of a value without being provided with a situation in which we can act upon it. The remarkable parallel between Mr. Richards's early theories of poetry and the recent theories of Mr. Morris need not detain us. It is enough to point out that Mr. Richards anticipated fifteen years ago everything that Mr. Morris's science of semiotic has to say about the language of poetry.

[6] *Science and Poetry*, pp. 28-29.

I have italicized a sentence, in the quotation from Mr. Richards, for two reasons: first, the vagueness of the language is significant; secondly, the idea of the coherent whole into which the "impulses" are organized has no experimental basis in terms of impulses. Mr. John Crowe Ransom remarks that Mr. Richards never shows us *how* this ordering act of poetry upon our minds takes place, and then proceeds to discern the reason for Mr. Richards's vague statements about the conduct of poetic stimulation and response:

> Most readers will retort, of course, that in the very large majority of cases the spiritual happenings are the only happenings we have observed, and *the neural happenings are simply what the behaviorists would like to observe.* [Italics mine.] At present the mental datum is the fact and the neural datum is the inference.[7]

In throwing out the mental fact Mr. Richards in his early writings preceded Mr. Morris in his rejection of the cognitive powers of the mind. I do not suggest any direct influence from Mr. Richards upon Mr. Morris, although Mr. Morris has acknowledged the work of his predecessor: it is easier to relate these men to a much wider movement. That movement is positivism, and it is more than a strict scientific method.

It is a general attitude towards experience. If it is not, why should Mr. Richards have attempted in his early criticism to represent the total poetic experience and even the structure of poetry in one of the positivist languages—experimental psychology? It was representation by analogy. The experimental basis for such a representation was wholly lacking. Mr. Richards, had we listened hard enough, was saying in *The Principles of Literary Criticism* and *Science and Poetry* that here at last is what poetry would be if we could only reduce it to the same laboratory technique that we use in

[7] "A Psychologist Looks at Poetry," *The World's Body*, p. 147. This essay is the most searching examination of Mr. Richards's position—or positions—that I have seen; but it does somewhat less than full justice to Mr. Richards's insights.

psychology; and without warning to the unwary reader, whose credulity was already prepared by his own positivist *zeitgeist*, Mr. Richards went on to state "results" that looked like the results of an experiment; but the experiment had never been made. It had been inferred. The "impulses" that we feel in response to a poem, says Mr. Richards, "do not show themselves as a rule." There is no scientific evidence that they have ever shown themselves to Mr. Richards or to any-body else. Mr. Richards like a good positivist was the victim of a deep-seated compulsive analogy, an elusive but all-engrossing assumption that all experience can be reduced to what is actually the very limited frame of reference supplied by a doctrine of correlation, or of the relevance of stimulus to response. This early procedure of Mr. Richards's was not even empiricism, for in empiricism the cognitive intelligence is not eliminated in the pursuit of verifiable facts. Mr. Richards, like Mr. Morris after him, eliminated cognition with-out demonstrating experimentally the *data* of his behavior-istic poetics. So this doctrine was not empiricism: it came out of the demi-religion of positivism. The poetry had been absorbed into a pseudo-scientific jargon, no more "relevant" to poetry than the poetic pseudo-statement was relevant to the world: the net result was zero from both points of view.

I have put this brief commentary on Mr. Richards's early poetics in the past tense because it is no longer his poetics. From 1926, the year of *Science and Poetry,* he has come a long way. It is perhaps not an extravagant claim to make for Mr. Richards's intellectual history, that it will probably turn out to be the most instructive, among critics, of our age. His great intellectual powers, his learning, his devotion to poetry —a devotion somewhat frustrated but as marked fifteen years ago as now—are qualities of an intellectual honesty rare in any age. In exactly ten years, from 1926, he arrived, in *The Philosophy of Rhetoric* (1936), at such a statement as this:

> So far from verbal language being a "compromise for a language of intuition"—a thin, but better-than-nothing,

substitute for real experience—language, well used, is a *completion* and does what the intuitions of sensation by themselves cannot do. Words are the meeting points at which regions of experience which can never combine in sensation or intuition, come together. They are the occasion and means of that growth which is the mind's endless endeavor to order itself. That is why we have language. *It is no mere signalling system.* [Italics mine] It is the instrument of all our distinctively human development, of everything in which we go beyond the animals. [Pp. 130-131.]

These words should be read and re-read with the greatest care by critics who still cite the early Richards as the continuing head of a positivist tradition in criticism. There is, in this passage, first of all, an implicit repudiation of the leading doctrine of *The Principles of Literary Criticism*. The early doctrine did look upon poetic language as a "substitute for real experience," if by experience is meant responses relevant to scientifically ascertained facts and situations: this early doctrine, as I have indicated, anticipated in psychological terms Mr. Morris's poetic doctrine of designation without *denotatum*, of value without consummation of value, of interpretant without an interpreter. Mr. Richards's more familiar equivalents of the semiotic terms were: pseudo-statement without referents; poetry as the orderer of our minds, as the valuer, although the ordering mysteriously operated in fictions irrelevant to the real world; a response, a behavioristic "readiness for action," without a knowing mind.

Language, says Mr. Richards, "is no mere signalling system." With that sentence the early psychological doctrine is discreetly put away. Is it too much to assume that the adjective "signalling" may indicate the relation of Mr. Richards's present views to the pragmatic bias of Mr. Morris's aesthetics? He speaks of the inadequacy of "sensation" and "intuition," and of the equal inadequacy of "intuitions of sensation." Is not the mere sensation Mr. Morris's interpretant, the intuition of sensation his iconic sign? What is the "completion" which language "well used" can achieve beyond sensation and intuition?

It is doubtless knowledge of a kind that we can discuss only if we assume the action of a knowing mind. Of what is it the completion? In the paragraph following the passage that I have just quoted, Mr. Richards cites Coleridge:

> Are not words parts and germinations of the plant? And what is the law of their growth? In something of this sort I would destroy the old antithesis of Words and Things: elevating, as it were, Words into Things and living things too.

This attribution to the language of poetry of a special kind of "life" goes back to Mr. Richards's *Coleridge on Imagination* (1935), the most ambitious attempt of a modern critic to force into unity the antithesis of language and subject, of pleasure and truth. It is an antithesis which, as we have seen, has harassed critical theory since the time of Coleridge. Mr. Richards's book may be looked upon as an effort to finish Coleridge's own uncompleted struggle with this neo-classical dilemma. This is not the place to describe the entire nature and scope of his effort, or to estimate it. A single chapter of the book, "The Wind Harp," contains the clearest presentation of the antithesis that I have seen by a modern critic.

There are "two doctrines," he says, which have tended to flourish independently—"And yet, neither is intelligible, apart from Imagination." He continues:

> The two doctrines can be stated as follows:
> 1. The mind of the poet at moments . . . gains an insight into reality, reads Nature as a symbol of something behind or within Nature not ordinarily perceived.
> 2. The mind of the poet creates a Nature into which his own feelings, his aspirations and apprehensions, are projected.

Now the positivist sciences have denied all validity to the first doctrine: as a proposition, in the many forms in which it may be stated, it is strictly meaningless. For the sole effective procedure towards nature is the positivist. The second doctrine is the standard poetics of our time: projection of feeling. The confusion and contradiction that we saw in Mr. Morris and in the early Richards came of trying to square a theory of interest-value with a theory of emotional projection which was not firmly based upon positivist knowledge. That contradiction is the clue to the "unintelligibility" of the doctrines if held separately. If you take the first alone, eliminating the second, you eliminate the "mind," and you get pure positivism: in thus eliminating cognition you lose "everything in which we go beyond the animals." If you take the second alone, and eliminate the external world in any of the four meanings [8] that Mr. Richards gives to the phrase, you have a knowing mind without anything that it can know.

Before the development of the positivist procedures towards nature, the pressure of this dilemma was not seriously felt. We have seen in Matthew Arnold (the determined anti-dialectician) the belief that the subject is external to the language—a merely common-sense view inherited from neoclassical theory. The poetic subject was the world of ordinary experience; but as soon as the subject—Nature—became the field of positivism, the language of poetry ceased to represent it; ceased, in fact, to have any validity, or to set forth anything real. (The world of positivism is a world without minds to know the world; and yet Mr. Morris does not hesitate to assert that his Unified Science will save the world. For whom will it be saved?)

What is this Imagination which Mr. Richards says will make the two doctrines intelligible? No doubt it becomes in his hands something different from Coleridge's conception of it: it closely resembles an Hegelian synthesis, which joins the opposites in a new proposition in which their truths, no longer contradictory, are preserved.

[8] *Coleridge on Imagination*, pp. 157-8.

They are [says Mr. Richards of the two doctrines] neither consequences of *a priori* decisions, nor verifiable as the empirical statements of science are verifiable; and all verifiable statements are independent of them. But this does not diminish in the least their interest, or that of the other senses in which they may be true.

With that we are almost ready to leave Mr. Richards, who offers no final solution of the problem of the unified imagination. "It is the privilege of poetry," he says finely, "to preserve us from mistaking our notions either for things or for ourselves. *Poetry is the completest mode of utterance.*"⁹ It is neither the world of verifiable science nor a projection of ourselves; yet it is *complete*. And because it is complete knowledge we may, I think, claim for it a unique kind of responsibility, and see in it at times an irresponsibility equally distinct. The order of completeness that it achieves in the great works of the imagination is not the order of experimental completeness aimed at by the positivist sciences, whose responsibility is directed towards the verification of limited techniques. The completeness of science is an abstraction covering an ideal of co-operation among specialized methods. No one can have an experience of science, or of a single science. For the completeness of *Hamlet* is not of the experimental order, but of the experienced order: it is, in short, of the mythical order. And here Mr. Richards can give us a final insight. Myths, he says,

> . . . are no amusement or diversion to be sought as a relaxation and an escape from the hard realities of life. They are these hard realities in projection, their symbolic recognition, co-ordination and acceptance. . . . The opposite and discordant qualities in things in them acquire a form. . . . Without his mythologies man is only a cruel animal without a soul . . . a congeries of possibilities without order and aim.¹⁰

⁹ *Ibid.*, p. 163.
¹⁰ *Ibid.*, pp. 171-172.

Man, without his mythologies, is an interpretant. Mr. Richards's books may be seen together as a parable, as a mythical and dramatic projection, of the failure of the modern mind to understand poetry on the assumptions underlying the demi-religion of positivism. We do not need to reject the positive and rational mode of inquiry into poetry; yet even from Mr. Morris we get the warning lest we substitute the criticism for the poem, and thus commit ourselves to a "learned ignorance." We must return to, we must never leave, the poem itself. Its "interest" value is a cognitive one; it is sufficient that here, in the poem, we get knowledge of a whole object. If rational inquiry is the only mode of criticism, we must yet remember that the way we employ that mode must always powerfully affect our experience of the poem. I have been concerned in this commentary with the compulsive, almost obsessed, application of an all-engrossing principle of pragmatic reduction to a formed realm of our experience, the distinction of which is its complete knowledge, the full body of the experience ᵗʰat it offers us. However we may see the completeness of poetry, it is a problem less to be solved than, in its full import, to be preserved.

# MISS EMILY
# AND THE BIBLIOGRAPHER [1]

## 1940

THE scene is a seminar room at a large American university. It is the first meeting of the year. The eager young man asks the professor a question. "What," he says, "is the ultimate purpose of graduate research in English literature?" The professor, whose special field is English bibliography of the decade 1840-1850, does not hesitate. "To lay the foundations of literary criticism," he replies. The eager young man is pleased because secretly and discreetly he hopes that some day he may hope to be a critic. A month later the bibliographer assigns the group a paper. "Gentlemen," he says, "we must maintain in these papers the graduate point of view. There must be no impressionism. There must be no literary criticism. Anybody can write that."

I came upon this tale about a year ago but a year before that I had read one like it in an essay written by Mr. John Crowe Ransom some time before the incident that I relate occurred. I began to wonder if Mr. Ransom had made it up; then I began to hope that he had, so that the witnessed fact should stand as proof of an insight. Without the witnessed fact Mr. Ransom (I assume for my purpose that he invented

[1] This paper was read before the English Club of Princeton University, April 10, 1940.

the tale) would be in the position of William Faulkner after
his story, "A Rose for Emily," appeared. You will remember
Mr. Faulkner's story. Miss Emily, a curious spinster, conceals
the dead body of her lover in an upstairs bedroom until con-
cealment is no longer possible. Nobody believed this tale;
it was one of Mr. Faulkner's outrageous lies; it just couldn't
have happened. Then it happened. This evidence of the
decadence of the South emerged about three years later from
a farmhouse in upstate New York. A middle-aged woman
had killed her lover and kept the body.

For both Mr. Ransom and Mr. Faulkner the later facts
confirmed the previous insights. Yet I must confess that for
another reason altogether the analogy between the scholar
and the spinster teases my fancy. Both tales are tales of
horror, and I submit that the greater horror, for me, is in
the scholar's insincerity. The analogy, like a good one, holds
on more than one level. Must we not suspect that Miss Emily
had a time of it conducting her intrigue in a provincial
American community and that she probably, with the lover's
last breath, breathed her sigh of relief? The need of judging
him as a living man had been happily removed with the
removal of his breath; the contingencies of personality were
happily gone; she could have him without any of the social
dangers of having him. She could now proceed without
interruption to the reconstruction of the history of her love.
But there was always the body, and the body wrecks the
analogy. Miss Emily's historical method recognized that
it was the history of something it could not ignore and had
to return to. But the specialist in English bibliography of the
decade 1840-1850 would doubtless bury the body at once,
concealing it forever; and he would never afterwards have
to be reminded what he was doing the bibliography of. Or
if you will give this figure yet another turn, the analogy is
wrecked again, again in favor of Miss Emily. The body has
got to decompose, and its existence will become shockingly
known—a crisis that the historical scholars conspire among
themselves to postpone indefinitely; and if the wild discour-

tesy of the real world reminds them of it they say, "No, you are mistaken; we buried it long ago." But have they? Can they? And that is why Miss Emily remains a somewhat endearing horror for me. It is better to pretend with Miss Emily that something dead is living than to pretend with the bibliographer that something living is dead.[2]

The bibliographer's belief that "anybody can write that" I wish to discuss later, when I get to some of the more dialectical phases of the question. Here I should like to set off against my frivolity what many literary critics have called the insincerity of the academic mind. Between the frivolity and the insincerity, between the ignorance and the irrelevant learning, the outlook for a literary criticism in our time is dark. But as a matter of fact, whatever may be said of the party of ignorance, it would be hard to maintain that anything like personal insincerity motivates the activities of the historical scholars. Every point of view entails upon its proponents, in the act of overreaching it, its own kind of insincerity. Yet the evidence for the insincerity of our bibliographer is damaging: what, if not insincerity, lies back of his professed purpose which he, when he is pressed, shamelessly repudiates? How can he spend years laying the foundations of literary criticism when he thinks that anybody can write it? If anybody can write it does it need the collaboration of many generations of scholarship to lay its foundations?

There is insincerity here no doubt; for it is plainly an instance of a professed intention that one never expects to carry out or that one vaguely expects the future to perform for us. Does this not have an ominous and familiar sound? We hear it in the world at large and on nearly every level of our experience.

We hear it in politics, and the political voice has its counterpoint in the uneasy speculation of the journalist critics

---

[2] The reader will suspect that I have had in mind all along the phrase "the *corpus* of English literature," widely used by scholars and their way no doubt of laying literature out for burial.

about the future of literature: some ten years ago we got from England a whole series of little books called *The Future of—;* and it is seldom that we get an essay on the present state of letters or even on a single book that does not look far beyond the occasion. We are asked as citizens to live only for the future, either in the preservation of democracy or in the creation of the classless society. Mr. T. S. Eliot has discussed this question in "Literature and the Modern World," an essay which I believe has not been reprinted in any of his books; he examines the point of view of H. G. Wells and sees in it the widespread eschatology of a secular, naturalistic philosophy. As individuals today we must subordinate our spiritual life and our material satisfactions to the single purpose of gaining superior material satisfactions in the future, which will be a naturalistic Utopia of mindless hygiene and Tom Swift's gadgets. There is no doubt that the most powerful attraction offered us by the totalitarian political philosophies is the promise of irresponsible perfection in the future, to be gained at the slight cost of our present consent to extinguish our moral natures in a group mind.

The moral nature affirms itself in judgment, and we cannot or will not judge. Because the scholars as much as other people today are involved in the naturalistic temper, they also refuse to judge. The historical scholar says that we cannot judge the literature of our time because we do not know whether the future will approve of it. Is he not obviously evading his moral responsibility? I do not say he evades it as a father or as a citizen; but he does evade it in the specific field in which he ought to exercise it, since of that field he professes knowledge.

He has reasons for the Great Refusal, and the reasons are of curious interest and at the same time of critical importance. In order to express my sense of their significance I must go a long way round. I should like to begin by citing certain critical views held by Mr. Edmund Wilson, a brilliant historian of literature, who because he puts literature above research may be expected to exhibit some of the values of the historical method when it is actually applied in criticism.

Let me first make a distinction—so broad that if it is true it will be virtually a truism. Let us assume that English critics from the late Renaissance to Coleridge had a firm sense of the differences among the *genres* of literature and that they tried constantly to state those differences critically. Whether they succeeded in this task, from our point of view, is not the question; it is rather that they tried to look upon works of literature as objective existences with respect to the different forms.

Taking up this defeated critical tradition we still from time to time consider the relation of poetry to prose fiction. Our approach to this problem was adumbrated by Coleridge in a fashion that would have been unintelligible a century before his time: in Chapter XIV of *Biographia Literaria* he remarks that a work of prose fiction will often have the imaginative qualities of poetry, no essential difference between poetry and fiction being discernible.[3] There are concealed in this view certain metaphysical assumptions, which we still use without awareness of the metaphysics. (In the study of "English" we are forbidden to "use" philosophy— which means that we are using it badly.) We say today that there is poetry in prose fiction and, wherever you have narrative, fiction in poetry. But it ought to be easy to see that the murk enveloping the question when we try to carry it further than this arises from a certain kind of fallacy of abstraction. We are thinking in terms of substance, or essence. Those who believe that poetry and prose fiction differ in some fundamental sense assume that poetry is a distinct essence; whether prose has an essence is irrelevant since it could not have the essence of poetry; and therefore, prose fiction being a kind of prose, it is essentially different from poetry.

Now Mr. Wilson easily disposes of this argument in a famous essay called "Is Verse a Dying Technique?" (by which I understand him to mean: Is verse becoming an

[3] For a more detailed discussion of this problem see pp. 35-40.

unpopular technique?). He boldly denies to poetry an essence distinct from the essence of prose. In denying a difference he affirms the same essence of both: he thinks in terms of essence. He shows that *Madame Bovary* contains a great deal of "poetry" and concludes that the only interesting difference between a work like Flaubert's masterpiece and the *Aeneid* is that the one is in prose, the other in verse. That is certainly a difference; it is, according to Mr. Wilson, strictly a difference of "technique"; and he assumes the likenesses in terms of a common essence. Here we get the deepest assumption of the literary historian: the subject matter alone has objective status, the specific form of the work being external and mechanical—mere technique. This essence common to all literature is human life. Both Flaubert and Virgil were concerned with it in its largest implications.

Nobody will deny this; but it is critically irrelevant to affirm it. Within the terms of this affirmation critical thought is impossible, and we succumb to the documentary routine which "correlates" this de-formed substance with its origin, which by convention is called history.

Now the writers who see in works of literature not the specific formal properties but only the amount and range of human life brought to the reader are expressionists. Back of the many varieties of expressionist theory lies the assumption of the common or the distinct essence. If I say that the essence of *Madame Bovary* is different from the essence of the *Aeneid* and Mr. Wilson says that the essences are the same, we merely shout our opinions at each other, and the louder voice prevails. The historical method will not permit us to develop a critical instrument for dealing with works of literature as existent objects; we see them as expressive of substances beyond themselves. At the historical level the work expresses its place and time, or the author's personality, but if the scholar goes further and says anything about the work, he is expressing himself. Expressionism is here a sentiment, forbidding us to think and permitting us to feel as we please. When the bored expressionist tires of the pure artistic essence he turns into the inquisitive literary historian; or he may be both at once, as indeed he often is.

The great historical scholars of our time are notoriously deficient critics, but critics they are nevertheless. I am far from believing that the bibliographer's defense of scholarship is acceptable to all the scholars, many of whom are certain that they are already doing for criticism all that is necessary. Do you want a critic? Why, we already have one —in John Livingston Lowes. Has he not given us *Convention and Revolt?* He has; but in the course of a few pages I cannot do justice to the historical scholarship that gave us the facile seesaw picture of the history of poetry, or to the poetic learning that permitted Mr. Lowes to take seriously the late Amy Lowell. The mere literary critics took Miss Lowell seriously for a while, but the literary critics were not scholars. If you will think of *Convention and Revolt* along with *The Road to Xanadu* you will see that the literary dilettante and the historical scholar can flourish, without much communication between them, in one man.

Are we not prepared here for one of the remarkable insights of the late Irving Babbitt? His *Literature and the American College,* published in 1908, is still quoted, but there is no reason to believe that its message has ever been taken seriously by the men who most need it. At that time the late J. E. Spingarn had not imported into American criticism the term expressionism. Mr. Babbitt called the dilettantes Rousseauistic impressionists; the historical scholars Baconian naturalists. Both dilettante and scholar repudiated the obligations of judgment because both alike were victims of a naturalistic philosophy. Perhaps Mr. Babbitt did not consider the possibility of their being the same man. He saw on the one hand the ignorant journalist critics, "decadent romantics," for whom intensity of feeling was the sole critical standard; and on the other hand the historical scholars, who had no critical standard at all but who amassed irrelevant information. It was—and still is—a situation in which it is virtually impossible for a young man to get a critical, literary education. If he goes to a graduate school he comes out incapacitated for criticism; if he tries to be a critic he is not unlike the ignorant impressionist who did not go to the graduate school. He cannot discuss the literary object in terms of its specific form; all that he can do is to give you its history or tell you how he feels about it. The concrete form of the play, the poem, the novel, that gave rise to the history or the feeling lies neglected on the hither side of the Styx, where Virgil explains to Dante that it is scorned alike by heaven and hell.

Mr. Babbitt saw in the aesthete and the historical scholar the same motivation. The naturalism of the scholar lies in his mechanical theory of history, a theory in which the literary object is dissolved into the determinism of forces surrounding it. The naturalism of the aesthete operates on the psychological plane; he responds to the aesthetic object in terms of sensation and if the sensation is intense the aesthetic object is good.

Mr. Babbitt scolded these erring brothers for not making a moral judgment, and it is just here that the limitations of his method appear. The moral obligation to judge does not necessarily obligate us to make a moral judgment. Mr. Babbitt's humanism contains some concealed naturalism in its insistence upon the value of the mere substance or essence of literature: the subject matter itself must be decorous in order to pass the humanist examination. The specific property of a work of literary art which differentiates it from mere historical experience he could never understand; and it is this specific property, this particular quality of the work, that puts upon us the moral obligation to form a judgment. Mr. Yvor Winters remarks that Mr. Babbitt never understood "how the moral intelligence gets into poetry." It gets in not as moral abstractions but as form, coherence of image and metaphor, control of tone and of rhythm, the union of these features. So the moral obligation to judge compels us to make not a moral but a total judgment.

The question in the end comes down to this: What as literary critics are we to judge? As literary critics we must first of all decide in what respect the literary work has a specific objectivity. If we deny its specific objectivity then not only is criticism impossible but literature also. We have got to decide what it is about the whole of a work of literature which distinguishes it from its parts—or rather the parts we can abstract from this whole and then distribute over the vast smudge of history, whence they presumably were derived. It is a question of knowing before we talk what as critics we are talking about.

From my point of view the formal qualities of a poem are the focus of the specifically critical judgment because they partake of an objectivity that the subject matter, abstracted from the form, wholly lacks. The form of "Lycidas" is Milton's specific achievement as a poet in the convention of the pastoral elegy; but this convention, which is his substance, represents in itself only a subjective selection from Milton's historical situation. Would it not be simpler to seize at once the specific quality of "Lycidas" and try to understand it than to grapple with that aspect which fades into the immense perspective of history?

It would be simpler, if not easier, to discuss the form if we had a way of discussing it; yet before we can understand a literary problem we must first confess the problem exists. We no longer admit the problem because we no longer believe in the specific quality of the work of literature, the quality that distinguishes it from a work of history or even of science. As men of letters we no longer, in fact, believe in literature; we believe rather that the knowledge offered us in even the most highly developed literary forms has something factitious and illusory about it, so that before we can begin to test its validity we must translate it into an analogy derived from the sciences. The historical method is an imitation of scientific method: we entertain as interesting and valuable that portion of the literary work to which we can apply the scientific vocabularies.

Not being a literary historian I do not know when the

literary profession lost confidence in literature; I suppose it was a gradual loss; we see its beginnings in the English romantics, and we do not yet see the end. The rise of the sciences, their immense practical successes, even their moral failures, intimidated the scholars and I seem to hear them say, at first secretly and late at night when black questions cannot be gainsaid: "Milton's science is false, and the scientists say that his moral and religious ideas have no empirical validity. But if I give up Milton I give up my profession, so I had better bestir myself to study scientifically Milton's unscientific science. We must get in on the wonderful scientific triumphs of the age. Nobody believes today that the arts give us a sort of cognition at least equally valid with that of scientific method; so we will just take the arts as fields of data for more scientific investigation."

The historical method is in the long run the unhistorical method. The literary historians are not first of all historians. We seldom get from them anything like Taine on English literature; no American literary scholar has produced a work of the distinction of Carl Becker's *The Heavenly City of the Eighteenth Century Philosophers*, a book written not in the historical method but out of the historical imagination. It is a work of literature by a mind informed with a mature point of view and seasoned with exact knowledge (by knowledge I do not mean documentation) in many fields. Could Mr. Becker have written the book had he been trained in the belief that philosophy, for example, not being "English," has no place in historical writing? Could he have written it had he been compelled to suppress all the resources of his intelligence but the single one employed in the mechanical "correlation" of literature with the undigested lump of history? Is there not an instructive moral in the distinction of Mr. Becker's prose style?

I am not attacking the study or the writing of history for use in the criticism of literature. I am attacking the historical method. I trust everybody understands what this method is. It reflects at varying distances the philosophies of monism current in the nineteenth century and still prevailing today. Because the literary scholar in his monistic naturalism cannot discern the objectivity of the forms of literature, he can only apply to literature certain abstractions which he derives, two stages removed, from the naturalistic sciences; that is to say he gets these abstractions from the historians who got them from the scientists. In the period when physics was the popular science we got historical studies of influences, conceived in terms of forces, causes, and effects; then came the biological analogies that gave us organic periods where we attended to growths and developments; and today we have a broadening of the historical method which reflects the vast extension of scientific procedure in the semi-sciences—psychology, economics, and sociology.

That this method is, in a definite sense, unhistorical it would not be hard to show. Under whatever leading analogy we employ the historical method—organism, mechanism, causality—it has the immediate effect of removing the historian himself from history, so that he cannot participate as a living imagination in a great work of literature. Even those scholars, usually men interested in the eighteenth century, who are concerned with the meaning of tradition conceive of tradition itself in terms of scientific analogies, so that there is something remote and mechanical about a tradition; and the tradition that we are interested in is almost always seen as a traditional "body" of literature, not operative today— not living, as the very word body implies.

This removal of the historian from living history has curious consequences. Because it is difficult—or too easy in some respects—to get historical documents for works of the present or recent past we refuse to study them. And we also refuse to study them because their reputations are not fixed. There is here the assumption, as I think the illusion, that the reputation of any writer is ever fixed. These two illusions—the necessity of documents for the study of literature and the fixed hierarchy of the past—are not necessarily consequences of the historical method: Milton complained of similar routines of pedantry at Cambridge. Yet perhaps more today than ever we get a systematic, semi-philosophical sanction for our refusal to study literature.

I take the somewhat naïve view that the literature of the past began somewhere a few minutes ago and that the literature of the present begins, say, with Homer. While there is no doubt that we need as much knowledge of all kinds, from all sources, as we can get if we are to see the slightest lyric in all its richness of meaning, we have nevertheless an obligation, that we perilously evade, to form a judgment of the literature of our own time. It is more than an obligation; we must do it if we would keep on living. When the scholar assumes that he is judging a work of the past from a high and disinterested position, he is actually judging it from no position at all but is only abstracting from the work those qualities that his semi-scientific method will permit him to see; and this is the Great Refusal.

We must judge the past and keep it alive by being alive ourselves; and that is to say that we must judge the past not with a method or an abstract hierarchy but with the present, or with as much of the present as our poets have succeeded in elevating to the objectivity of form. For it is through the formed, objective experience of our own time that we must approach the past; and then by means of a critical mastery of our own formed experience we may test the presence and the value of form in works of the past. This critical activity is reciprocal and simultaneous. The scholar who tells us that he understands Dryden but makes nothing of Hopkins or Yeats is telling us that he does not understand Dryden.

Perhaps the same scholar acknowledges the greatness of Dryden and the even more formidable greatness of Milton and Shakespeare; and if you ask him how they became great he will reply, as I have heard him reply, that History did it and that we have got to wait until History does it, or declines to do it, to writers of our own time. Who is this mysterious person named History? We are back again with our old friend, the Great Refusal, who thrives upon the naturalistic repudiation of the moral obligation to judge. If we wait for history to judge there will be no judgment; for if we are not history then history is nobody. He is nobody when he has become the historical method.

One last feature of this illusion of the fixed hierarchy I confess I cannot understand. It is the belief that the chief function of criticism is the ranking of authors rather than their use. It is the assumption that the great writers of the past occupy a fixed position. If we alter the figure slightly, admitting that History has frozen their reputations, we must assume also that the position from which we look at them is likewise fixed; for if it were not we should see them in constantly changing relations and perspectives, and we should think their positions were changing too. If you will now see this same figure as a landscape of hills, trees, plains, you will quickly become fearful for the man who from a fixed point surveys the unchanging scene; for the man, the only man, who cannot change his position is a dead man: the only man for whom the greatness of the great poets is fixed is also dead. And so, if we may look at this Homeric simile with the eyes of Bishop Berkeley, we must conclude that the great authors are dead too, because there is nobody to look at them. I have adapted this figure from one of the Prefaces of Henry James because it seems to me to be a good way of saying that the literature of the past can be kept alive only by seeing it as the literature of the present. Or perhaps we ought to say that the literature of the past lives in the literature of the present and nowhere else; that it is all present literature.

# THE FUNCTION

# OF THE CRITICAL QUARTERLY

## *1936*


IF THE quarterly journal has ceased forever to be our popular magazine, may it still be said that the specialized critical quarterly has a "use"? *Use* is a term too slippery to invite definition. Since the time I became aware of the literary magazine, nearly twenty years ago, the declining usefulness of the critical quarterly has been taken for granted. It now increasingly serves the end of acquainting unpopular writers with one another's writings. That is a "use" that I, for one, am not prepared to deride. But the reader is entitled to his own sense of usefulness. He is the cultivated layman who felt at one time, say a hundred years ago, that the high places of literature were not beyond his reach: he saw himself and the author in a communion of understanding in which the communicants were necessary to each other.

It is a communion lost to us. The weekly and the monthly, renovated for modern speed of the eye, have captured the intelligent layman entirely.[1] And for a good reason. At his best he likes his "theory," as he educatedly names ideas, mixed unobtrusively into the "practice" of his times: he likes to believe that the literary news of his period can bring him

[1] Since this was written, *Life, Look, Pic, Click,* and other picture magazines have appeared.

a sufficient criticism of it. And this was precisely what was procured for him, at a high level of excellence, by the British quarterlies in the day of Lockhart, Jeffrey, and Wilson. The layman found out what was happening at the same time that he was told what it meant.

Doubtless our own splitting off of information from understanding, this modern divorce of action from intelligence, is general, and not particular to the arts of literature. If it is a problem that on every hand confronts us, it must affect the policy of the critical review—and tremendously determine it. For the critical review stands for one-half of the modern dilemma, the purer half: the intelligence trying to think into the moving world a rational order of value.

The critical review, then, must severely define its relation first to a public and then to its contributors. The editor's attitude towards his contributors, his choice of contributors, and his direction of their work, depend upon the kind of influence that he has decided to exercise.

Our best quarterlies have readers but not enough readers to pay the "cost of production." The quarterly must be subsidized; it either runs on a subsidy or does not run. It cannot define its "use" in terms of the size of its public; and it assumes that the public needs something that it does not want, or—what is the same thing—that a minority wants what the greater public needs. The leading quarterlies are subsidized by universities or are backed, like the late *Hound and Horn,* by persons whose fortunes and interests may be expected to change. The fate of *The Symposium,* the best critical quarterly published in America up to its time (1929-1933), offers timely warning to the founder of a review that cannot count upon a subsidy or a private fortune.

There is no record of success for a quarterly review that, in recent times, has tried to compete with the weekly or the monthly. The weekly reader gets the news of books and affairs while it is still, I imagine, hot; and if he asks for a little meditation upon the passing shadows, he will take not much more of this than he can get out of the pages of the

monthly—regretting that the meditation is a month old and
that something new to be meditated upon has, last week or
yesterday, risen to invalidate the old meditation. Of course
we ought to enjoin the reader to suspect the monthly meditation; it was perhaps not sufficiently considered and fundamental. We ought, in fact, to tell him that the critical quarterly, devoted to principles, can alone give him a meditation
of such considered depth that it will illuminate the risen
event of yesterday, or the rising event of tomorrow. But
unfortunately the modern reader's synthesizing powers are
limited, and nothing is applicable to nothing, and the gap
between idea and event leaves the reader and the quarterly
somewhat high and dry with respect to each other. The
quarterly is always too late, even if its standards are not
stubbornly too high. If the quarterly imitates the freshness
of the weekly, its freshness is necessarily three months stale,
refrigerated but not new; and if it tries for the liveliness of
monthly commentary, its peril is the sacrifice of leisured
thought. In either instance the quarterly sacrifices its standards only to attempt a work that it cannot hope to do.

But if the quarterly editor is not forced by poverty to run
a monthly *manqué,* his problem at once becomes simpler
and more difficult; simpler, because he does not need to find
out by trial and error what a paying public will read; more
difficult, because he must become himself a first-rate critic
in the act of organizing his material, four times a year, into
coherent criticism.

The critical performance of the quarterly lies no more
in the critical essays than in the "creative" department; good
creative work is a criticism of the second rate; and the critical
department ought to be run for the protection of that which
in itself is the end of criticism. If this observation be extended
to society and social criticism, the complete function of the
quarterly will emerge. For only the social criticism that
instances the value of concrete social experience may be
termed properly critical. Literature in this broadest sense
tells us the meaning of experience, what it is and has been,

and it is there that the political and aesthetic departments join.

It is a formidable union, and the difficulty of consummating it may well appal the stoutest editorial heart. Given the freedom to engage the difficulty, the editor is immediately assailed by a series of questions. Is there a critical task that might be done effectively by the quarterly? Can it be done at the present time? If it can, how can it best be done?

Though it would be untrue to say that good critical essays never appear in the monthly magazines, yet an effective critical program cannot, in that medium, be maintained. The monthly is too close to the weekly, the weekly to the newspaper, for any of these kinds of organ to maintain a critical program in the midst of the more pressing need to report the "scene." If one use of criticism is to make the reader aware of himself through the literature of his time, and aware, through this literature, of the literature of the past, the critical program must have an objective, and not be contented with partial glimpses or mere reports of points of view. The reader needs more than the mere news that a given point of view exists; he must be initiated into the point of view, saturated with it. The critical program must, then, supply its readers with coherent standards of taste and examples of taste in operation; not mere statements about taste. Mere reporting enjoins the editor to glance at all points of view. The reader gets a "digest" of opinion, not critical thought; he is encouraged to sample everything and to experience nothing.

A sound critical program has at least this one feature: *it allows to the reader no choice in the standards of judgment.* It asks the reader to take a post of observation, and to occupy it long enough to examine closely the field before him, which is presumably the whole field of our experience. This, one supposes, is dogmatism, but it is arguable still that dogma in criticism is a permanent necessity: the value of the dogma will be determined by the quality of the mind engaged in constructing it. For dogma is coherent thought in the pursuit of principles. If the critic has risen to the plane of principle, and refuses to judge by prejudice, he will, while allowing no quarter to critical relativity, grant enormous variety to the specific arts. For it must be remembered that prejudice is not dogma, that the one has no toleration of the other. If prejudice were dogma, the *New York Times Book Review* would be a first-rate critical organ. It allows the narrowest possible range of artistic performance along with the widest latitude of incoherent opinion and of popular success —simply because it uses, instead of principle, prejudice.

To deny the use of the critical quarterly today is to deny the use of criticism. It is a perilous denial. For criticism is not merely a way of saying that a certain poem is better than another; it gives meaning to the awareness of differences only in so far as it instructs the reader in three fundamentals of mounting importance: the exercise of taste, the pursuit of standards of intellectual judgment, and the acquisition of self-knowledge. If the reader is not encouraged in self-knowledge—a kind of knowing that entails insight into one's relation to a moral and social order that one has begun, after great labor, to understand—then taste and judgment have no center, and are mere words.

If this is the task of criticism, and if the task of criticism can be accomplished only in the quarterly, what is to prevent its being carried out? There are obstacles. To distinguish cause and effect is neither easy nor, fortunately, obligatory: living evidence of the divorce of fact and understanding, of action and intelligence, is the mass-produced monthly. It is a kind of journalism that includes both the fashionable Hearst magazines and the "quality" group. The Hearst readers have always existed potentially; the "quality" readers number in their ranks many new recruits, but quite as many must surely be persons with an education that formerly qualified them to read the critical quarterly. Such readers have a certain sensibility, but not being actively critical themselves, they take what comes; and the monthly magazine, being efficiently because profitably distributed, is what they take. The inference to be studied here, if the inference were not already visible as fact, is that the quarterly must be heavily subsidized.

There is still another obstacle to successful quarterly publication: the task of getting suitable contributors. Or perhaps the obstacle is the effect of the monthly magazine on writers who might, but for its existence, be constantly available to the quarterly editor. The quality group, for example, can pay better rates for manuscripts than the most flourishing quarterly can ever pay. The monthly can command first choice of the work of writers who would otherwise put their best effort into the more considered, and to them more satisfactory, performance demanded by the more critical journal. If the quarterly pay five dollars a page, critics trying to set forth a program, and "creative" writers who wish to exhibit their work in terms of the coherent standards of those critics, will accept the five dollars a page—provided the lure of a bigger price does not meanwhile keep them from doing their better and more serious work. The menacing possibility of eight or ten dollars a page is, by writers of all sorts, gratefully embraced. The writer is offering a commodity for sale, and he, like every other producer, must get the highest price.

It is a law of "capitalism." There is no moral theory that can place a stigma upon this procedure. If it were possible for good writers deliberately to lower their quality, that would be a horse of another color; but the leveling comes from the market itself, which asks for a superficial, fragmentary performance that may, within the assigned limits, be excellent work. In the long run it is futile work, because it cannot be systematic and comprehensive. The writer, if he happen to be a critic, must begin his program over again with every essay, and journalize his thought out of existence: he cannot develop continuity of thought because he cannot count upon the attention of the same readers over a number of years: he is selling on the open market, and he cannot be sure that his product will be bought by the same *entrepreneur* a second time. He fidgets in this insecure, disorderly position because he must—or starve—seek the highest money reward for his work.

If the quarterly shall be less fragmentary than the monthly, it must maintain a policy that not only demands the leisured, considered performance; it has got to make the performance possible to its contributors. I suggest that the quarterly pay the highest rate it can—cheapening perhaps the quality of its paper and printing—but not that it try to compete in prices with the monthly. There is, I think, a compromise. And the compromise, a concession to the writer and an eventual benefit to the editor, consists in breaking the law of capitalism already referred to. One article of this law grows out of the merely cash nexus between producer and distributor—between writer and editor—and it urges the distributor to be as disloyal as possible—for a purpose—to the producer of the commodity which he sells. The distributor's purpose is to keep the producer insecure and humble, so that, should the strain of competition permit, he can give the producer the lowest possible price. For here it may be said that the monthly pays a better price than the quarterly, not because it is by good luck more prosperous and by nature more generous, but because competition forces it to pay ten dollars a page for work that might go to another editor for nine.

The quarterly must be loyal to its contributors in two indispensable ways, and both these ways involve another kind of "nexus" between writer and editor than the cash. A genuine critical objective cannot be attained if the editor waits on the market for what may arrive in the mail. If he has a mind, he must make up his mind what he wants, and decide that there are certain contributors whom he would rather have than others. There will be perhaps a dozen of these and the editor has got to be loyal to them. If he is a second-rate man, and fears that, by giving rein over a long stretch to a talented group of men, he will be personally overshadowed, he had better write the entire contents of his magazine —a feat that, being a second-rate man, he will not be equal to.

Whether he be first- or second-rate, his first proof of loyalty is the highest price that he can pay. If the editor wants to enlist a regular staff of contributors whom he can call upon at a moment's notice, he should pay them a little more than he will pay for the casual manuscript, however good, that he found on his desk this morning. Authors are as responsive to kind treatment as other labor. They will feel for this editor a corresponding loyalty. They will let him have for five dollars a page, for instance, a manuscript that, after a little blood-letting, they might easily sell for ten to a quality magazine. They will do this all the more eagerly if the editor is willing to let the writer continue the work in three or four more essays, or stories, or poems; if, in short, the writers are encouraged in their programs.

That, in fact, is the editor's second loyalty—to take most of the output of his selected, inner circle of contributors. He must assume, if he does not actually know, that his contributors are not men of independent income. He must take a responsible view of their welfare. If he does not, the lure of high prices will attract their work into the open market. If the quarterly editor's attitude is indistinguishable from that of the commercial editor, he is doomed to fail.

For, let his literary standards be the highest, his relation to his contributors is still commercial, even if he is not trying "to make money." He is only a less effective part of a system that the writer cannot afford to be loyal to. Both the serious writer and the critical quarterly are thus defeated. I could name a dozen leading writers, north and south, who remember the quarterlies for manuscripts that they cannot sell elsewhere at high prices. The quarterly review gets what is left in the trunk.

There is no use blinking these facts. It is futile to discuss the higher aims of the critical review without facing them. There is, of course, a very small group of writers—the present writer is doubtless one of them—whose aims are directed towards the limited audience of the critical review. It is not an exalted purpose that so confines them; it is only the accident of concentration. If the quarterly editor's attitude is the same as his commercial colleague's, the performance of his critical minority is not more effective than the scattered performance of the hack writer seeking the open market. The minority suffers the restriction of audience without enjoying the satisfaction of taking part in a literature, and without getting the higher pay of competition.

Given the right relation between the editor and his contributors, what work may they together be expected to do? The question is rhetorical; but I think it is clear that nothing useful can be done without that right relation. Modern experiments in quarterly publication achieve moderate success; they win readers, a very few, year after year. The best quarterlies indirectly affect the "quality" reader, for the "quality" writer is often formed by the quarterly that his public never sees. But the quarterly that would justify the name of criticism must have a set purpose—not merely to publish the "best" that drifts into its office; its internal organization and its outward policy must be sharply defined.

The great magazines have been edited by autocrats. Within the memory of our time the great editors were Henley and Ford; in our own age, the late A. R. Orage and T. S. Eliot. Ford Madox Ford had notable success with *The English Review*, as early as 1909, because he knew what men to bring to the front: he gave concentration of purpose, the conviction of being part of a literature, to at least half of the distinguished writers who survived the War and who have deeply influenced our own age. He, more than any other modern editor, enrolled his contributors in the profession of letters—in a time when, under finance-capitalism, editors had already become employers who felt as little responsibility to their labor as manufacturers are able to feel towards theirs.

*The Criterion* under T. S. Eliot has been the best quarterly of our time.[2] It has become the fashion to deride it: its intellectualism, its traditionalism, its devotion to "lost causes," expose it to an attack that for my purpose here need not be

[2] It suspended publication with the January 1939 issue.

discussed. The value of its critical program does not concern me at the moment. It has been important because it does have a critical program: the editor from the beginning set out to develop critical issues. For a brief period, around 1926 or 1927, *The Criterion* became a monthly; it soon reverted to quarterly appearance. In the reduced size of the monthly the editor could not print contributions long enough to carry considered critical discussion.

If the task of the quarterly is to impose an intelligible order upon a scattering experience that the monthly and the weekly may hope only to report, the task of the editor must be one 'of difficulty and responsibility. We must expect him to have power and influence. His power should be concentrated if—it is worth repeating again—he is not merely to do what the monthly can do better. There can be little doubt that the success of *The Criterion*—it has never, I believe, had more than two thousand subscribers—has been due to concentrated editorship functioning through a small group of regular contributors. By group I do not mean the personal friends of the editor, or persons enlisted in some movement, for a movement is not always a program. By a group I mean a number of writers who agree that certain fundamental issues exist and who consent, under direction of the editor, to discuss them with a certain emphasis. The editor may not believe in Marxism or neo-Thomism, but he will see it as an issue, and he will seek discussion of Marxism or neo-Thomism from a point of view.

I have described the high aims of the critical quarterly as if financial backing were not a problem; as if the editor were at liberty to develop his program unhampered by the need of cash subscribers; as if his magazine were free to find whatever public may exist for it. All writing seeks an audience. But the editor has a responsibility that he must discharge as perfectly as the contingencies of backing and public will permit. He owes his first duty to his critical principles, his sense of the moral and intellectual order upon which society ought to rest, whether or not society at the moment has an interest in such an order or is even aware of a need for it. For the ideal task of the critical quarterly is not to give the public what it wants, or what it thinks it wants, but what— through the medium of its most intelligent members—it ought to have. At a time when action has become singularly devoid of intelligence, there could not be a "cause" more disinterested. The way to give the public what it resentfully needs is to discredit the inferior ideas of the age by exposing them to the criticism of the superior ideas.

# TENSION IN POETRY

## 1938

MANY poems that we ordinarily think of as good poetry—
and some, besides, that we neglect—have certain common
features that will allow us to invent, for their sharper apprehension, the name of a single quality. I shall call that quality
tension. In abstract language, a poetic work has distinct
quality as the ultimate effect of the whole, and that whole
is the "result" of a configuration of meaning which it is the
duty of the critic to examine and evaluate. In setting forth
this duty as my present procedure I am trying to amplify a
critical approach that I have used on other occasions, without wholly giving up the earlier method, which I should describe as the isolation of the general ideas implicit in the
poetic work.

Towards the end of this essay I shall cite examples of
"tension," but I shall not say that they exemplify tension
only, or that other qualities must be ignored. There are all
kinds of poetry, as many as there are good poets, as many
even as there are good poems, for poets may be expected to
write more than one kind of poetry; and no single critical
insight may impute an exclusive validity to any one kind.
In all ages there are schools demanding that one sort only
be written—their sort: political poetry for the sake of the

cause; picturesque poetry for the sake of the home town; didactic poetry for the sake of the parish; even a generalized personal poetry for the sake of the reassurance and safety of numbers. This last I suppose is the most common variety, the anonymous lyricism in which the common personality exhibits its commonness, its obscure yet standard eccentricity, in a language that seems always to be deteriorating; so that today many poets are driven to inventing private languages, or very narrow ones, because public speech has become heavily tainted with mass feeling.

Mass language is the medium of "communication," and its users are less interested in bringing to formal order what is sometimes called the "affective state" than in arousing that state.

> Once you have said that everything is One it is obvious that literature is the same as propaganda; once you have said that no truth can be known apart from the immediate dialectical process of history it is obvious that all contemporary artists must prepare the same fashionplate. It is clear too that the One is limited in space as well as time, and the no less Hegelian Fascists are right in saying that all art is patriotic.

What Mr. William Empson calls patriotic poetry sings not merely in behalf of the State; you will find it equally in a lady-like lyric and in much of the political poetry of our time. It is the poetry of the mass language, very different from the "language of the people" which interested the late W. B. Yeats. For example:

> What from the splendid dead
> We have inherited—
> Furrows sweet to the grain, and the weed subdued—
> See now the slug and the mildew plunder.
> Evil does overwhelm
> The larkspur and the corn;
> We have seen them go under.

From this stanza by Miss Millay we infer that her splendid ancestors made the earth a good place that has somehow gone bad—and you get the reason from the title: "Justice Denied in Massachusetts." How Massachusetts could cause a general desiccation, why (as we are told in a footnote to the poem) the execution of Sacco and Vanzetti should have anything to do with the rotting of the crops, it is never made clear. These lines are mass language: they arouse an affective state in one set of terms, and suddenly an object quite unrelated to those terms gets the benefit of it; and this effect, which is usually achieved, as I think it is here, without conscious effort, is sentimentality. Miss Millay's poem was admired when it first appeared about ten years ago, and is no doubt still admired, by persons to whom it communicates certain feelings about social justice, by persons for whom the lines are the occasion of feelings shared by them and the poet. But if you do not share those feelings, as I happen not to share them in the images of desiccated nature, the lines and even the entire poem are impenetrably obscure.

I am attacking here the fallacy of communication in poetry. (I am not attacking social justice.) It is no less a fallacy in the writing of poetry than of critical theory. The critical doctrine fares ill the further back you apply it; I suppose one may say—if one wants a landmark—that it began to prosper after 1798; for on the whole nineteenth-century English verse is a poetry of communication. The poets were trying to use verse to convey ideas and feelings that they secretly thought could be better conveyed by science (consult Shelley's *Defense*), or by what today we call, in a significantly bad poetic phrase, the Social Sciences. Yet possibly because the poets believed the scientists to be tough, and the poets joined the scientists in thinking the poets tender, the poets stuck to verse. It may scarcely be said that we change this tradition of poetic futility by giving it a new name, Social Poetry. May a poet hope to deal more adequately with sociology than with physics? If he seizes upon either at the level of scientific procedure, has he not abdicated his position as poet?

At a level of lower historical awareness than that exhibited by Mr. Edmund Wilson's later heroes of the Symbolist school, we find the kind of verse that I have been quoting, verse long ago intimidated by the pseudo-rationalism of the Social Sciences. This sentimental intimidation has been so complete that, however easy the verse looked on the page, it gave up all claim to sense. (I assume here what I cannot now demonstrate, that Miss Millay's poem is obscure but that Donne's "Second Anniversarie" is not.) As another example of this brand of obscurity I have selected at random a nineteenth-century lyric, "The Vine," by James Thomson:

> The wine of love is music,
>     And the feast of love is song:
> When love sits down to banquet,
>     Love sits long:
>
> Sits long and rises drunken,
>     But not with the feast and the wine;
> He reeleth with his own heart,
>     That great rich Vine.

The language here appeals to an existing affective state; it has no coherent meaning either literally or in terms of ambiguity or implication; it may be wholly replaced by any of its several paraphrases, which are already latent in our minds. One of these is the confused image of a self-intoxicating man-about-town. Now good poetry can bear the closest literal examination of every phrase, and is its own safeguard against our irony. But the more closely we examine this lyric, the more obscure it becomes; the more we trace the implications of the imagery, the denser the confusion. The imagery adds nothing to the general idea that it tries to sustain; it even deprives that idea of the dignity it has won at the hands of a long succession of better poets going back, I suppose, to Guinizelli:

> *Al cor gentil ripara sempre Amore*
> *Come alla selva augello in la verdura . . .*

What I want to make clear is the particular kind of failure, not the degree, in a certain kind of poetry. Were we interested in degrees we might give comfort to the nineteenth century by citing lines from John Cleveland or Abraham Cowley, bad lyric verse no better than "The Vine," written in an age that produced some of the greatest English poetry. Here are some lines from Cowley's "Hymn: to light," a hundred-line inventory of some of the offices performed by the subject in a universe that still seems to be on the whole Ptolemaic; I should not care to guess the length the poem might have reached under the Copernican system. Here is one of the interesting duties of light:

> Nor amidst all these Triumphs does thou scorn
> The humble glow-worm to adorn,
> And with those living spangles gild,
> (O Greatness without Pride!) the Bushes of the Field.

Again:

> The Violet, springs little Infant, stands,
> Girt in thy purple Swadling-bands:
> On the fair Tulip thou dost dote;
> Thou cloath'st it in a gay and party-colour'd Coat.

This, doubtless, is metaphysical poetry; however bad the lines may be—they are pretty bad—they have no qualities, bad or good, in common with "The Vine." Mr. Ransom has given us, in a remarkable essay, "Shakespeare at Sonnets" [1] (*The World's Body*, 1938), an excellent description of this kind of poetry: "The impulse to metaphysical poetry . . . consists in committing the feelings in the case . . . to their determination within the elected figure." That is to say, in metaphysical poetry the logical order is explicit; it must be coherent; the imagery by which it is sensuously embodied must have at least the appearance of logical determinism: perhaps the appearance only, because the varieties of am-

---

[1] His rejection of Shakespeare's sonnets seems to be a result of deductive necessity in his premises, or of the courage of mere logic; but the essay contains valuable insights into the operation of the metaphysical "conceit."

biguity and contradiction possible beneath the logical surface are endless, as Mr. Empson has demonstrated in his elucidation of Marvel's "The Garden." Here it is enough to say that the development of imagery by extension, its logical determinants being an Ariadne's thread that the poet will not permit us to lose, is the leading feature of the poetry called metaphysical.

But to recognize it is not to evaluate it; and I take it that Mr. Ransom was giving us a true Aristotelian definition of a *genus,* in which the identification of a type does not compel us to discern the implied values. Logical extension of imagery is no doubt the key to the meaning of Donne's "Valediction: forbidding mourning"; it may equally initiate inquiry into the ludicrous failure of "Hymn: to light," to which I now return.

Although "The Vine" and "Hymn: to light" seem to me equally bad poetry, Cowley's failure is somewhat to be preferred; its negative superiority lies in a firmer use of the language. There is no appeal to an affective state; the leading statement can be made perfectly explicit: God is light, and light is life. The poem is an analytical proposition exhibiting the properties inherent in the major term; that is, exhibiting as much of the universe as Cowley could get around to before he wearied of logical extension. But I think it is possible to infer that good poetry could have been written in Cowley's language; and we know that it was. Every term, even the verbs converted into nouns, denotes an object, and in the hands of a good poet would be amenable to controlled distortions of literal representation. But here the distortions are uncontrolled. Everything is in this language that a poet needs except the poetry, or the imagination, or what I shall presently illustrate under the idea of tension.

I have called "Hymn: to light" an analytical proposition. That is the form in which the theme must have appeared to Cowley's mind; that is to say, simple analysis of the term *God* gave him, as it gave everybody else in Christendom, the proposition: God is light. (Perhaps, under neo-Platonic influence, the prime Christian symbol, as Professor Fletcher and others have shown in reducing to their sources the powers of the Three Blessed Ladies of *The Divine Comedy*.) But in order to write his poem Cowley had to develop the symbol by synthetic accretion, by adding to light properties not inherent in its simple analysis:

> The Violet, springs little Infant, stands,
> Girt in thy purple Swadling-bands . . .

The image, such as it is, is an addition to the central figure of light, an assertion of a hitherto undetected relation among the objects, light, diapers, and violets—a miscellany that I recommend to the consideration of Mr. E. E. Cummings, who could get something out of it that Cowley did not intend us to get. If you will think again of "The Vine," you will observe that Thomson permits, in the opposite direction, an equal license with the objects *de*noted by his imagery, with the unhappy results that we have already seen.

"The Vine" is a failure in denotation. "Hymn: to light" is a failure in connotation. The language of "The Vine" lacks objective content. Take "music" and "song" in the first two lines; the context does not allow us to apprehend the terms in extension; that is, there is no reference to objects that we may distinguish as "music" and "song"; the wine of love could have as well been song, its feast music. In "Hymn: to light," a reduction to their connotations of the terms *violet, swadling-bands*, and *light* (the last being represented by the pronoun *thou*) yields a clutter of images that may be unified only if we forget the firm denotations of the terms. If we are going to receive as valid the infancy of the violet, we must ignore the metaphor that conveys it, for the metaphor renders the violet absurd; by ignoring the diaper, and the two terms associated with it, we cease to read the passage, and begin for ourselves the building up of acceptable denotations for the terms of the metaphor.

Absurd: but on what final ground I call these poems absurd I cannot state as a principle. I appeal to the reader's experience, and invite him to form a judgment of my own. It is easy enough to say, as I shall say in detail in a moment, that good poetry is a unity of all the meanings from the furthest extremes of intension and extension. Yet our recognition of the action of this unified meaning is the gift of experience, of culture, of, if you will, our humanism. Our powers of discrimination are not deductive powers, though they may be aided by them; they wait rather upon the cultivation of our total human powers, and they represent a special application of those powers to a single medium of experience—poetry.

I have referred to a certain kind of poetry as the embodiment of the fallacy of communication: it is a poetry that communicates the affective state, which (in terms of language) results from the irresponsible denotations of words. There is a vague grasp of the "real" world. The history of this fallacy, which is as old as poetry but which towards the end of the eighteenth century began to dominate not only poetry, but other arts as well—its history would probably show that the poets gave up the language of denotation to the scientists, and kept for themselves a continually thinning flux of peripheral connotations. The companion fallacy, to which I can give only the literal name, the fallacy of mere denotation, I have also illustrated from Cowley: this is the poetry which contradicts our most developed human insights in so far as it fails to use and direct the rich connotation with which language has been informed by experience.

## II

WE RETURN to the inquiry set for this discussion: to find out whether there is not a more central achievement in poetry than that represented by either of the extreme examples that we have been considering. I proposed as descriptive of that achievement, the term *tension*. I am using the term not as a general metaphor, but as a special one, derived from lopping the prefixes off the logical terms *extension* and *intension*. What I am saying, of course, is that the meaning of poetry is its "tension," the full organized body of all the extension and intension that we can find in it. The remotest figurative significance that we can derive does not invalidate the extensions of the literal statement. Or we may begin with the literal statement and by stages develop the complications of metaphor: at every stage we may pause to state the meaning so far apprehended, and at every stage the meaning will be coherent.

The meanings that we select at different points along the infinite line between extreme intension and extreme extension will vary with our personal "drive," or "interest," or "approach": the Platonist will tend to stay pretty close to the end of the line where extension, and simple abstraction of the object into a universal, is easiest, for he will be a fanatic in morals or some kind of works, and will insist upon the shortest way with what will ever appear to him the dissenting ambiguities at the intensive end of the scale. The Platonist (I do not say that his opponent is the Aristotelian) might decide that Marvel's "To His Coy Mistress" recommends immoral behavior to the young men, in whose behalf he would try to suppress the poem. That, of course, would be one "true" meaning of "To His Coy Mistress," but it is a meaning that the full tension of the poem will not allow us to entertain exclusively. For we are compelled, since it is there, to give equal weight to an intensive meaning so rich that, without contradicting the literal statement of the lover-mistress convention, it lifts that convention into an insight into one phase of the human predicament—the conflict of sensuality and asceticism.

I should like to quote now, not from Marvel, but a stanza from Donne that I hope will reinforce a little what I have just said and connect it with some earlier remarks.

> Our two soules therefore, which are one,
>     Though I must goe, endure not yet
> A breach, but an expansion,
>     Like gold to aiery thinnesse beate.

Here Donne brings together the developing imagery of twenty lines under the implicit proposition: the unity of two lovers' souls is a nonspatial entity, and is therefore indivisible. That, I believe, is what Mr. John Crowe Ransom would call the logic of the passage; it is the abstract form of its extensive meaning. Now the interesting feature here is the logical contradiction of embodying the unitary, non-spatial soul in a spatial image: the malleable gold is a plane whose surface can always be extended mathematically by one-half towards infinity; the souls are this infinity. The finite image of the gold, in extension, logically contradicts the intensive meaning (infinity) which it conveys; but it does not invalidate that meaning. We have seen that Cowley compelled us to ignore the denoted diaper in order that we might take seriously the violet which it pretended to swathe. But in Donne's "Valediction: forbidding mourning" the clear denotation of the gold contains, by intension, the full meaning of the passage. If we reject the gold, we reject the meaning, for the meaning is wholly absorbed into the image of the gold. Intension and extension are here one, and they enrich each other.

Before I leave this beautiful object, I should like to notice two incidental features in further proof of Donne's mastery. "Expansion"—a term denoting an abstract property common to many objects, perhaps here one property of a gas: it expands visibly the quality of the beaten gold.

>             . . . endure not yet
>     a breach . . .

But if the lovers' souls are the formidable, inhuman entity that we have seen, are they not superior to the contingency of a breach? Yes and no: both answers are true answers; for by means of the sly "yet" Donne subtly guards himself against our irony, which would otherwise be quick to scrutinize the extreme metaphor. The lovers have not endured a breach, but they are simple, miserable human beings, and they may quarrel tomorrow.[2]

Now all this meaning and more, and it is all one meaning, is embedded in that stanza: I say more because I have not exhausted the small fraction of significance that my limited powers have permitted me to see. For example, I have not discussed the rhythm, which is of the essential meaning; I have violently isolated four lines from the meaning of the whole poem. Yet, fine as it is, I do not think the poem the greatest poetry; perhaps only very little of Donne makes that grade, or of anybody else. Donne offers many examples of tension in imagery, easier for the expositor than greater passages in Shakespeare.

But convenience of elucidation is not a canon of criticism. I wish now to introduce other kinds of instance, and to let them stand for us as a sort of Arnoldish touchstones to the perfection that poetic statement has occasionally reached. I do not know what bearing my comment has had, or my touchstones may have, upon the larger effects of poetry or upon long poems. The long poem is partly a different problem. I have of necessity confined both commentary and illustration to the slighter effects that seemed to me commensurate with certain immediate qualities of language. For, in the long run, whatever the poet's "philosophy," however wide may be the extension of his meaning—like Milton's Ptolemaic universe in which he didn't believe—by his language shall you know him; the quality of his language is the valid limit of what he has to say.

I have not searched out the quotations that follow: they at once form the documentation and imply the personal bias

---

[2] Mr. F. O. Matthiessen informs me that my interpretation here, which detaches the "yet" from the developing figure, is not the usual one. Mr. Matthiessen refers the phrase to the gold, for which in his view it prepares the way.

from which this inquiry has grown. Only a few of the lines will be identified with the metaphysical technique, or, in Mr. Ransom's fine phrase, the metaphysical strategy. Strategy would here indicate the point on the intensive-extensive scale at which the poet deploys his resources of meaning. The metaphysical poet as a rationalist begins at or near the extensive or denoting end of the line; the romantic or Symbolist poet at the other, intensive end; and each by a straining feat of the imagination tries to push his meanings as far as he can towards the opposite end, so as to occupy the entire scale. I have offered one good and one bad example of the metaphysical strategy, but only defective examples of the Symbolist, which I cited as fallacies of mass language: Thomson was using language at its mass level, unhappily ignorant of the need to embody his connotations in a rational order of thought. (I allude here also, and in a quite literal sense, to Thomson's personal unhappiness, as well as to the excessive pessimism and excessive optimism of other poets of his time.) The great Symbolist poets, from Rimbaud to Yeats, have heeded this necessity of reason. It would be a hard task to choose between the two strategies, the Symbolist and the metaphysical; both at their best are great, and both are incomplete.

These touchstones, I believe, are not poetry of the extremes, but poetry of the center: poetry of tension, in which the "strategy" is diffused into the unitary effect.

> Ask me no more whither doth hast
> The Nightingale when *May* is past:
> For in your sweet dividing throat
> She winters, and keeps warm her note.

                    *  *  *

> O thou Steeled Cognizance whose leap commits
> The agile precincts of the lark's return . . .

                    *  *  *

That time of year thou mayst in me behold
When yellow leaves, or none, or few do hang
Upon those boughs which shake against the cold,
Bare ruined choirs where late the sweet birds sang.

&ast; &ast; &ast;

Beauty is but a flower
Which wrinkles will devour;
Brightness falls from the air,
Queens have died young and fair,
Dust hath closed Helen's eye.
I am sick, I must die
   Lord, have mercy upon us!

&ast; &ast; &ast;

And then may chance thee to repent
The time that thou hast lost and spent
   To cause thy lovers sigh and swoon;
Then shalt thou know beauty but lent,
   And wish and want as I have done.

&ast; &ast; &ast;

We have lingered in the chambers of the sea
By seagirls wreathed with seaweed red and brown
Till human voices wake us and we drown.

&ast; &ast; &ast;

I am of Ireland
And the Holy Land of Ireland
And time runs on, cried she.
Come out of charity
And dance with me in Ireland.

&ast; &ast; &ast;

And my poor fool is hanged! No, no, no life!
Why should a dog, a horse, a rat, have life
And thou no breath at all? Thou'lt come no more,
Never, never, never, never, never!—
Pray you undo this button; thank you, sir.—

Do you see this? Look on her,—look,—her lips,—
Look there, look there!

           ◦   ◦   ◦

'Tis madness to resist or blame
The force of angry heavens flame:
   And, if we would speak true,
   Much to the Man is due,
Who, from his private Gardens, where
He liv'd reserved and austere,
   As if his highest plot
   To plant the Bergamot,
Could by industrious Valour climbe
To ruin the great Work of Time,
   And cast the Kingdome old
   Into another Mold.

           ◦   ◦   ◦

Cover her face; mine eyes dazzle; she died young.

## III

THERE are three more lines that I wish to look at: a tercet
from *The Divine Comedy*. I know little of either Dante or
his language; yet I have chosen as my final instance of tension
—the instance itself will relieve me of the responsibility of the
term—not a great and difficult passage, but only a slight and
perfect one. It is from a scene that has always been the de-
light of the amateur reader of Dante; we can know more
about it with less knowledge than about any other, perhaps,
in the poem. The damned of the Second Circle are equivo-
cally damned: Paolo and Francesca were illicit lovers but
their crime was incontinence, neither adultery nor pander-
ing, the two crimes of sex for which Dante seems to find any
real theological reprobation, for they are committed with
the intent of injury.

You will remember that when Dante first sees the lovers
they are whirling in a high wind, the symbol here of lust.

When Francesca's conversation with the poet begins, the wind dies down, and she tells him where she was born, in these lines:

> *Siede la terra dove nata fui*
> *Sulla marina dove il Po discende*
> *Per aver pace co' seguaci sui.*

Courtney Landon renders the tercet:

> The town where I was born sits on the shore,
> Whither the Po descends to be at peace
> Together with the streams that follow him.

But it misses a good deal; it misses the force of *seguaci* by rendering it as a verb. Professor Grandgent translates the third line: "To have peace with its pursuers," and comments: "The tributaries are conceived as chasing the Po down to the sea." Precisely; for if the *seguaci* are merely followers, and not pursuers also, the wonderfully ordered density of this simple passage is sacrificed. For although Francesca has told Dante where she lives, in the most directly descriptive language possible, she has told him more than that. Without the least imposition of strain upon the firmly denoted natural setting, she fuses herself with the river Po near which she was born. By a subtle shift of focus we see the pursued river as Francesca in Hell: the pursuing tributaries are a new visual image for the pursuing winds of lust. A further glance yields even more: as the winds, so the tributaries at once pursue and become one with the pursued; that is to say, Francesca has completely absorbed the substance of her sin —she is the sin; as, I believe it is said, the damned of the *Inferno* are plenary incarnations of the sin that has put them there. The tributaries of the Po are not only the winds of lust by analogy of visual images; they become identified by means of sound:

> . . . *discende*
> *Per aver pace co' seguaci sui.*

The sibilants dominate the line; they are the hissing of the wind. But in the last line of the preceding tercet Francesca has been grateful that the wind has subsided so that she can be heard—

*Mentre che il vento, come fa, si tace.*

After the wind has abated, then, we hear in the silence, for the first time, its hiss, in the susurration to the descending Po. The river is thus both a visual and an auditory image, and since Francesca is her sin and her sin is embodied in this image, we are entitled to say that it is a sin that we can both hear and see.

# THREE TYPES OF POETRY

## 1934

IN THIS essay I propose to discuss three kinds of poetry that bring to focus three attitudes of the modern world. I do not say all three attitudes, because there are more than three attitudes. And there are more than three kinds of poetry.

The first attitude is motivated by the practical will: in poetry until the seventeenth century it leaned upon moral abstractions and allegory; now, under the influence of the sciences, it has appealed to physical ideas. It looks from knowledge to action. The second attitude has been developed from the second phase of the first; it is a revolt against the domination of science; and in poetry it has given us the emotion known as "romantic irony." The third attitude is nameless because it is perfect, because it is complete and whole. Criticism may isolate the imperfect, and formulate that which is already abstract; but it cannot formulate the concrete whole. There is no philosophical or historical name for the kind of poetry that Shakespeare wrote. I shall call it, in this essay, the creative spirit. I use the term for convenience, and ask the reader to forget its current uses by the followers of the Expressionist school.

We happen to be dominated at the moment by the scientific spirit of the practical will. A hundred and fifty years ago rose the thin cry of romantic irony—the poet's self-pity upon the rack of science, which he mistook for reality. Most notably in the sixteenth century we had the creative spirit.

The reader is asked to keep in mind two more general statements with some brief commentary:

First, the power of seizing the inward meaning of experience, the power of poetic creation that I shall call here the vision of the whole of life, is *a quality of the imagination.* The apologists of science speak as if this were the scientific attitude, but the aim of science is to produce a dynamic whole for the service of the practical will. Our experience of nuclear energy seems to be very different from our capacity to control it. For the imaginative whole of life is the wholeness of vision at a particular moment of experience; it yields us the quality of the experience.

It may be conveyed in a poem of four or six lines or in an epic of twelve books; or the twelve books may contain less of it than the four lines. Blake's "To the Accuser" is the total vision in eight lines; Darwin's "The Loves of the Plants" is the aimlessly statistical aggregation of fact—pseudo-botany or semi-science—in a number of lines that I have not counted.

Second, there is a surer grasp of the totality of experience in Wyat's "To His Lute" than in Shelley's "Adonaïs." This is the center of my argument. We must understand that the lines

> Life like a dome of many-colored glass
> Stains the white radiance of eternity

are not poetry; they express the frustrated individual will trying to compete with science. The will asserts a rhetorical proposition about the whole of life, but the imagination has not seized upon the materials of the poem and made them into a whole. Shelley's simile is imposed upon the material from above; it does not grow out of the material. It exists as explanation external to the subject: it is an explanation of "life" that seems laden with portent and high significance, but *as explanation* it necessarily looks towards possible action, and it is there that we know that the statement is meaningless. Practical experimental knowledge can alone fit means to ends.

If the simile of the dome were an integral part of a genuine poem, the question of its specific merit as truth or falsehood would not arise. Yet Shelley's dome, as an explanation of experience, is quite as good as Edgar's reflection on his father's downfall:

> Ripeness is all.

But the figure rises from the depth of Gloucester's situation. It is a summation not only of Gloucester's tragedy but of the complex tensions of the plot before the catastrophe in the last scene. Possibly *King Lear* would be as good without Edgar's words; but it would be difficult to imagine the play without the passage ending in those words. They are implicit in the total structure, the concrete quality, of the whole experience that we have when we read *King Lear*. The specific merit of Edgar's statement as general truth or falsehood is irrelevant because it is an *experienced statement*, first from Edgar's, then from our own, point of view; and the statement remains experienced, and thus significant and comprehensible, whether it be true or false.

The truth or falsity of Shelley's figure is the only issue that it raises. This bit of Platonism must be accepted before we can accept the material of the poem "Adonaïs"; for it must be a true idea to afford to the poet a true explanation. He must have an explanation for a material that he cannot experience. The idea of the dome is asserted to strengthen a subject that the poet has not implicitly imagined.

It was this quality of modern poetry that Arnold had in mind, or doubtless should have had in mind, when he remarked that the romantics "did not know enough." We have not known enough since their time. Arnold wrote later that the Victorian critics permitted the poet "to leave poetic sense ungratified, provided that he gratifies their rhetorical sense and their curiosity." If the term rhetoric must have an in-

vidious meaning, I think we may understand Arnold somewhat in this manner: that rhetoric is a forcing of the subject,
which is abstractly conceived, not implicitly seized upon.
It is external and decorative in the early romantics of the
mid-eighteenth century; it is hysterical, and evasive of the
material, in the great romantics—and it excites the "curiosity"
of the reader, who dwells on the external details of the poem
or pities the sad poet. The reader is not given an integral
work of art. How could criticism since Shelley and Wordsworth be anything but personal?—strive for anything but
evaluation of personality? It has been given little else to
evaluate. And why should not criticism fail in evaluating
Shakespeare's personality? And is this not the glory of
Shakespeare?

The reader's curiosity is motivated by his will. In the lowest terms, he seeks information (even from a poet); then,
more purposefully, he seeks for the information an explanation that, if it is good, is some branch of science. But like
the recent neo-Humanists he tries to get explanations from
the poets.

"For what is rhetoric," wrote W. B. Yeats nearly fifty years
ago, "but the will trying to do the work of the imagination?"
Mr. Yeats, with insight as profound as it is rare in our time,
went straight to the problem. Rhetoric is the pseudo-explana-
tion of unimagined material. The "right" explanation—the
exhibit of workable relations among different parts of any
material—although always provisional, is the scientific explanation. When the will tries to do the work of the imagination, it fails, and only succeeds in doing badly the work of
science. When the will supplants the imagination in poetry,
the task of the poet, because his instrument is not adequate
to his unconscious purpose, which is that of a science, is
bound to be frustrated. We get the peculiar frustration of
the poet known as romantic irony.

The pure scientific spirit I shall call here without much
regard for accuracy, a positive Platonism, a cheerful confidence in the limitless power of man to impose practical ab-

stractions upon his experience. Romantic irony is a negative Platonism, a self-pitying disillusionment with the positive optimism of the other program: the romantic tries to build up a set of fictitious "explanations," by means of rhetoric, more congenial to his unscientific temper. The creative spirit occupies an aloof middle ground—it is in no sense a compromise, as the late Irving Babbitt conceived it to be—between these positions. Its function is the quality of experience, the total revelation—not explanation for the purpose of external control by the will.

## II

DANTE distinguished two kinds of allegory. Religious allegory is both literally and figuratively true: we are to believe that the events of the story happened. But poetical allegory is true only in the figurative sense. The derivative meanings, called by Dante the moral and the anagogical, are legitimate, indeed they are the highest meanings; but they lean upon no basis of fact. Although fictional allegory is not popular today, it is the only sort that we can conceive. When the medieval allegorist used the Bible, it never entered his head that he was not using historical fact; and he brought the same mentality to bear upon material that even we, who are sophisticated, recognize as historical.

But a modern poet, attempting allegory, undoes the history. We accept his figures and images as amiable make-believe, knowing that historical fact and poetic figure have no real connection, simply because there is nothing true but fact. About this fact science alone can instruct us, not with a fundamentally different kind of instruction from that of the allegorist, but with the same kind, more systematic and efficient. When the author of the popular poem, "John Brown's Body," shows us the machine age growing out of Brown's body, we know that nothing of the sort happened, and we ask for the more enlightened view of the facts available in the scientific historians.

It is the kind of poetry that is primarily allegorical that

seems to me to be inferior. It is inferior as science, and it is inferior as poetry. Mere allegory is a vague and futile kind of science. And because its primary direction is towards that oversimplification of life which is the mark of the scientific will, it is a one-sided poetry, ignoring the whole vision of experience. Although *The Divine Comedy* is allegorical, it would not be one of the great poems of all time if Dante had not believed its structure of action to be true. It came out of an age whose mentality held the allegorical view of experience as easily as we hold the causal and scientific; so, in Dante, allegory never rises to an insubordinate place, but consistently occupies an implicit place, from which we must derive it by analysis.

There is a general sense in which all literature may be apprehended as allegory, and that sense explains the popular level of literary appreciation. When certain moral ideas preponderate over others in any kind of literature, the crudely practical reader abstracts them, and contents himself with the illusion that they are the total meaning of the work. The naïve Roman Catholic may see only this phase of Dante, who for him might as well have written a tract. Now when the preponderance of meanings receives from the author himself the seal of his explicit approval, in face of the immense complication of our experience, then the work tends towards allegory. The work is written in the interest of social, moral, and religious ideas apart from which it has little existence or significance. It becomes aesthetic creation at a low level of intensity. If the intention is innocent, the result is didacticism. If it is deliberate and systematic, and calculated to move people into some definite course of action, we get what is called in our time propaganda.

Didactic and propagandist works frequently have great artistic merit and power. Fiction different as *The Pilgrim's Progress* and *An American Tragedy* is overwhelming evidence of this. The perception of merit in this kind of writing has become a pretext, in our age, for believing that its defects, chiefly the defect of "propaganda," are a primary motive of all literature in all times. When the deficiency or impurity of inspiration is not forthright, it is nevertheless assumed as present but concealed: this is the kind of propaganda that is supposedly written from the security of a ruling class.

Pure allegory differs from this kind of writing in that the preponderance of meaning is wholly revealed; the characters, images, symbols, ideas, are simple, and invite restatement in paraphrases that exhaust their meaning; they stand, not in themselves, but merely for something else. *The Faerie Queene* belongs to this class of allegory. The summary remarks that I shall make about that great poem by no means encompass it; for there is more to be said that would not be to my purpose.

The structural feature that first impresses the reader of the poem is the arbitrary length of each canto: there is no reason inherent in the narrative why a canto should not be longer or shorter than it is. The characters remain homogeneous throughout; that is to say, they suffer no dramatic alteration; an episode ends when they have acted out enough of the moral to please the poet. The action has no meaning apart from the preconceived abstractions, which we may call Renaissance Platonism or any other suitable name, so long as we remember that the ideas suffer no shock and receive no complication in contact with the narrative. The narrative lacks inner necessity; it is all illustration. The capacity of the poet to allegorize the "philosophy" was illimitable, and terminated only with his death, which prevented completion of the poem.

One must remember that this sort of allegory has predominated in our tradition. Anglo-American literature, with the possible exception, at his high moments, of Nathaniel Hawthorne, has not given us allegory of the Dantesque order. I allude here to Dante's ability to look into a specific experience and to recreate it in such a way that its meaning is nowhere distinct from its specific quality. The allegorical interpretation is secondary. We get a genuine creation of the imagination. We get, in the Spenserian allegory, a projection of the will.

The quality and intention of the allegorical will are the intention and quality of the will of science. With allegory the image is not a complete, qualitative whole; it is an abstraction calculated to force the situation upon which it is imposed toward a single direction. In the sixteenth century science proper had achieved none of its triumphs. The allegorist had before him no standard by which he could measure the extent of his failure to find the right abstractions for the control of nature. He could spin out his tales endlessly in serene confidence of their "truth." But by the end of the eighteenth century his optimism had waned; it had passed to the more efficient allegorist of nature, the modern scientist.

Now in a poet like Dante we may say that there is an element of "science" in so far as the allegorical interpretation is possible: *The Divine Comedy* has something to say, not only to the naïve Roman Catholic, but to the ordinary man whose prepossessions are practical, and whose literary appreciation is limited by the needs of his own will. The poem has a moral, a set of derivative ideas that seem to the reader to be relevant to practical conduct. But to say this is not to say, with most schools of modern criticism, that it is the primary significance of the work. For Dante is a poet; the didactic element is in solution with the other elements, and may be said barely to exist in itself, since it must be isolated by the violence of the reader's own will.

There is therefore a distinction to be drawn between a kind of writing in which allegorical meanings are fused with the material, and pure and explicit allegory. It is the difference between works of the creative imagination and the inferior works of the practical will. The reader will recall my first proposition: the power of creating the inner meaning of experience is a quality of the imagination. It is not a construction of the will, that perpetual modernism through which, however vast may be the physical extent of the poet's range, the poet ignores the whole of experience for some special interest. This modern literature of Platonism— a descriptive term used to set apart a kind of work in which the meanings are forced—carries with it its own critical apparatus. It is known at present as the revolutionary or social point of view. Since the rise of science it has been also the "capitalist" point of view. For our whole culture seems to be obsessed by a kind of literature that is derivative of the allegorical mentality.

By the time of Dryden allegory of the medieval variety had lost its prestige; we get the political fables of "The Hind and the Panther," of "Absalom and Achitaphel," where the intention is pleasantly fictitious and local, with little pretense of universal truth. By the end of the next century the Platonic conquest of the world, the confident assertion of control over the forces of nature, had contrived a system of abstractions exact enough to assume the new name of science. So, in poetry, the allegorical mentality, which had hitherto used all the crude science available, lost confidence in its unexperimental ideas. The poetical assertion of the will took the form of revolt from its more successful counterpart, science. We find here two assertions of the same erring will, diverging for the first time: science *versus* romanticism.

## I I I

WITH the decline then of pure allegory, we see the rise of a new systematic structure of entities called science, which makes good the primitive allegorist's futile claim to the control of nature. Between allegorist and scientist there exists the illusion of fundamental opposition. They are, however, of one origin and purpose.[1] For the apparent hostility of science to the allegorical entities is old age's preoccupation with the follies of its youth.

---

[1] "Always science has grown up on religion . . . and always it signifies nothing more or less than an abstract melioration of these doctrines, considered as false because less abstract." Spengler: *The Decline of the West.*

When this situation became fully developed, the poets, deprived of their magical fictions, and stripped of the means of affirming the will allegorically, proceeded to revolt, pitting the individual will against all forms of order, under the illusion that all order is scientific order. The order of the imagination became confused. Thus arose romanticism, not qualitatively different from the naturalism that it attacked, but identical with it, and committed in the arts to the same imperfect inspiration.

This summary will, I believe, be illuminated by a passage from Taine, who is discussing Byron:

> Such are the sentiments wherewith he surveyed nature and history, not to comprehend them and forget himself before them, but to seek in them and impress upon them the image of his own passions. He does not leave the objects to speak for themselves, but forces them to answer him.

We have the endless quest of the romantic, who ranges over nature in the effort to impose his volitional ego as an absolute upon the world. Compare Taine's analysis of Byron with a sentence from Schopenhauer:

> While science, following the unresting and inconstant stream of the fourfold forms of reason and consequent, with each end attained sees further, and can never reach a final goal nor attain full satisfaction any more than by running we can reach the place where the clouds touch the horizon; art, on the contrary, is everywhere at its goal.

For the will of science and the will of the romantic poet (the frustrated allegorist) are the same will. Romanticism is science without the systematic method of asserting the will. Because it cannot participate in the infinite series of natural conquests, the romantic spirit impresses upon nature the image of its own passions:

> Make me thy lyre, even as the forest is:
> What if my leaves are falling like its own!
> The tumult of thy mighty harmonies
>
> Will take from both a deep autumnal tone,
> Sweet though in sadness. Be thou, Spirit fierce,
> My spirit! Be thou me, impetuous one!

It is the "will trying to do the work of the imagination." The style is inflated and emotive. The poet, instead of fixing his attention upon a single experience, instead of presenting dramatically the plight of human weakness—the subject of his poem—flies from his situation into a rhetorical escape that gives his will the illusion of power. (It may be observed that at the culmination of French romanticism in Rimbaud, the poet, still caught upon the dilemma of the will, carried this dilemma to its logical and most profound conclusion—the destruction of the will.)

The momentary illusion of individual power is a prime quality of the romantic movement. In the intervals when the illusion cannot be maintained, arise those moments of irony that create the subjective conflict of romantic poetry. In generalizing about such a quality one must take care; it differs with different poets. I have just pointed out incidentally how the individual will receives, in a late, and perhaps the greatest, romantic a self-destructive motivation. Yet the dramatic effect is similar in poets as different as Rimbaud and Shelley. Throughout the nineteenth century, and in a few poets today, we get an intellectual situation like this: there is the assumption that Truth is indifferent or hostile to the desires of men; that these desires were formerly nurtured on legend, myth, all kinds of insufficient experiment; that, Truth being known at last in the form of experimental science, it is intellectually impossible to maintain illusion any longer, at the same time that it is morally impossible to assimilate the inhuman Truth.

The poet revolts from Truth; that is, he defies the cruel and naturalistic world to break him if it can; and he is broken. This moral situation, transferred to the plane of drama or the lyric, becomes romantic irony—that is, an irony of his position of which the poet himself is not aware:

> I fall upon the thorns of life! I bleed!

His will being frustrated by inhospitable Truth, Shelley is broken; falls into disillusionment; and asks the west wind to take him away and make him its lyre. In a contemporary poet, whose death two years ago was probably the climax of the romantic movement in this country, we get the same quality of irony. Invoking a symbol of primitive simplicity, Pocahontas, Crane says:

> Lie to us! Dance us back our tribal morn!

The poet confesses that he has no access to a means of satisfying his will, or to a kind of vision where the terms are not set by the demands of the practical will. He returns to a fictitious past. There he is able to maintain, for a moment, the illusion that he might realize the assertion of his will in a primitive world where scientific truth is not a fatal obstacle.

At this point we must notice a special property of the romantic imagination. It has no insight into the total meanings of actual moral situations; it is concerned with fictitious alternatives to them, because they invariably mean frustration of the will. This special property of escape is the Golden Age, used in a special fashion. The romantic poet attributes to it an historical reality. In a great poet like Shakespeare, notably in *The Tempest*, we get the implications of the poetic convention of the Golden Age; properly looked at, it is more than a poetic convention, it is a moral necessity of man. The use to which Shakespeare puts it is not involved in the needs of his personal will; it assists in defining the quality of his insight into the permanent flaws of human character. For the Golden Age is not a moral or social possibility; it is a way of understanding the problem of evil, being a picture of human nature with the problem removed It is a qualitative fiction, not a material world, that permits the true imagination to recognize evil for what it is.

Now the romantic and allegorical poet, once he is torn with disbelief in the adequacy of the poetic will, sees before him two alternatives. After falling upon the thorns of life, he may either ask the west wind to take him up, or cry for his tribal morn in the Golden Age: this is the first alternative —disillusionment with life after defeat of the will. He will seize this escape provided that he lacks the hardihood of a Rimbaud, who saw that, given the satisfaction of will as a necessity of the age, the poet must either destroy his will or repudiate poetry for a career of action. But Rimbaud is the exceptional, because he is the perfect, romantic poet.

The other ordinary alternative of the modern allegorist lies in the main Spenserian tradition of ingenuous tale-telling; it is the pure Golden Age of the future, which the poet can envisage with complacency because his will has not gone off into the frustration of romantic irony. He enjoys something like the efficient optimism of science; he asks us to believe that a rearrangement of the external relations of man will not alone make him a little more comfortable, but will remove the whole problem of evil, and usher in perfection. It is this type of crude, physical imagination that we find in Tennyson:

> Till the war-drums sound no longer, and the battleflags
> are furled
> In the Parliament of Man, the Federation of the World.

The cult of the will is a specially European or Western cult; it rose after the Middle Ages; and it informs our criticism of society and the arts. For, given the assumption that poetry is only another kind of volition, less efficient than science, it is easy to believe in the superiority of the scientific method. I myself believe in it. For the physical imagination of science is, step by step, perfect, and knows no limit.

The physical imagination of poetry, granting it an unlimited range, is necessarily compacted of futile and incredible fictions, which we summarily reject as inferior instruments of the will. And rightly reject, if we assume two things—and our age is convinced that it is impossible to assume anything else: (1) that the only kind of imagination is that of the will, which best realizes its purposes in external constructions or in the control of the external relations of persons and things; (2) that this sole type of imagination will be disillusioned or optimistic, according as it is either imperfectly informed, as in mere poetry, or adequately equipped by science with the "fourfold forms of reason and consequent." That is the view held by a leading school of critics in this country, the most influential of whom has been Mr. Edmund Wilson in *Axel's Castle*, a book written on the assumption that *all* poetry is only an inferior kind of social will.

The critical movement so ably represented by Mr. Wilson is the heresy that I am opposing throughout this essay. That the kind of imaginative literature demanded by this school is the third, and I think necessarily the final, stage in the history of allegory in Western culture, may not be immediately clear.

The school preoccupied with what is called the economic determinism of literature is in the direct line of descent from the crudely moralistic allegory of the Renaissance. The notion that all art is primarily an apology for institutions and classes, though it is now the weapon of the Marxists against "capitalist" literature, has been explicit in our intellectual outlook since the time of Buckle in England, and Taine and Michelet in France. It is an article of faith in the "capitalist" and utilitarian dogma that literature, like everything else, must be primarily, and thus solely, an expression of the will. From such allegory as:

> With him went Danger, clothed in ragged weeds,
>   Made of bear's skin, that him more dreadful made,

> Yet his own face was dreadful, ne did need
>   Strange horror, to deform his grisly shade;
>   A net in th' one hand, and a rusty blade
> In th' other was, this Mischief, that Mishap . . .

—from this it is only a step to the sophisticated entities and abstractions of the agitation for social reform, whose vocabulary is an imitation, and an application to conduct, of the terms of physical science. Or rather, I should say, two steps; for the intermediate stage of allegory is the romantic irony of the age of Byron and Shelley. The contemporary allegorists have regained something of the easy confidence of their early forerunners; they believe as fully in the positive efficacy of the Marxian dialectic, as Spenser in the negative example of the Seven Deadly Sins.

Yet, the Seven Deadly Sins being now a little threadbare, our new allegorists are quite clear in their recognition that the arts, more especially poetry, have no specific function in society. The arts offer to society a pusillanimous instrument for the realization of its will. The better the art, one must add, the more pusillanimous. For art aims at nothing outside itself, and, in the words of Schopenhauer, "is everywhere at its goal." There is no goal for the literature of the will, whose new objective must be constantly redefined in terms of the technology, verbal or mechanical, available at the moment.

The significance of this movement in modern society is perfectly plain: by seizing exclusively those aspects of the total experience that are capable of being put to predictable and successful use, the modern spirit has committed itself to the most dangerous program in Western history. It has committed itself exclusively to this program. We should do well to consider a specimen, by Phelps Putnam, of contemporary romantic irony; the "He" in the passage is the Devil:

> He leaned his elbows on two mountain tops
> And moved his head slowly from side to side,
> Sweeping the plain with his unhurried eyes.
> He was the phoenix of familiar men,

> Of husbands I have known, the horns and all,
> But more, much more—O God, I was afraid.
> I would have hid before the eyes had come.
> Then they were there, and then
> My guts grew warm again in my despair
> And I cried "Pour la Reine" and drew my sword.
> But, Christ, I had no sword.

He had no science; the fictitious sword of the allegorical will that the hero "drew" was incompetent to deal with his desperately practical situation. Our new scientific allegorists rest their case against poetry there. What they neglect to provide for is the hero's failure in case he has a genuine sword of science. For the recognition of that other half of experience, the realm of immitigable evil—or perhaps I had better say in modern abstraction, the margin of error in social calculation—has been steadily lost. The fusion of human success and human error in a vision of the whole of life, *the vision itself being its own goal*, has almost disappeared from the modern world.

## I V

I HAVE set forth two propositions about poetry. I will now ask the reader to examine a little more narrowly the second, in the attempt to discriminate between a poetry of the will and a poetry of genuine imagination. We have seen that the poetry of the will takes two forms. There is the romantic, disillusioned irony of Shelley, or for that matter of a poet like Mr. Robinson Jeffers; there is the crude optimism of Tennyson, a moral outlook that has almost vanished from poetry,[2] surviving today as direct political and social propaganda supported by the "social" sciences. My second proposition was a brief commentary on the lines by Shelley:

> Life like a dome of many-colored glass
> Stains the white radiance of eternity

[2] I make exception for Mr. Stephen Spender, the English poet.

The will asserts a general proposition about the whole of life, but there is no specific, imagined context to support the assertion. As a product of the imagination the passage is incomprehensible; as a practical, that is to say, as a scientific generalization, it is open to the just contempt of the scientific mind. What, then, is the exact purpose and function of such poetry?

In purpose it competes with science; as to function it supports the illusion of moral insight in persons who are incapable of either scientific discipline or poetic apprehension. It is an affirmation of the will in terms that are not a legitimate vehicle of the will. The proper mode of the will—proper, that is, in efficiency, but not necessarily in morals, for the question whether the will should be so expressed at all is a distinct problem—the right mode of the will is some kind of practical effort adequately informed by exact science.

Most modern schools of criticism assume that all poetry is qualitatively the same as the lines by Shelley; they assume this negatively, for the positive assumption is that poetry must of necessity be like science, a quantitative instrument for mastery of the world. This is the interesting theory of Mr. I. A. Richards: because poetry is compacted of "pseudo-statements" it cannot compete with "certified scientific statements," and must be discredited as science moves on to fresh triumphs. This point of view is doubtless inevitable in a scientific age; but it is not an inevitable point of view.

Mr. Richards's theory of the relation between poetry and our beliefs about the world appears novel to some critics. It is the latest version of the allegorical, puritan and utilitarian theory of the arts—a theory that is rendered, by Mr. Richards, the more plausible because it seems to give to the arts a very serious attention. The British utilitarians, a century ago, frankly condemned them. So, with less candor, does Mr. Richards: his desperate efforts to make poetry, after all, useful, consist in justly reducing its "explanations" to nonsense, and salvaging from the wreck a mysterious agency for "ordering our minds." Poetry is a storehouse of ordered emotional energy that properly released might re-educate the public in the principles of the good life. For brevity, I paraphrase Mr. Richards; it should be observed that the idea is set forth in terms of the will.[8]

Yet there is, even according to Mr. Richards, little hope for this kind of education. The "certified scientific state-ments" about the world make the metaphors, the images, the symbols, all the varieties of "pseudo-statements"—similes like the dome of many-colored glass—look extremely foolish, because in the more exact light of science, they are patently untrue. I do not intend here to discuss this theory as a whole, nor to do justice to Mr. Richards's poetic taste, which is su-perior. One part of the theory, I believe, may be dismissed at once. How can poetry, a tissue of lies, equip the public with "relevant responses" to an environment? Our responses must work; they must be, in at least a provisional sense, scientifically true. What is this mysterious emotional func-tion of poetry that orders our minds with falsehood?

Mr. Richards is, I believe, talking about the unstable fringe of emotion that I have called romantic irony: we have seen that this is what is left to the poet—a lugubrious residue —after he realizes that science is truth and that his own fic-tions are lies. This residue, alas, organizes and orders nothing whatever. Mr. Richards's underlying assumption about poetry is, like Mr. Edmund Wilson's, embedded in the humanitarian mentality of the age, where it lies too deep for examination.

If the pseudo-statement is motivated by the will (the only intention for it that Mr. Richards can conceive), it is false, and Mr. Richards is right: the poet of this sort expects po-tatoes to grow better when planted in the dark of the moon.

If, on the other hand, a genuine poet uses the pseudo-statement, it is neither true nor false, but is a quality of the total created object: the poem. The power to perceive

---

[8] The discussion here is based upon Mr. Richards's two principal books: *The Principles of Literary Criticism*, 1924, and *Practical Criticism*, 1929. For discussion of Mr. Richards's later views see "Literature as Knowledge," pp. 41-48.

this total quality has almost disappeared from modern criticism. For all the arts are assumed to be necessarily assertions of the will.

Mr. Richards, like the romantic poet of the age of Byron and Shelley, sees that science has contrived a superior instrument of the will; again like them, he tries to rescue poetry by attributing to it functions of practical volition, functions that he cannot define but which, in the true "liberal" tradition, he asserts in some realm of private hope against the "truths" of science.

Now it seems to me that the foundations of poetry, and possibly of the other creative arts, are somewhat different. We cannot understand them until we shall have eliminated from our thinking the demands of the category of will with its instrument, the practical intellect.

Let us look at Mr. Richards's famous terms: "certified scientific statement" (science) and "pseudo-statement" (poetry). I will try to show briefly that, for poetry, the certified scientific statement is the half-statement. The pseudo-statement may be, as I have just said, neither true nor false, but a feature of the total quality of the poem. The lines

> Out, out brief candle!
> Life's but a walking shadow; a poor player
> That struts and frets his hour upon the stage,
> And then is heard no more . . .

are certainly not "true": we know that life is not a shadow, it is a vast realm of biological phenomena; nor is it a player. Neither are the lines false: they represent a stage in the dynamic unfolding of Macbeth's character, the whole created image of which is the whole play *Macbeth*, which in its turn is neither true nor false, but *exists as a created object*. None of the pseudo-statements in the play, representing the conflict of will that forms the plot, is either approved or disapproved by the poet. He neither offers us a practical formula for action nor rejects any of the volitional purposes of the characters. He creates the total object of which the pseudo-statements of the will are a single feature, and are therefore neither true nor false. What Mr. Richards's theory (and others like it) comes down to is the uneasy consciousness that such a passage as I have just quoted does not tell us how to keep out of the sort of mess that Macbeth got himself into. The ideal connection of this theory with the traditions of moralistic allegory is quite evident.

Before we may see the certified scientific statement as the half-statement, a further point of Mr. Richards's theory must be noticed. Poets, being ignorant of science and their general ideas false, ought to write poems in which appear no beliefs whatever, but in which, presumably, there is that mysterious ordering of our minds. "The Waste Land" is such a poem— supposedly. But is it? According to the poet himself and to my own simple powers of inspection, it is full of beliefs. Mr. Richards, with admirable aplomb, has seized upon a poem in which large generalizations do not appear, as an instance of his theory: that poets, to keep our respect, must order our minds without lies; that, in order to avoid saying wrong things, they must say nothing. And this "nothing" is only another species of half-statement. It leads straight to a defense of the recent school of "pure poets" in France,[4] a school that had its meeker followers in England and this country.

This half-statement may be in the pure poets an immersion in the supposedly pure sensations of experience. But in the older romantics of the nineteenth century, it is due to a sentimental escape from the abstractions of science. And indeed both fallacies are due to a misunderstanding of the exact nature of the "certified scientific statement." We saw, in the second section of this essay, how the romantics revolted from science, or one kind of half-statement, giving us romantic irony. This irony has dwindled, in our day, to the other half-statement (to the other activity of the same will) of "pure poetry." It is significant that at the present time we

[4] See *La Poésie Pure*. By Henri Bremond. Paris, 1926.

get, from both scientist and pure poet, a renunciation of poetry because it cannot compete with the current version of our objective world, a version that is pre-empted by the demands of the will with its certified scientific statements.

It must be remembered that this kind of statement is invariably the half-statement. It is the statement about a thing, a person, an experience, which relates it to something else, not for the purpose of giving us intensive knowledge of the thing, person, or experience, in itself and as a whole; but to give us, in varying degrees depending upon the exactness of the science under which it is viewed, the half-knowledge that limits us to the control of its extensive relations. If I feed a horse corn every day at noon, I may expect him to do more work in the afternoon than he would do without it. I am controlling the relation between grain and horse under the general proposition: Regular feeding of grain increases an animal's capacity for work. The statement must be either true or false.

But the statements in a genuine work of art are neither "certified" nor "pseudo-"; the creative intention removes them from the domain of practicality. "In aesthetics," wrote Mr. Leo Stein a few years ago in an excellent book, "we have to do with complex wholes which are never in a rigid state of adjustment." [5] This integral character of the work of art forever resists practical formulation. The aesthetic whole invites indefinitely prolonged attention; whereas the half-statement of science arrests our attention at those features of the whole that may be put to the service of the will. In the following verses the horse cannot be *used*, but as an object arousing prolonged contemplation in its particular setting it may be *known:*

> I set her on my pacing steed,
> And nothing else saw all day long,
> For sidelong she would bend, and sing
>    A faëry's song.

[5] *The ABC of Æsthetics.* By Leo Stein. New York, 1927.

The stanza is neither true nor false; it is an object that exists.

I think it ought to be clear by this time that theories like Mr. Richards's, theories covertly or avowedly developed in the interest of social schemes, are not guides to the study of the immense qualitative whole of works of art; they are scientific (more or less) charts, relating the art-object to other objects at the command of the practical will. So it may be said that such theories belong to that perpetually modern impulse to *allegorize* poetry, to abstract for use those features that are available for immediate action, and to repudiate the rest.

It ought to be clear that this is the regular course of science in the whole universe of objects; that with the arts science proceeds consistently, on principle; that society has developed an instinctive approach to the arts appropriate to the scientific temper of the age.

A man lives in a beautiful house in a beautiful place. Let him discover oil under his land. The oil has been there all the time as a feature of the total scene. But he violates the integrity of the scene by "developing" the oil. Where the house and land had previously existed as a whole of which utility was only one aspect, he abstracts one feature of it for immediate use by means of Mr. Richards's certified scientific half-statements; and destroys its wholeness. Perhaps he was a dreaming kind of man: suppose he had always meant to get out the oil, and had gone about it with an improper method. Suppose that all he could do was to write a poem, like the "Ode to the West Wind," in which he said: "O Oil, make me thy conduit, even as the earth is!" It would be a poem of the will, and Mr. Richards would have a perfect right to test the scientific efficiency of the formula urged by the poem.

It is not with this kind of poetry, but with another kind that is not a poetry of the will, that I have been concerned; and I have been offering a few commonplaces about its neglect by our advanced critics. Genuine poetry has been written in most ages—including the present—but it is a sort of poetry that was written most completely by Shakespeare. It is the sort of poetry that our "capitalist" and "communist" allegorists have forgotten how to read.

I have sketched some aspects of the poetry of the will, which in the last century and a half has taken two directions that I will summarize again. First, the optimism of science, either pure or social science, an uncritical and positive Platonism. Secondly, the negative Platonism of the romantic spirit, a pessimistic revolt of the individual against the optimism of the scientific will. The quality of volition is practical in both kinds of Platonism. But for isolated figures like Landor, Hopkins and Dickinson in the last century, and a few today, the creative spirit has been shunted off into obscurity by the heresy of the will.

The quality of poetic vision that I have already in this essay named, with respect to the two forms of will, the middle ground of vision, and, with respect to itself, the vision of the whole, is not susceptible of logical demonstration. We may prepare our minds for its reception by the logical elimination of error. But the kind of criticism that dominates our intellectual life is that of the French mathematician who, after reading a tragedy by Racine, asked: *"Qu'est ce que cela prouve?"* It proves nothing; it creates the totality of experience in its quality; and it has no useful relation to the ordinary forms of action.

Since I have not set out to prove an argument, but to look into arguments that seem to me to be wrong. I will state a conclusion as briefly as possible: that poetry finds its true usefulness in its perfect inutility, a focus of repose for the will-driven intellect that constantly shakes the equilibrium of persons and societies with its unremitting imposition of partial formulas. When the will and its formulas are put back into an implicit relation with the whole of our experience, we get the true knowledge which is poetry. It is the "kind of knowledge which is really essential to the world, the true content of its phenomena, that which is subject to no change, and therefore is known with equal truth for all time." Let us not argue about it. It is here for those who have eyes to see.

# UNDERSTANDING MODERN POETRY

## *1 9 4 0*

ABOUT every six months I see in the *New York Times Book Review* the confident analogy between the audience of the modern poet and the audience that the English Romantics had to win in the early nineteenth century. Only wait a little while, and T. S. Eliot will be as easy for high-school teachers as "The Solitary Reaper." There may be some truth in this; but I think there is very little truth in it, and my reasons for thinking so will be the substance of this essay. There is a great deal of confusion about this matter, and not a little of it comes from the comfortable habit of citing a passage in the "Preface" to *Lyrical Ballads,* in which Wordsworth says that, as soon as the objects of modern life (meaning the physical changes wrought in society by the Industrial Revolution) become as familiar to the people as the old mythologies of poetry, the difficulties of apprehension and communication will disappear. But this has not happened. It is true that no modern poet has succeeded in knowing all the physical features of modern industrial society; but neither has "society" succeeded in knowing them. It may be doubted that any poet in the past ever made a special point of studying the "techniques of production" of his time or of looking

self-consciously at the objects around him as mere objects.
Wordsworth himself did not.

Dante knew the science of the thirteenth century, and he
was intensely aware of the physical features of his time—
the ways of living, the clothing, the architecture, the imple-
ments of war, the natural landscape. But it was not a question of his becoming "familiar" with objects, though it cannot be denied that a relatively unchanging physical background, since it can be taken for granted, is an advantage
to any poet. It is rather that *all* that he knew came under a
philosophy which was at once dramatic myth, a body of
truths, and a comprehensive view of life.

Now Wordsworth's point of view is still the point of view
of the unreflecting reader, and it is a point of view appropriate and applicable to the poets of the Romantic movement
who are still, to the general reader, all that poets ought to
be or can be. But the modern poetry that our general reader
finds baffling and obscure is a radical departure from the
Romantic achievement; it contains features that his "education" has not prepared him for; neither in perception nor in
intellect is he ready for a kind of poetry that does not offer
him the familiar poetical objects alongside the familiar
poetical truths.

Let us say, very briefly and only for the uses of this discussion, that the Romantic movement taught the reader to
look for inherently poetical objects, and to respond to them
"emotionally" in certain prescribed ways, these ways being
indicated by the "truths" interjected at intervals among the
poetical objects.

Certain modern poets offer no inherently poetical objects,
and they fail to instruct the reader in the ways he must feel
about the objects. All experience, then, becomes potentially
the material of poetry—not merely the pretty and the agree-
able—and the modern poet makes it possible for us to "respond" to this material in all the ways in which men everywhere may feel and think. On the ground of common sense
—a criterion that the reader invokes against the eccentric

moderns—the modern poet has a little the better of the argument, for to him poetry is not a special package tied up in pink ribbon: it is one of the ways that we have of knowing the world. And since the world is neither wholly pretty nor wholly easy to understand, poetry becomes a very difficult affair, demanding both in its writing and in its reading all the intellectual power that we have. But it is very hard for people to apply their minds to poetry, since it is one of our assumptions that come down from the early nineteenth century that our intellects are for mathematics and science, our emotions for poetry.

Who are these modern poets? Some twenty years ago they were supposed to be Mr. Lindsay, Mr. Masters, and Mr. Carl Sandburg. When Mr. Sandburg's poetry first appeared, it was said to be both ugly and obscure; now it is easy and beautiful to high-school students, and even to their teachers, whose more advanced age must have given them a prejudice in favor of the metrical, the pretty, and the "poetical" object. Doubtless the "obscure" moderns are the poets whom Mr. Max Eastman has ridiculed in *The Literary Mind,* and whom Mr. Cleanth Brooks, in *Modern Poetry and the Tradition,* distinguishes as the leaders of a poetic revolution as far-reaching as the Romantic revolution brought in by *Lyrical Ballads* in 1798.

The volumes by Mr. Eastman and Mr. Brooks are of uneven value, but I recommend them to be read together; and I would suggest that it is exceedingly dangerous and misleading to read Mr. Eastman alone. Yet, although Mr. Eastman is aggressive, sensational, and personal in his attacks, he has been widely read; while Mr. Brooks, who is sober, restrained, and critical, will win one reader for Mr. Eastman's fifty. Mr. Eastman is a debater, not a critic; and he is plausible because, like the toothpaste manufacturer, he offers his product in the name of science. Reading his book some years ago, I expected on every page to see the picture of the white-coated doctor with the test tube and the goatee, and under it the caption: "Science says . . ." But why science? Simply because Mr. Eastman, being still in the Romantic movement, but not knowing that he is, insists that the poet get hold of some "truths" that will permit him to tell the reader what to think about the new poetical objects of our time: he must think scientifically or not at all. Eastman's *The Literary Mind* is an interesting document of our age; Brooks's *Modern Poetry and the Tradition* will probably survive as an epoch-making critical synthesis of the modern movement.

The poets of the new revolution range all the way from the greatest distinction to charlatanism—a feature of every revolution, literary or political. Mr. Eastman can make the best moderns sound like the worst—as no doubt he could make the great passages of "The Prelude" sound like "Peter Bell" if he set his hand to it; and he found, as he confesses with candor and chagrin, that certain passages in the later works of Shakespeare strongly resemble some of the poetry of the modern "Cult of Unintelligibility"; but this hot potato, because he doesn't know what to do with it, he quickly drops. It is not my purpose to make Mr. Eastman the whipping-boy of a school of critics; of his school, he is one of the best. What I wish to emphasize is the negative of his somewhat sly contention that an admirer of Eliot's *Ash Wednesday* must also be an admirer of Miss Stein's *Geography and Plays*, that there is only a great lump of modernist verse in which no distinctions are possible. By such tactics we could discredit Browning with quotations from Mrs. Hemans. I notice this palpable nonsense because Mr. Eastman has been widely read by professors of English, who are really rather glad to hear this sort of thing, since it spares them the trouble of reading a body of poetry for which there are no historical documents and of which generations of other professors have not told them what to think.

In this essay I cannot elucidate a great many modern poems—a task that at the present time would be only a slight service to the reader; for in the state of his education and mine, we should have to undertake the infinite series of elucidations. We have no critical method; we have no principles to guide us. Every poem being either a unique expression of personality or a response to an environment, we should know at the end of the tenth difficult poem only what we knew at the end of the first; we could only cite the personalities and the environments. What I wish to do here, then, is not to explain certain modern poems but rather to discuss the reasons, as I see them, why certain kinds of poetry are difficult today.

The most pervasive reason of all is the decline of the art of reading—in an age in which there is more print than the world has seen before. If you ask why this is so, the answer is that impressionistic education in all its varieties, chiefly the variety known as "progressive education," is rapidly making us a nation of illiterates: a nation of people without letters. For you do not have to attend to the letters and words on the page in order to "read" what is there. In an essay entitled "The Retreat of the Humanities" (*English Journal*, February, 1939, p. 127), Mr. Louis B. Wright quotes an interesting passage from another essay, "Supervising the Creative Teaching of Poetry," whose author Mr. Wright mercifully leaves anonymous:

> The teaching of poetry divides itself naturally into two areas of enterprise, each with its essential conditioning validities. . . . Comprehending a poem need not involve any intellectual or formal concern with its technique, prose content, type, moral, diction, analysis, social implications, etc. Comprehending a poem is essentially an organic experience, essentially a response to the poetic stimulus of the author. Poetic comprehension may be verbalized or it may not.

In short, poetic comprehension does not involve anything at all, least of all the poem to be comprehended. Mr. Wright remarks that this is "equivalent to the emotion that comes from being tickled on the ear with a feather. . . . Before such ideas and such jargon, sincere advocates of learning sometimes retreat in despair." Yes; but for the sake of the good people whose "education" has doomed them to teach poetry with this monstrous jargon, I wish to examine the quotation more closely, and more in contempt than in despair. We have here, then, an offensive muddle of echoes ranging from business jargon through sociological jargon to the jargon of the Watsonian behaviorists. One must be more pleased than disappointed to find that poetry "naturally divides" itself, without any intellectual effort on our part, into "areas" having "conditioning validities" that are "essential"—an adjective that our Anonymity repeats twice adverbially in a wholly different non-sense. Now, if technique, diction, analysis, and the others are irrelevant in the reading of poetry, in what respect does poetry differ from automobiles: cannot one be conditioned to automobiles? No, that is not the answer. One is conditioned by responding to the "poetic stimulus of the author." One gets the poet's personality; and there's no use thinking about the poet's personality, since one cannot think, "verbalization" now being the substitute for thought—as indeed it is, in our Anonymity.

I am sure that thoughtful persons will have perceived, beyond this vulgar haze, an "idea" curiously resembling something that I have already alluded to in this essay: it is astonishing how regularly the pseudo-scientific vocabularies are used in order to reach a poetic theory that the most ignorant "man in the street" already holds. That theory I call "decadent Romanticism," but I should like it to be plainly understood that I am not attacking the great Romantic poets. Romanticism gave us the "Ode to a Nightingale"; decadent Romanticism is now giving us the interminable ballads and local-color lyrics of Mr. Coffin and Mr. Stephen Benét—as it gave us, some twenty-five years ago, Joyce Kilmer's "Trees," the "favorite poem" of the American people, taught piously by every high-school teacher, and sometimes aggressively by college professors when they want to show what poetry ought to be; surely one of the preposterously bad lyrics in any language.

What I said earlier that I should like to call attention to

again is: The weakness of the Romantic sensibility is that it gave us a poetry of "poetical" (or *poetized*) objects, pre-digested perceptions; and in case there should be any misunderstanding about the poetical nature of these objects, we also got "truths" attached to them—truths that in modern jargon are instructions to the reader to "respond" in a certain way to the poetical object, which is the "stimulus." And in the great body of nineteenth-century lyrical poetry—whose worst ancestor was verse like Shelley's "I arise from dreams of thee"—the poet's personal emotions became the "poetic stimulus." The poem as a formal object to be looked at, to be studied, to be construed (in more than the grammatical sense, but first of all in that sense), dissolved into biography and history, so that in the long run the poetry was only a misunderstood pretext for the "study" of the sexual life of the poet, of the history of his age, of anything else that the scholar wished to "study"; and he usually wished to study anything but poetry.

Now our Anonymity has said that prose content, morals, and social implications are irrelevant in reading poetry, and it looks as if there were a fundamental disagreement between him and the biographical and historical scholars. There is no such disagreement. Once you arrive with Anonymity at the "poetic stimulus of the author," you have reached his biography and left his poetry behind; and, on principle, Anonymity cannot rule out the morals and the social implications (however much he may wish to rule them out), because morals and social implications are what you get when you discuss personality.

At this point I ought to enter a *caveat* to those persons who are thinking that I would dispense with historical scholarship. It is, in fact, indispensable; it is pernicious only when some ham actor in an English department uses it to wring tears from the Sophomores, by describing the sad death of Percy Shelley. Let me illustrate one of its genuine uses. Here are the first two stanzas of Donne's "Valediction: forbidding mourning":

As virtuous men passe mildly away,
   And whisper to their soules, to goe,
Whilst some of their sad friends doe say,
   The breath goes now, and some say, no:

Soe let us melt, and make no noise,
   No teare-floods, nor sigh-tempests move,
T'were prophanation of our joyes
   To tell the layetie our love.

The elaborate simile here asserts on several planes the analogy between the act of love and the moment of death. But if you happen to know that in Middle English and down through the sixteenth century the verb *die* has as a secondary meaning, "to perform the act of love," you are able to extend the analogy into a new frame of reference. The analogy contains a concealed pun. But we are detecting the pun not in order to show that a man in the late sixteenth century was still aware of the early, secondary meaning of *die;* we are simply using this piece of information to extend our knowledge of what happens in the first eight lines of the poem. It is of no interest to anybody that Donne knew how to make this pun; it is of capital interest to know what the pun does to the meaning of the poem.

I have seemed to be talking about what I consider bad poetic theory; but I have also been talking about something much larger, that cannot here be adequately discussed: I have been talking about a bad theory of education. If only briefly, I must notice it because it abets the bad poetic theory and is at the bottom of the popular complaint that modern poetry is difficult. The complainant assumes that he understands all English poetry up to, say, about 1917—a date that I select because in that year Eliot's *Prufrock and Other Observations* was published. But, as a matter of fact, the complainant does not understand Marvel and Donne any better than he understands Eliot; and I doubt that he can read Sidney any better than he can read Pound; he could not read Raleigh at all, and he has never heard of Fulke Greville.

So it is not "modern" poetry which is difficult; it is rather a certain kind of poetry as old, in English, as the sixteenth century, and, in Italian, much older than that. It is a kind of poetry that requires of the reader the fullest co-operation of all his intellectual resources, all his knowledge of the world, and all the persistence and alertness that he now thinks only of giving to scientific studies.

This kind of poetry must have the direct and *active* participation of a reader who today, because he has been pampered by bad education, expects to lie down and be *passive* when he is reading poetry. He admits, for some obscure reason, that poetry is a part of his education; but he has been taught to believe that education is *conditioning:* something is being done to him, he is not doing anything himself. And that is why he cannot read poetry.

A conditioning theory of education may be good enough for animals in the zoo, but it is not good enough for human beings; and it is time that this symptom of decadence were known for what it is, and not as enlightenment, "science," liberalism, and democracy. I do not know whether we are living in a democracy; it is, at any rate, an anomaly of democratic theory that it should produce, in education, a theory that we are bundles of reflexes without intelligence.

The theory assumes, first of all, that education is a process of getting adjusted to an environment. Something known as "personality" is making *responses* to things known as *stimuli*. In the educational environment there are *stimuli* called "poems," to which you make responses.

Now while you are making a response, you are not doing more than a chimpanzee or a Yahoo would be doing. But should you do more than respond, you might perform an act of intelligence, of knowing, of cognition. In the conditioning theory there is no cognition because there is no intelligence. Of what use is intelligence? It does not at all help to describe the "behavior" of persons who are getting responses from the *stimuli* of poems. What the poem is in itself, what it says, is no matter. It is an irrelevant question. But if you can imagine it not to be irrelevant, if you can imagine "Lycidas" to be something more than the stimulation of "drives," "appetites," "attitudes," in certain "areas," then you have got to use your intelligence, which, after you have been progressively educated, you probably no longer have.

As I conceive this gloomy situation, it is far more complicated than the violent synopsis of it that I have just sketched. The complications would distribute the blame to many historical villains, of whom the teachers'-college racketeers (some of them misguided idealists) are only a conspicuous contemporary group. The trouble goes far back, farther even than the Romantic movement, when, for the first time in Western art, we had the belief that poetry is chiefly or even wholly an emotional experience.

Does poetry give us an emotional experience? What is an "emotional experience"? And what is an "intellectual experience"?

These are difficult questions. We are proceeding today as if they were no longer questions, as if we knew the answers, and knew them as incontestable truths. If by "an emotional experience" we mean one in which we find ourselves "moved," then we mean nothing; we are only translating a Latin word into English: a tautology. If by "an intellectual experience" we mean that we are using our minds on the relations of words, the relation of words and rhythm, the relation of the abstract words to the images, all the relations together—and if, moreover, we succeed in reducing all these things to the complete determination of logic, so that there is nothing left over, then this intellectual experience is a tautology similar to that of the emotional experience: we are intellectually using our intellects, as before we were emotionally being moved. But if on the other hand, as in the great seventeenth-century poets, you find that exhaustive analysis applied to the texture of image and metaphor fails to turn up any inconsistency, and at the same time fails to get all the meaning of the poem into a logical statement, you are participating in a poetic experience. And both intellect and emotion become meaningless in discussing it.

I have had to make that statement abstract, or not at all; it needs many pages of illustration. I can cite only three examples of poetry, which I hope will somewhat illuminate it. The first example is William Browne's slight "Epitaph on the Countesse Dowager of Pembroke," a favorite anthology piece, and one that is neither in the metaphysical style of its period nor romantically modern:

> Underneath this sable Herse
> Lyes the subject of all verse:
> Sydney's sister, Pembroke's Mother:
> Death, ere thou hast slaine another
> Faire and learned and good as she,
> Time shall throw a dart at thee.

I find this poem perennially moving (exciting, interesting), and it is plain that we cannot be moved by it until we understand it; and to understand it we have got to *analyze* the meaning of the difference here asserted as existing between Time and Death, who are dramatically personified and in conflict. Since, in one of the major modes of poetry, Death is conceived as the work of Time, we must perform a dissociation of ideas, and see Time as turning against himself, so that the destruction of Death is actually the destruction of Time. However far you may take these distinctions, no inconsistency appears; nothing contradicts anything else that is said in the poem; yet we have not reduced the poem to strict logic. Browne has offered certain particulars that are irreducible: the Sydney and Pembroke families (for the sake of whose dignity this upheaval of the order of nature will occur); and then there is the dart, a dramatic and particular image that does not contradict, yet cannot be assimilated into, a logical paraphrase of the poem. Is this poem an emotional experience? And yet it is not an "intellectual" experience.

The second quotation must be slighted, but it is so familiar that a few lines will bring the whole poem before the reader

—Shelley's "When the lamp is shattered"; I quote the last stanza:

> Its [Love's] passions will rock thee,
> As the storms rock the ravens on high:
>     Bright reason will mock thee,
> Like the sun from a wintry sky.
>         From thy nest every rafter
> Will rot, and thine eagle home
>     Leave thee naked to laughter,
> When leaves fall and cold winds come.

The general "argument" is that the passing of spiritual communion from lovers leaves them sad and, in this last stanza, the prey of lust and self-mockery, and even of the mockery of the world ("naked to laughter"). The first line sets the tone and the "response" that the reader is to maintain to the end: we are told in advance what the following lines will mean: an abstraction that will relieve us of the trouble of examining the particular instances. Indeed, when these appear, the development of their imagery is confused and vague. The ravens in the second line are eagles in the sixth; but, after all, they are only generically birds; greater particularity in them would have compromised their poeticism as objects, or interfered with the response we are instructed to make to them. I pass over "Bright reason," the self-mockery, for the mockery of the world. Are we to suppose that other birds come by and mock the raven (eagle), or are we to shift the field of imagery and see "thee" as a woman? Now in the finest poetry we cannot have it both ways. We can have a multiple meaning through ambiguity, but we cannot have an incoherent structure of images. Shelley, in confusion, or carelessness, or haste, could not sustain the nest-bird metaphor and say all that he wished to say; so, in order to say it, he changed the figure and ruined the poem. The more we track down the implications of his imagery, the greater the confusion; the more we track down the implications of the imagery in the best verse of Donne, Marvel, Raleigh, Milton, Hopkins,

Yeats, Eliot, Ransom, Stevens, the richer the meaning of the poem. Shelley's poem is confused. Are we to conclude that therefore it offers an emotional experience?

In conclusion, one more poem—this one by W. H. Auden:

> Our hunting fathers told the story
>    Of the sadness of the creatures,
> Pitied the limits and the lack
>    Set in their finished features;
> Saw in the lion's intolerant look,
>    Behind the quarry's dying glare
> Love raging for the personal glory
>    That reason's gift would add,
> The liberal appetite and power,
>    The rightness of a god.
>
> Who nurtured in that fine tradition
>    Predicted the result,
> Guessed love by nature suited to
>    The intricate ways of guilt;
> That human company could so
>    His southern gestures modify
> And make it his mature ambition
>    To think no thought but ours,
> To hunger, work illegally,
>    And be anonymous?

In this poem there is an immense complication of metaphor, but I do not propose to unravel it. I would say just this: that all the complications can be returned without confusion or contradiction to a definite, literal, and coherent field of imagery; that when the poet wishes to extend his meaning, he does it by means of this field of metaphor, not by changing the figure, which is: the hunter debases his human nature (Love) in his arrogant, predatory conquest of the world, and Love itself becomes not merely morally bad but evil. The field of imagery, to which all the implications refer, is that of the hunting squire, who by a deft ambiguity quickly becomes predatory man.

I halt the analysis here because, as I have already said, we need something more fundamental in reading poetry than the occasional analyses of poems. I would say then, in conclusion, that modern poetry is difficult because we have lost the art of reading any poetry that will not read itself to us; that thus our trouble is a fundamental problem of education, which may be more fundamental than education. We may be approaching the time when we shall no longer be able to read anything and shall be subject to passive conditioning. Until this shall happen, however, we might possibly begin to look upon language as a field of study, not as an impressionistic debauch. If we wish to understand anything, there is only the hard way; if we wish to understand Donne and Eliot, perhaps we had better begin, young, to read the classical languages, and a little later the philosophers. There is probably no other way.

# TECHNIQUES OF FICTION

## *1944*

THERE must be many techniques of fiction, but how many?
I suppose a great many more than there are techniques of
poetry. Why this should be so, if it is, nobody quite knows,
and if we knew, I do not know what use the knowledge would
have. For the great disadvantage of all literary criticism is
its practical ignorance, which in the very nature of its aims
must be incurable. Even the aims of criticism are unknown,
beyond very short views; for example, in the criticism of the
novel, Mr. Percy Lubbock tells us that the secret of the art is
the strategy of "point of view"; Mr. E. M. Forster that the
novelist must simply give us "life," or the illusion of "bounc-
ing" us through it—which looks like a broader view than Mr.
Lubbock's, until we pause to examine it, when it turns out
to be worse than narrow, since to look at everything is to see
nothing; or again Mr. Edwin Muir holds that "structure" is
the key to the novelist's success or failure. There is no need
here to explain what these critics mean by "point of view,"
or "life," or "structure"; but they all mean something useful
—in a short view, beyond which (I repeat) critics seem to
know little or nothing.

What the novelists know may be another thing altogether,
and it is that knowledge which ought to be our deepest con-

cern. You will have to allow me the paradox of presuming to know what the novelists know—or some of them at any rate—while as a critic I profess to know nothing. The presumption might encourage us to predict from the very nature of the critic's ignorance the nature and quality of the knowledge possible to good writers of fiction. The novelist keeps before him constantly the structure and substance of his fiction as a whole, to a degree to which the critic can never apprehend it. For the first cause of critical ignorance is, of course, the limitations of our minds, about which we can do little, work at them as we will. It is the special ignorance by which we, as critics, are limited in the act of reading any extended work of the imagination. The imaginative work must always differ to such a great degree as almost to differ in kind from philosophical works, which our minds apprehend and retain almost as wholes through the logical and deductive structures which powerfully aid the memory. Who can remember, well enough to pronounce upon it critically, all of *War and Peace,* or *The Wings of the Dove,* or even *Death in Venice,* the small enclosed world of which ought at least to do something to aid our memories? I have reread all three of these books in the past year; yet for the life of me I could not pretend to know them as wholes, and without that knowledge I lack the materials of criticism.

Because Mr. Lubbock seems to know more than anybody else about this necessary ignorance of the critic, and for other important reasons, I believe him to be the best critic who has ever written about the novel. His book, *The Craft of Fiction,* is very nearly a model of critical procedure. Even in so fine a study as Albert Thibaudet's *Gustave Flaubert* there is nothing like the actual, as opposed to the merely professed, critical modesty of numerous statements like this by Lubbock: "Our critical faculty may be admirable; we may be thoroughly capable of judging a book justly, if only we could watch it at ease. But fine taste and keen perception are of no use to us if we cannot retain the image of the book; and the image escapes and evades us like a cloud." Where, then, does Lubbock get the material of his criticism? He gets as much of it as any critic ever gets by means of a bias which he constantly pushes in the direction of extreme simplification of the novel in terms of "form," or "point of view" (after James's more famous phrase, the "post of observation"), or more generally in terms of the controlling intelligence which determines the range and quality of the scene and the action. It is the only book on fiction which has earned unanimous dislike among other critics (I do not know three novelists who have read it), and the reason, I think, is that it is, in its limited terms, wholly successful; or, if that is too great praise, it is successful in the same sense, and to no less degree than the famous lecture notes on the Greek drama taken down by an anonymous student at the Lyceum in the fourth century B.C. The lecture notes and *The Craft of Fiction* are studies of their respective arts in terms of form; and I think that Lubbock had incomparably the more difficult job to do. The novel has at no time enjoyed anything like the number and the intensity of objective conventions which the drama, even in its comparatively formless periods, has offered to the critic. The number of techniques possible in the novel are probably as many as its conventions are few.

Having said so much in praise of Mr. Lubbock, I shall not, I hope, seem to take it back if I say that even-his intense awareness of what the novelist knows fails somehow, or perhaps inevitably, to get into his criticism. Anybody who has just read his account of *Madame Bovary* comes away with a sense of loss, which is the more intense if he has also just read that novel; though what the loss is he no more than Mr. Lubbock will be able to say. Yet no critic has ever turned so many different lights, from so many different directions, upon any other novel (except perhaps the lights that are called today the social and the historical); and yet what we get is not properly a revelation of the techniques of *Madame Bovary* but rather what I should call a marvelously astute chart of the operations of the central intelligence which binds all the little pieces of drama together into the pictorial

biography of a silly, sad, and hysterical little woman, Emma
Bovary. It is this single interest, this undeviating pursuit of
one great clue, this sticking to the "short view" till the last
horn blows and night settles upon the hunting field, which
largely explains both the greatness of Mr. Lubbock's book
and the necessary and radical ignorance of criticism. We
cannot be both broad and critical, except in so far as knowledge of the world, of ideas, and of man generally is broadening; but then that knowledge has nothing to do specifically
with the critical job; it only keeps it from being inhuman.
That is something; but it is not criticism. To be critical is to
be narrow in the crucial act or process of judgment.

But after we gather up all the short views of good critics,
and have set the limits to their various ignorances, we are
confronted with what is left out or, if you will, left over:
I have a strong suspicion that this residue of the novel or
the story is what the author knew as he wrote it. It is what
makes the little scenes, or even the big ones, "come off."
And while we no doubt learn a great deal about them when,
with Mr. Muir, we study the general structure, or the relation of scenes, or, with Mr. Lubbock, follow the godlike
control of the mind of Flaubert or of James through all the
scenes to the climax—while this knowledge is indispensable,
I should, myself, like to know more about the making of the
single scene, and all the techniques that contribute to it;
and I suspect that I am not asking the impossible, for this
kind of knowledge is very likely the only kind that is actually
within our range. It alone can be got at, definitely and at
particular moments, even after we have failed, with Mr.
Lubbock (honorable failure indeed), to "retain the image
of the book."

It sounds very simple, as no doubt it is essentially a simple
task to take a scene from a novel apart, and to see what
makes it tick; but how to do it must baffle our best inten-
tions. Suppose you want to understand by what arts Tolstoy,
near the beginning of *War and Peace*, before the ground
is laid, brings Peter, the bastard son of old Count Bezuhov,

into the old Count's dying presence, and makes, of the atmosphere of the house and of the young man and the old man, both hitherto unknown to us, one of the great scenes of fiction: you would scarcely know better than I where to take hold of it, and I have only the merest clue. Suppose you feel, as I do, that after Rawdon Crawley comes home (I believe from jail—it is hard to remember Thackeray) and finds Becky supping alone with Lord Steyne—suppose you feel that Thackeray should not have rung down the curtain the very moment Becky's exposure was achieved, but should have faced up to the tougher job of showing us Becky and Rawdon alone after Lord Steyne had departed: Is this a failure in a great novelist? If it is, why? The negative question, addressed to ourselves as persons interested in the techniques of an art, may also lead us to what the novelists know, or to much the same thing, what they should have known. And, to come nearer home, what is the matter with Ty Ty Walden's philosophical meditations, towards the end of *God's Little Acre*, which freezes up our credulity and provokes our fiercest denial? It is surely not that Ty Ty is merely expressing as well as he can the doctrine of the innate goodness of man in the midst of depravity. That doctrine will do as well as any other in the mouth of a fictional character provided his scene and his experience within the scene entitle him to utter it. but before we can believe that Ty Ty is actually thinking anything whatever, we have got in the first place to believe that Ty Ty is a man—which is precisely what Mr. Caldwell evidently did not think it important to make us do.

How shall we learn what to say about particular effects of the story, without which the great over-all structure and movement of the human experience which is the entire novel cannot be made credible to us? The professional critics pause only at intervals to descend to these minor effects which are of course the problems without which the other, more portentous problems which engage criticism could not exist. The fine artists of fiction, I repeat, because they produce these effects must understand them. And having produced them, they are silent about the ways they took to produce them, or paradoxical and mysterious like Flaubert, who told Maupassant to go to the station and look at the cab-drivers until he understood the typical cab-driver, and then to find the language to distinguish one cab-driver from all others in the world. It is the sort of *obiter dicta* which can found schools and movements, and the schools and movements often come to some good, even though the slogan, like this one, means little.

I suppose only the better novelists, like Defoe, Madame de La Fayette, Turgenev, Dickens, Flaubert, many others as great as these, some greater, like Tolstoy and Dostoevsky, knew the special secrets which I am trying, outside criticism, so to speak, to bring before you. There is almost a masonic tradition in the rise of any major art, from its undifferentiated social beginnings to the conscious aptitude which is the sign of a developed art form. Doubtless I ought to repeat once more that for some reason the moment the secrets of this aptitude come within the *provenance* of formal criticism, they vanish. They survive in the works themselves, and in the living confraternity of men of letters, who pass on by personal instruction to their successors the "tricks of the trade." The only man I have known in some twenty years of literary experience who was at once a great novelist and a great teacher, in this special sense, was the late Ford Madox Ford. His influence was immense, even upon writers who did not know him, even upon other writers, today, who have not read him. For it was through him more than any other man writing in English in our time that the great traditions of the novel came down to us. Joyce, a greater writer than Ford, represents by comparison a more restricted practice of the same literary tradition, a tradition that goes back to Stendhal in France, and to Jane Austen in England, coming down to us through Flaubert, James, Conrad, Joyce, Virginia Woolf and Ernest Hemingway.

It is a tradition which has its own secrets to offer; yet in saying that I am not claiming for it greater novelists than some other school can produce or novelists greater than those who just happen. There is Meredith (for those who, like Ramon Fernandez, can read him); there is Thomas Hardy, there is even the early H. G. Wells. But there is not Arnold Bennett; there is not John Galsworthy; not Hugh Walpole nor Frank Swinnerton. This is prejudice, not criticism. And these are all Britons, not Americans. I have no desire to play 'possum on the American question. Yet I am convinced that among American novelists who have had large publics since the last war, only Dreiser, Faulkner, and Hemingway are of major importance. There are "good" popular novelists who have done much to make us at home physically in our own country; they have given us our scenes, our people, and above all our history; and these were necessary to the preliminary knowledge of ourselves which we have been a little late in getting and which must be got and assimilated if we are going to be a mature people. Possibly the American novel had to accomplish the task that in Europe had been done by primitive chronicle, mémoire, ballad, strolling player. The American novel has had to find a new experience, and only in our time has it been able to pause for the difficult task of finding out how to get itself written. That is an old story with us, yet beneath it lies a complexity of feeling that from Hawthorne down to our time has baffled our best understanding. The illustration is infinite in its variety. At this moment I think of my two favorite historians, Herodotus and Joinville, and I am embarrassed from time to time because Herodotus, the pagan, seems nearer to my experience than Joinville, the Christian chronicler of St. Louis. It is perhaps easier for us to feel comfortable with the remote and relatively neutral elements of our culture. Those experiences of Europe which just precede or overlap the American experience bemuse us, and introduce a sort of chemical ambivalence into our judgment. Joinville is both nearer to me than Herodotus, and less immediate. What American could not be brought to confess a similar paradox? To our

European friends who are now beginning to know us, and who in all innocence may subscribe to the popular convention of The Simple American Mind, I would say, if it is not too impolite: Beware.

But the American novel is not my present subject, nor, thank heaven, the American mind. My subject is merely the technique of fiction which now at last I feel that I am ready to talk about, not critically, you understand, but as a member of a guild. Ford used to say that he wrote his novels in the tone of one English gentleman whispering into the ear of another English gentleman: how much irony he intended I never knew; I hope a great deal. I intend none at all when I say that these remarks are set down by an artisan for other artisans.

Gustave Flaubert created the modern novel. Gustave Flaubert created the modern short story. He created both because he created modern fiction. I am not prepared to say that he created all our fictional forms and structures, the phases of the art of fiction that interest Mr. Lubbock and Mr. Muir. He did not originate all those features of the short story which interest historians and anthologists. These are other matters altogether. And I do not like to think that Flaubert created modern fiction because I do not like Flaubert. It was the fashion in France, I believe, until the Fall, to put Stendhal above Flaubert. I am not sure but I suspect that a very tired generation felt more at ease with a great writer whose typical heroes are persons of mere energy and whose books achieve whatever clarity and form that they do achieve as an accident of the moral ferocity of the author. But without *Le Rouge et Le Noir,* or without what it put into circulation in French literary *milieu* after 1830, Flaubert could not have written *Madame Bovary.* I do not like to think that Stendhal did this because I do not like Stendhal. Both Stendhal and Flaubert had the single dedication to art which makes the disagreeable man. Doubtless it would be pleasanter if the great literary discoveries could be made by gentlemen like Henry James, who did make his share, and

who, of course, was a greater novelist than either of these
Frenchmen; or by English squires; but we have got to take
them, as Henry James would not do in the instance of Flaubert, as they come, and they often come a little rough.

A moment ago I introduced certain aspersions upon a few
English novelists of the recent past, but it was with a pur-
pose, for their limitations, sharply perceived by the late
Virginia Woolf in her famous essay *Mr. Bennett and Mrs.
Brown,* will make quite clear the difference between the
novelist who, with Mr. Forster, merely bounces us along
and the novelist who tries to do the whole job, the job that
Flaubert first taught him to do. Mrs. Woolf is discussing
Hilda Lessways, Arnold Bennett's heroine, and she says:

> But we cannot hear her mother's voice, or Hilda's voice;
> we can only hear Mr. Bennett's voice telling us facts
> about rents and freeholds and copyholds and fines. What
> can Mr. Bennett be about? I have formed my own
> opinion of what Mr. Bennett is about—he is trying to make
> us imagine for him. . . .

"Trying to make us imagine for him"—the phrase erects a
Chinese wall between all that is easy, pleasant, and perhaps
merely socially useful in modern fiction, and all that is
rigorous, sober, and self-contained. Mrs. Woolf, again, in
speaking of the novels of Galsworthy, Bennett and Wells,
says: "Yet what odd books they are! Sometimes I wonder if
we are right to call them books at all. For they leave one
with a strange feeling of incompleteness and dissatisfaction.
In order to complete them it seems necessary to do something—to join a society, or, more desperately, to write a
cheque."

That is very nearly the whole story: the novelist who
tries to make us imagine for him is perhaps trying to make
us write a check—a very good thing to do, and I am not
sure that even the socially unconscious Flaubert was deeply
opposed to it, though I shall not attempt to speak for him
on the question of joining societies. Let us see this matter as

reasonably as we can. All literature has a social or moral
or religious purpose: the writer has something that he has
got to say to the largest public possible. In spite of Flaubert's belief that he wrote only for himself, this is as true of
*Madame Bovary* as of *Uncle Tom's Cabin.* Is there a real
difference between these books that might justify us in
setting apart two orders of literature? Perhaps; for the difference is very great between getting it all inside the book
and leaving some of it irresponsibly outside. For even though
the check be written in a good cause it is the result of an
irresponsible demand upon the part of the novelist. But the
distinction is not, I think, absolute, nor should it be. And I
am sure that Sainte-Beuve was right when he wrote in his
review of *Madame Bovary* that not all young married women
in Normandy were like Emma: was there not the case of the
childless young matron of central France who, instead of
taking lovers and then taking arsenic, "adopted children
about her . . . and instructed them in moral culture"? Very
good; for it is obvious that persons who join societies and
write checks for moral culture are proper characters of
fiction, as indeed all human beings of all degrees of charity
or misanthropy are. But that is not the point at issue.

That point is quite simply that Flaubert, for the first time
consciously and systematically, but not for the first time in
the history of fiction, and not certainly of poetry—Flaubert
taught us how to put this overworked and allegorical check
*into* the novel, into its complex texture of scene, character
and action: which, of course, is one way of saying that he
did the complete imaginative job himself, and did not merely
point to what was going on, leaving the imaginative specification to our good will or to our intellectual vanity. (I pause
here to remark the existence of a perpetual type of critic who
prefers inferior literature, because it permits him to complete it. Flaubert understood the critics who, committed to
the public function of teacher, resent being taught.) This
completeness of presentation in the art of fiction was not,
I repeat, something new, but I gather that it had previously

appeared only here and there, by the sheer accident of genius: I think of Petronius; a few incidents in Boccaccio; half a dozen scenes by the Duke of Saint-Simon (the memorialists shade imperceptibly into the novelists); the great scene in which the Prince de Clèves tells his wife that he has refrained from expressing his love for her because he wished to avoid conduct improper to a husband; Emma Woodhouse with Mr. Knightly at the parlor table looking at the picture-album; countless other moments in early prose literature; but most of all that great forerunner, *Moll Flanders*, which is so much all of a piece in the Flaubertian canon that sometimes I think that Flaubert wrote it; or that nobody wrote either Defoe or Flaubert. For when literature reaches this stage of maturity, it is anonymous, and it matters little who writes it.

This is extravagant language. Or is it? It is no more than we are accustomed to when we talk about poetry, or music, or most of all the classical drama. The fourth-century lecture notes, to which I have already referred, some time ago licensed the most pretentious claims for the stage, and for poetry generally. I am only saying that fiction can be, has been, and *is* an art, as the various poetries are arts. Is this an extravagant claim? Only, I am convinced, in the minds of the more relaxed practitioners of this art, who excuse something less than the utmost talent and effort, and in the minds of critics who find the critical task more exacting than historical reporting, which reduces the novel to a news supplement. Was, as a matter of fact, Emma typical of young Norman womanhood? Are the Okies and Arkies just as Steinbeck represents them? What a triumph for the historians when it was found that there had actually been a young man whose end was like Julien Sorel's! And is it true what Mr. Faulkner says about Dixie? If it is, is what Mr. Stark Young says also true? This, I submit, is the temper of American criticism of fiction, with rare exceptions of little influence.

It is time now, towards the end of this *causerie*, to produce an image, an *exemplum,* something out of the art of fiction that underlies all the major problems of "picture and drama," symmetry, foreshortening, narrative pattern, pace and language—all those complexities of the novelist's art which Henry James, alone of the great fictionists, tried to explain (how much he coyly evaded!) in his famous Prefaces: problems that laid the ground for Mr. Lubbock's beautiful study. I am looking for something very simple and, in its direct impact, conclusive; a scene or an incident that achieves fullness of realization in terms of what it gives us to see and to hear. It must offer us fullness of rendition, not mere direction or statement. Don't state, says James, time and again —render! Don't tell us what is happening, let it happen! So I would translate James. For our purposes here it cannot be too great a scene, if we would see all round it: it must be a scene that will give us the most elementary instruction in that branch of the art of which the critics tell us little. What shall it be? Shall it be Prince André lying wounded under the wide heavens? Shall it be Moll Flanders peeping out of the upstairs window of the inn at her vanishing fourth (or is it fifth?) and undivorced husband, slyly avoiding him because she is in the room with her fifth or is it sixth? I could find perfect *exempla* in James himself. What could be better than Milly Theale's last soirée before she becomes too ill to appear again? Then there are James's fine "sitting-room scenes," the man and the woman talking out the destiny of one or both of them: Lambert Strether and Maria Gostrey, John Marcher and May Bartram, Merton Densher and Milly Theale. Or there is Strether looking down upon the boat in which Chad Newsome and Madame de Vionnet, unaware of Strether's scrutiny, betray that air of intimacy which discloses them for the first time to Strether as lovers.

Yet about these excellent scenes there is something outside our purpose, a clue that would sidetrack us into the terms of form and structure which I have virtually promised to neglect. Let us select an easy and perhaps even quite vulgar scene, a stock scene, in fact, that we should expect

to find in a common romantic novel, or even in a Gothic story
provided the setting were reduced to the bourgeois scale. Let
the situation be something like this: A pretty young married
woman, bored with her husband, a small-town doctor, has
had an affair of sentiment with a young man, who has by
this time left town. Growing more desperate, she permits
herself to be seduced by a neighboring landowner, a coarse
Lothario, who soon tires of her. Our scene opens with the
receipt of his letter of desertion. He is going away and will
not see her again. The young woman receives the letter with
agitation and runs upstairs to the attic, where having read
the letter she gives way to hysteria. She looks out the window
down into the street, and decides to jump and end it all. But
she grows dizzy and recoils. After a moment she hears her
husband's voice; the servant touches her arm; she comes to
and recovers.

It is distinctly unpromising: James would not have touched
it; Balzac, going the whole hog, might have let her jump, or
perhaps left her poised for the jump while he resumed the
adventures of Vautrin. But in any case there she stands, and
as I have reported the scene you have got to take my word
for it that she is there at all: you do not see her, you do not
hear the rapid breathing and the beating heart, and you
have, again, only my word for it that she is dizzy. What I
have done here, in fact, is precisely what Mrs. Woolf accused
the Georgian novelists of doing: I am trying to make you imagine for me, perhaps even covertly trying to make you write
a check for the Society for the Improvement of Provincial
Culture, or the Society for the Relief of Small Town Boredom, or for a subscription to the Book of the Month Club
which would no doubt keep the young woman at improv-
ing her mind, and her mind off undesirable lovers. I hope
that we shall do all these good things. But you must bear
in mind that the Book of the Month Club would probably
send her the kind of literature that I have just written for
you, so that she too might take to writing checks. Is there
any guarantee that they would be good checks? The question

brings us up short against certain permanent disabilities of
human nature, which we should do well to see as objectively
as possible, in the language of a greater artist; which is just
what we shall now proceed to do:

Charles was there; she saw him; he spoke to her; she
heard nothing, and she went on quickly up the stairs,
breathless, distraught, dumb, and ever holding this hor-
rible piece of paper, that crackled between her fingers
like a plate of sheet-iron. On the second floor she stopped
before the attic-door, that was closed.

Then she tried to calm herself; she recalled the letter;
she must finish it; she did not dare to. And where? How?
She would be seen! "Ah, no! here," she thought, "I shall
be all right."

Emma pushed open the door and went in.

The slates threw straight down a heavy heat that
gripped her temples, stifled her; she dragged herself to
the closed garret-window. She drew back the bolt, and
the dazzling light burst in with a leap.

Opposite, beyond the roofs, stretched the open country till it was lost to sight. Down below, underneath her,
the village square was empty; the stones of the pave-
ment glittered, the weathercocks on the houses were
motionless. At the corner of the street from a lower story,
rose a kind of humming with strident modulations. It
was Binet turning.

She leant against the embrasure of the window, and
reread the letters with angry sneers. But the more she
fixed her attention upon it, the more confused were her
ideas. She saw him again, heard him, encircled him with
her arms, and the throbs of her heart, that beat against
her breast like blows of a sledge-hammer, grew faster
and faster, with uneven intervals. She looked about her
with the wish that the earth might crumble into pieces.
Why not end it all? What restrained her? She was free.

She advanced, looked at the paving-stones, saying to herself, "Come! Come!"

The luminous ray that came straight up from below drew the weight of her body towards the abyss. It seemed to her that the floor dipped on end like a tossing boat. She was right at the edge, almost hanging, surrounded by vast space. The blue of the heavens suffused her, the air was whirling in her hollow head; she had but to yield, to let herself be taken; and the humming of the lathe never ceased, like an angry voice calling her.

"Emma! Emma!" cried Charles.

She stopped.

"Wherever are you? Come!"

The thought that she had just escaped from death made her faint with terror. She closed her eyes; then she shivered at the touch of a hand on her sleeve; it was Félicité.

"Master is waiting for you, madame; the soup is on the table."

And she had to go down to sit at table.

The English translation is not good; its failure to convey the very slight elevation of tone is a fundamental failure. It is not a rhetorical elevation, but rather one of perfect formality and sobriety. We are not looking at this scene through Emma's eyes. We occupy a position slightly above and to one side, where we see her against the full setting; yet observe that at the same time we see nothing that she does not see, hear nothing that she does not hear. It is one of the amazing paradoxes of the modern novel, whose great subject is a man alone in society or even against society, almost never with society, that out of this view of man isolated we see developed to the highest possible point of virtuosity and power a technique of putting man wholly into his physical setting. The action is not stated from the point of view of the author; it is rendered in terms of situation and scene. To have made this the viable property of the art of fiction was to have virtually made the art of fiction. And that, I think, is our debt to Flaubert.

But we should linger over this scene if only to try our hands at what I shall now, for the first time, call sub-criticism, or the animal tact which permits us occasionally to see connections and correspondences which our rational powers, unaided, cannot detect. What capital feature of the scene seems (if it does) to render the actuality more than any other? The great fact, I think, is the actuality, and your sense of it is all that is necessary. Yet I like to linger over the whirring lathe of old Binet, a lay figure or "flat character" who has done little in the novel and will never do much, and whose lathe we merely noted from the beginning as a common feature of a small town like Yonville. I should like to know when Flaubert gave him the lathe, whether just to tag him for us; whether, writing the present scene, he went back and gave it to him as a "plant" for use here later; or whether, having given him the lathe, he decided it would be useful in this scene.

What is its use? James said that the work of fiction must be "a direct impression of life," a very general requirement; but in the perspective of nearly ninety years since the publication of *Madame Bovary* and the rise of the Impressionist novel through Henry James, James Joyce, and Virginia Woolf, the phrase takes on a more specific sense. Mind you the phrase is not "direct representation," which only the stage can give us. But here, using this mechanic's tool, Flaubert gives us a direct *impression* of Emma's sensation at a particular moment (which not even the drama could accomplish), and thus by rendering audible to us what Emma alone could hear he charged the entire scene with actuality. As Emma goes to the window she merely notes that Binet's lathe is turning—*C'était Binet qui tournait.* Then she looks down at the street which seems to rise towards her—*Allons! Allons!* she whispers, because she cannot find the will to jump. We have had rendered to us visually the shock of violent suicide. Now comes the subtle fusion of the reaction and of the pull toward self-destruction, which is the humming in her head: how can Flaubert *render* it for us? Shall we not have to take his word for it? Shall we not have to imagine for him? No: *l'air circulait dans sa tête creuse,* he says; and then: *le ronflement du tour ne discontinuait pas, comme une voix furieuse qui l'appelait*—"the whirring of the lathe never stopped like a voice of fury calling her." The humming vertigo that draws the street towards her is rendered audible to us by the correlative sound of the lathe.

That is all, or nearly all, there is to it; but I think it is enough to set up our image, our *exemplum.* I leave to you, as I constantly reserve for myself, the inexhaustible pleasure of tracing out the infinite strands of interconnection in this and other novels, complexities as deep as life itself but ordered, fixed, and dramatized into arrested action. If I have made too much of Flaubert, or too much of too little of Flaubert, I can only say that I have not willfully ignored men as great, or greater. It is proper to honor France, and to honor the *trouvère,* the discoverer; for it has been through Flaubert that the novel has at last caught up with poetry.

# THE HOVERING FLY

*A Causerie on the Imagination and the Actual World*

*1943*

OF THE three great novels of Dostoevsky *The Idiot* has perhaps the simplest structure. In the center of the action there are only three characters. The development of the plot is almost exclusively "scenic" or dramatic; that is to say, a succession of scenes with episodic climaxes leads, with more than Dostoevsky's usual certainty of control, to the catastrophe at the end. There is very little summary or commentary by the author; here and there a brief lapse of time is explained, or there is a "constatation," a pause in the action in which the author assumes the omniscient view and reminds us of the position and plight of the other characters, who are complicating the problem of the hero. I emphasize here the prevailing scenic method because at the catastrophe the resolution of the dramatic forces is not a statement about life, or even about the life that we have seen in this novel: the resolution is managed by means of that most difficult of all feats, a narrow scene brought close up, in which the "meaning" of the action is conveyed in a dramatic visualization so immediate and intense that it creates its own symbolism. And it is the particular symbolism of the fly in the final scene of *The Idiot* which has provided the spring-board, or let us say the catapult, that will send us off into the unknown regions of "actuality," into which we have received orders to advance.[1]

What is *The Idiot* about? In what I have said so far I have purposely evaded any description of the novel; I have not tried to distinguish the experience which it offers, a kind of experience that might start a wholly different train of speculation upon actuality from that which will be our special concern in these notes. But now, before we get into the last scene, where the three main characters find themselves in a dark room, alone for the first time, we must drop them, and go a long way round and perhaps lose our way on a road that has no signs at the forks to tell us which turn to take.

## I I

WHEN we say poetry *and* something else—poetry and science, poetry and morality, or even poetry and mathematics—it makes little difference in dialectical difficulty what the co-ordinate field may be: all problems are equally hard and in the end they are much the same. The problem that I shall skirt around in these notes is a very old one, going back to the first records of critical self-consciousness. Aristotle was aware of it when he said that poetry is more philosophical than history. Although the same quagmire awaits us from whatever direction we come upon it, the direction itself and the way we tumble into the mud remain very important. Perhaps the crucial value of the critical activity—given the value of the directing mind, a factor that "systematic" criticism cannot find—will be set up or cast down by the kind of tact that we can muster for the "approach," a word that holds out to us a clue.

Armies used to besiege towns by "regular approaches"; or they took them by direct assault; or they maneuvered the enemy out of position, perhaps into ambuscade. These strategies are used today, for in war as in criticism the new is

[1] This essay was read as one of the *Mesures Lectures* at Princeton University, on April 8, 1943. The general subject of the series was "The Imagination and the Actual World."

usually merely a new name for something very old. When Caesar laid waste the country he was using a grand tactics that we have recently given a new name: infiltration, or the tactics of getting effectively into the enemy's rear. When you have total war must you also have total criticism? In our time critics are supposed to know everything, and we get criticism on all fronts. Does this not outmode the direct assault? When there are so many "problems" (a term equally critical and military) you have got to do a little here and a little there, and you may not be of the command that enters the suburbs of Berlin.

At any rate the world outside poetry, which continues to disregard the extent that it is also *in* poetry, resists and eludes our best understanding. When and why did it begin to behave in this way? When we had the Truce of God for three days a week, we attacked, with a great deal of military rhetoric and pageantry, the enemy, on the fourth day, and the attack was a frontal assault; both sides knew the rules. But we do not know them. And in the critical manual of war there has been nothing comparable to the rules since Arnold's doctrine of the "criticism of life" could still engage the non- or anti-poetic forces of the world head on.

But suppose there isn't an enemy? Suppose the war figure is misleading? Henry James (one of the great critics) wrote to Stevenson in 1891 that "No theory is kind to us that cheats us of seeing." What did he mean? In this instance he meant Stevenson's refusal to visualize his scene. "It struck me," says James, "that you either didn't feel—through some accident—your responsibility on this article quite enough; or, on some theory of your own, had declined it." We know that Stevenson did have a theory that made him generalize his scenes.

It is not necessary to find out here what Stevenson missed, or what, missing that, he did actually succeed in seeing. Every imaginative writer has a theory, whether he recognize it or not; it may operate for him at some dynamic level where it can liberate all that writer's power; but in so far

as it participates in the exclusive nature of theory, it must
entail upon some phase of his work very great risks, even
perils. "Thus Hardy," says William Empson, "is fond of
showing us an unusually stupid person subjected to very unusually bad luck, and then a moral is drawn, not merely by
inference but by solemn assertion, that we are all in the same
boat as this person whose story is striking precisely because
it is unusual." The "solemn assertion" in Hardy and in many
other writers, critics no less than novelists and poets, must
always either limit or somehow illegitimately extend what
the writer has actually seen.

What I want to end these beginning remarks with is an
observation that has been too little acknowledged. The art
of criticism must inevitably partake of the arts on which it
lives, and in a very special and niggling way. I refer to the
"approach," the direction of attack, the strategy; and in terms
of the strategy of this occasion, I mean the "point of view,"
as Percy Lubbock understands that phrase when he tells us
that very nearly the whole art of fiction is in it. From what
position shall the critic, who is convinced that the total
view is no view at all, the critic not being God, and convinced too that even if (which is impossible) he sees everything, he has got to see it from somewhere, like the painter
Philippoteaux who placed himself under a tree in his picture
of the Battle of Gettysburg to warn you that what you see
is only what he sees, under that tree: under what tree, then,
or from what hill, or under what log or leaf, shall the critic
take his stand, which may be less than an heroic stand, to
report what he sees, infers, or merely guesses? Merely to ask
this question is enough to indicate something of the post
which I am trying to find and hold. You may locate it far to
the sinister side of the line which divides the arts and the
sciences. Even if this spectator succeeds in holding his ground,
you may be sure that he will not be able to give you a scientific report.

### III

SUPPOSE we take two terms and relate them. The two terms for this occasion are, first, Poetry, and, second, the Actual World. Do we mean then by the actual world a world distinguished from one which is less actual or not actual at all? I suppose we mean both things; else we should say: Poetry and the World. We might again alter the phrase and get: Poetry and Actuality, which by omitting the world would give us a clue to its bearing in the preceding phrase; that is, world might then mean region, realm, field of observation or experience. So I take it that the bearing of the phrase "actual world" is towards something outside us, something objective, whose actuality is somehow an empirical one which tends to look after its own affairs without consulting us, and even at times resisting whatever it is in us which we like to call by names like subjective, private, human as opposed to non-human, although even the human and the subjective lie ready for objective scrutiny if we change our vantage-point and let them stand opposite us rather than let them oppose a third thing, a world, beyond them. It is, in fact, no mere quibble of idealism if we decide to call this subjective field not only the world but the actual world, taking our stand on the assumption that it sufficiently reflects or gathers in or contains all that we can ever know of any other world or worlds that appear to lie beyond it.

Are we prepared to take this stand? Perhaps we are if we are philosophers of a certain logical stubbornness; but as poets our zeal for subjectivism might seem to be good only at times, at certain places and moments. And are we, here in this kind of enquiry, either philosophers or poets? To ask that question is to diminish or perhaps to reduce to zero any degree of confidence that we may have enjoyed in trying to sort out, however provisionally, some of the bearings of our phrase "actual world." When we are sorting them out are we outside them, or inside, or partly inside and partly outside?

If we go back for another glimpse of a suggestion that I

merely threw down at the outset of this discussion, we shall drop to a degree somewhere below zero in our confidence of certainty in this enquiry. From what position is the critic looking at the object of his enquiry? That was our suggestion, but we have now identified the critic's object as the actual world, whatever that is, as that world is related to poetry, whatever that is.

If I seem to be making this matter obscure, let me plead my ignorance, and if you will, add your own ignorance to my plea; or if you like it better, add your skepticism to mine; and we shall examine together our riddle, so far as we can, as if nobody had seen it before: which, I take it, is the *action* of skepticism as distinguished from the mere feeling of the skeptic.

I suppose the easiest and, for all I know, the best way to establish our post of observation to look at the actual world, under our given condition, is to look at it through poetry. But here again we encounter difficulties as harassing as those we almost had to give up when we plumped ourselves down into the actual world. Even if we knew what poetry is, we should have to find it in particular poetic works: you see in that abstract phrase—"particular poetic works"—how difficult it is to face the paralyzing simplicity of our problem at this stage. We should have to find poetry in poems. Does not that make it look easier? It does, until we remember that even the man who may have read five thousand poems, an anthologist, for example, could lay claim to real mastery of not more than a few hundred.

What, then, is poetry? The innocence of the question ought to excuse it. Were we German idealists of the past century, or their disciples of today, we might easily begin poetry with a capital P, and putting initial capitals before actual and world, start Poetry and the Actual World off on their historic merry-go-round; or perhaps Poetry could pursue the Actual World as the Lord, in the Gullah sermon, chased Adam and Eve "round and round dat Gyarden, round and round"; or again there are the standard clowns in the bestiary of the animatéd cartoon that chase each other's tail until at last all that is left on the screen is a whirling vortex. Any of these similes will do that testify to our helplessness before the fenced-in apriorism of the merely philosophical approach: its conclusions are impressive and are usually stated at length, but I have never seen one of them that increased my understanding of the XXVIIIth Canto of the *Paradiso,* or even of "Locksley Hall."

But if we cannot say philosophically what poetry is, or even how it functions, how shall we know from any point of view what post of observation we are taking when we decide to look at the actual world through poetry? From now on this is what I shall be trying to get at. We shall certainly not be looking on as a spectator who has no stake in the scene; and yet to say that as a man who has written verse I have a special tact which will lead me to the right hill and turn my eyes in the right direction smacks a little of our national reliance upon expert testimony. For even if a poet, some other poet, seems in his verse to have given us flashes of what we may provisionally call actuality, he is not, as he talks about poetry, inside his verse, but outside it; and his report is as much under the obligation to make good as yours.

## I V

I AM sorry to introduce another complication before we go further. I must introduce a broader term, and the broader term usually lifts the spirits for a brief span, until somebody reminds us that it may be an evasion of the harder distinctions enjoined by the narrower term. The broader term is Imagination. If we say that we are trying to discover the relation between the Imagination and the Actual World, we find ready to run to our aid a host of comforting saws that could easily turn this vacillating discourse into an oration— and may actually do so before we are done. The Imagination is superior to Reality. Imagination is the rudder, Fancy the sails. Imagination is the esemplastic power. There are others as good, perhaps even better; and I do not deny the probability that before I am through I shall have spoken in substance one of these doctrines.

Yet I have brought in the Imagination for a more empirical reason. The great prose dramatists and novelists are makers and thus poets, and they give us something that is coherent and moving about human life which partakes of actuality but which is not actuality as it is reported to me by my senses as I look about me at a given moment. How does their report differ from mine? How does it differ from the report of the poet who writes, either lyrically or dramatically, in verse? Perhaps we had better take the risk and decide that the two reports seem to differ, verse being the occasion of the difference but not its explanation; and yet bearing in mind a few of the examples and comparisons which I shall produce or refer to in a few minutes, I make a large reservation about a categorical difference between the imagination in prose and the imagination in verse: Whether verse be expressive or formal in its function, it nevertheless becomes a sort of medium through which the poet may convey a deeper and wider heterogeneity of material than the prose vehicle will ordinarily carry. My reservation about this difference simply acknowledges the probability that it may be only a difference of degree, of intensity, of scope, with respect to the material; or if it is a real distinction, it cannot be said to hold all the time, but only as a rule. I admire, for example, the late Robert Bridges's poetry, but I see in it a failure or, if you will, a refusal to go all the way for as much of the richness of image as his magnificent control of verse-technique would have justified. On the other hand, if you will recall the cutting up of the whale in *Moby Dick* you will see at once the long reach of a prose style that is probably richer and more fluent than any verse style of its century, and far more dynamic than the style of *Dawn in Britain*, which perhaps alone in nineteenth-century poetry equals *Moby Dick* in rhetorical ambition. Bridges and Melville, then, might be seen as the exceptions in their respective mediums; and

yet, in order to see them that way, we should have to establish a middle point at which the prose imagination and the
verse imagination pass each other on the way to their proper
extremes; and no such point exists except in books on the
differential calculus.

But if we look at this matter empirically, not claiming too
much for any differences or for our more confident distinctions, we may succeed in taking up an attitude towards a
very real problem; for I take it that nobody denies the value
of what seems to go on in sound works of the imagination.
In what respects does this value belong to an actual world?
In that spirit, we may phrase the question more narrowly,
even finically, and ask it in terms of motion or process, or as
Mr. Kenneth Burke would have it, of drama. In what ways,
then, does an actual world *get into* the imagination?

Thus I turn to another line of speculation, with an observation that ought to arrest some of the vacillation of my opening trial flights, and at the same time fix our point of view.
If we think of the actual world as either a dead lump or a
whirling wind somewhere outside us, against which we
bump our heads or which whirls us around, we shall never
be able to discover it: we have got to try to find it in terms
of one of our chief interests. Let us call that interest the
imagination.

## V

THERE is now raging in one of our best journals a controversy about a human crisis which the editors of that journal
call "The Failure of Nerve." [2] The full implications of the
controversy are irrelevant to the end of my discussion; yet
there is one issue, perhaps the central issue, of that controversy which may instruct us, or at any rate prepare us for
what follows. Professors Dewey, Hook, and Nagel are anxious
and at moments even a little angry about the disorderly re-
birth of certain beliefs about man that tend to reject scientific positivism and the reliance upon what they, in their

[2] *Partisan Review,* vol. X, nos. 1-4.

tradition of thought, are pleased to call reason. The answers to these challenging blasts are scarcely developed; the editors of *Partisan Review* have so far relegated them to their correspondence columns; and I do not know whether or not there will be more considered replies. As an old anti-positivist I cannot do less than to point out a standard objection to the positivist program, reminding its adherents that our supposed "failure of nerve" might actually turn out to be the positivists' failure to allow for all that our nerve-ends are capable of taking in.

The positivist program for the complete government of man may perhaps be a form of what Scott Buchanan has called "occultation," a term that I should apply to positivism somewhat as follows: Positivism offers us a single field of discourse which may be briefly labeled as physicalism; and it pretends that this is the sole field of discourse, all the others being illusion, priestcraft, superstition, or even Nazism. Now as this single field of discourse is directed towards works of the imagination it carries with it a certain test of validity, which is usually the semantical test; and I hold that when this test becomes the pragmatic test and usurps the business of other tests, from other fields of discourse, pretending to be the sole test, it is performing an act of occultation upon these tests—a hiding away, an ascription of dark motives, even an imputation of black art.

Is there failure of nerve in a recognition of the failure of positivism even at its subtlest level to deliver all the goods? Are men the victims of a failure of nerve if, standing on a precipice from which there is no retreat, they prepare to make the best jump possible, and refuse to mumble to themselves that their fall will only exemplify the laws of gravity? There is no doubt that the fall will offer this confirmation of positivism; for positivism is a highly efficient technique of our physical necessities; it is the creation of the practical reason which organizes our physical economy, without which we cannot live. But under the rule of a positivism which has become a group of self-sufficient sciences, the organization

has grown exclusive. What is it that is excluded? What is
*occulted?*

There are two answers to this question which are two ways
of giving the same answer. But before I try to give this single-
double answer I ought to say that my purpose here is not to
berate the sciences but only the positivist religion of scientists. I am even more concerned with what it leaves out, or
at least to "point" towards that omitted thing, as one nods
in the direction of a good landscape which one might have
missed, driving by it at seventy miles an hour.

What is excluded, what is occulted? First, the actual
world; second, Dostoevsky's hovering fly; I shall be saying
presently that in terms of the dramatic imagination the
world and the fly are the same thing. Our skepticism—and as
I say it I have my own doubt—our doubt of this identification
proceeds from what we ordinarily call our common sense, a
good thing to have, but not good enough if it is all we have.
Let me put the matter somewhat differently. We may *look* at
the hovering fly; we can to a degree *know* the actual world.
But we shall not know the actual world by looking at it; we
know it by looking at the hovering fly.

I am sorry that this sounds a little gnomic; and it is time
to remember James's remark again: No theory is kind to us
that cheats us of seeing. But it is also time to amend James:
No theory is kind to us that cheats us of seeing what path we
ought to be on. What is our path? When we do not know, we
may get a vision, and then hope that all visions appear on
the road to Damascus. Before we may build our hope so
high we had better confront Pascal: "We run carelessly to
the precipice, after we have put something before us to
prevent us seeing it."

## V I

THE fly appears out of nowhere in the last scene in *The
Idiot:* out of nowhere, but only if we limit our apperception
of place to the scale of the human will. There are, as I have
said, three persons in the scene, but one of them is dead, and

her place is taken by the hovering fly. Nastasya Filippovna has appeared less directly in the action than other women characters of the story; but she is the heroine; for it is she who creates for the hero his insoluble problem. She is a beautiful and gifted orphan of good family who has been seduced by her guardian, a libertine of high political and social connections at the court. There is Rogozhin, who, as the story opens, has just inherited a fortune; he is in love with Nastasya and he offers her the worldly solution of money and marriage, a solution that she will not accept; and it is he, of course, who murders her at the end, since in no other way may he possess her. From the beginning Prince Myshkin, our hero, has been in his special way in love with Nastasya. He is the "idiot," the man whom epilepsy has removed from the world of action. I am not prepared to add to our critical knowledge of Myshkin. He has a marvelous detachment and receptivity, and a profundity of insight into human motives which I believe nobody but Dostoevsky has ever succeeded so perfectly in rendering dramatically. (It is always easy for the novelist to *say* that a character is profound; it is quite another matter to dramatize the profundity, to make it *act*.) Nastasya's agony of guilt, the conviction of sin, mirrors an almost Christ-like perception of the same potentialities on the part of Myshkin; and it is Nastasya who creates Myshkin's problem. Nastasya is tortured by those oscillating extremes, personal degradation and nobility of motive; and Myshkin alone in his world knows that she is not a "bad woman." But she will not marry Myshkin either. Marriage to Myshkin would be the symbolic signal that the pressure of her conflict had abated, and that Myshkin's problem had found solution in Nastasya's solution of her own. She cannot marry Rogozhin because she is too noble; she cannot marry Myshkin because she is too degraded. Thus we get in Rogozhin's murder of Nastasya the deeply immoral implications of Rogozhin's character, and the dramatically just irony of the good in her being destroyed by the lover who was indifferent to it. When the murder is done, Myshkin

feels no resentment: he can accept that too. The lovers stand
over the dead body of the murdered girl:

> [Myshkin's] eyes were by now accustomed to the dark-
> ness, so that he could make out the whole bed. Someone
> lay asleep on it, in a perfectly motionless sleep; not the
> faintest stir, not the faintest breath could be heard. The
> sleeper was covered over from head to foot with a white
> sheet and the limbs were vaguely defined; all that could
> be seen was that a human figure lay there, stretched at
> full length. All around in disorder at the foot of the bed,
> on chairs beside it, and even on the floor, clothes had
> been flung; a rich white silk dress, flowers, and ribbons.
> On a little table at the head of the bed there was the
> glitter of diamonds that had been taken off and thrown
> down. At the end of the bed there was a crumpled heap
> of lace and on the white lace the toes of a bare foot
> peeped out from under the sheet; it seemed as though
> it had been carved out of marble and it was horribly
> still. Myshkin looked and felt that as he looked, the room
> became more and more still and death-like. Suddenly
> there was the buzz of a fly which flew over the bed and
> settled on the pillow.

I assume that the minimum of exposition is necessary; it is
one of the great and famous scenes of modern literature; and
I hope that seeing it again you recalled the immense drama
preceding it and informing it and stretching the tensions
which are here let down, eased, and resolved for us. I am
not sure that the power of the scene would be diminished
by the absence of the fly; but at any rate it is there; and its
buzz rises like a hurricane in that silent room, until, for me,
the room is filled with audible silence. The fly comes to stand
in its sinister and abundant life for the privation of life, the
body of the young woman on the bed. Here we have one of
those conversions of image of which only great literary talent
is capable: life stands for death, but it is a wholly different
order of life, and one that impinges upon the human order

only in its capacity of scavenger, a necessity of its biological situation which in itself must be seen as neutral or even innocent. Any sinister significance that the fly may create for us is entirely due to its crossing our own path: by means of the fly the human order is compromised. But it is also extended, until through a series of similar conversions and correspondences of image the buzz of the fly distends, both visually and metaphorically, the body of the girl into the world. Her degradation and nobility are in that image. Shall we call it the actual world?

Or is there another adjective that we could apply to this world? There doubtless is; but I cannot, for my purpose, find it short of an adjectival essay, which this essay largely is, of another sort. With some propriety we might call it *an* actual world, which resembles other worlds equally actual, like Dante's or some of Shakespeare's, in its own final completeness, its coherence, depth, perspective. Yet I suspect that this side of the very great men we seldom get magnitude with actuality. We get magnitude in Thackeray and actuality in James; but not both in either. We get both in Tolstoy; but I take it that we accept his magnitude because it is actual, not because it is large. Thackeray's hurly-burly over the Battle of Waterloo is pleasant, empty, and immemorable; Prince André lying wounded under the infinite sky is all the world so lying; and we suspect that Tolstoy's magnitude is only a vast accumulation of little actualities—young Rostov on his horse at the bridgehead, the "little uncle" serving tea to the young people, Natasha weeping over Anatol in her room.

Whither do these casual allusions take us? They might take us far, on some other occasion, at a time when we had the heart for the consideration of actual worlds. But now we are in an occult world, from which actualities, which in their nature are quiet and permanent, are hard to find. As we face the morning's world we see nothing, unless we have the peculiar though intermittent talent for it, so actual as Dostoevsky's fly or Prince André's empty heavens. For if the drift of this essay have anything of truth in it, then our daily suffering, our best will towards the world in which we with difficulty breathe today, and our secret anxieties, however painful these experiences may be, must have something of the occult, something of the private, even something of the willful and obtuse, unless by a miracle of gift or character, and perhaps of history also, we command the imaginative power of the relation of things.

## VII

IT IS a gift that comes and goes; its story is so long that neither time nor understanding has permitted me to tell it here. Yet I think that the risk, the extreme risk that I have so far faced, of some general commitments concerning the function of the imagination as a black art will be worth taking, if only to challenge a fierce denial. It ought to be plain to us, who share a common experience of two conflicts in a single war and who continue to wonder at the ingenious failure of our time, that although human powers are by no means depleted, something has gone wrong with their direction. No man but acknowledges this commonplace; yet how shall we imbed it, ground it, in some conceivable knowledge of the actuality of a world?

It must be plain also that the very instruments of our daily economy have more and more dictated our ends, or at best have suggested to an obscure power within us how we shall conduct our lives. The possibilities latent in our situation must make us falter. The obscure power within us we have made into an occult power; we are no longer conscious of its limits, its function, its purposes. Is that not the meaning of an occult power? One that we sway under but cannot know?

Here again I come up against formidable hazards, and I feel as if I had gone round the flank only to lose direction and to be cut off; but these perils will be plain enough although I shall not describe them. This occult power that seems to overwhelm us must, in times past, have enjoyed the fullness of light; but even underground it will not be gainsaid. If it does not have the privilege of its rational place in the order of human experience, it will take irrational toll of that order. Human violence is an historical constant; yet how shall we come to terms with a violence that is rationally implemented, an efficient, a total violence? It seems to me that the answer of our time to this problem is at present the historical answer of the dead-end, of the stalemate, of the facile optimism of decay. In a time like ours you may be sure of this: that men will be easy and hopeful, and will try a little of the medicine of the bridge-expert along with the elixirs of the innumerable Gerald Heards. Why? Because, although historically man may be a social being before he is a religious being, he is, after he achieves society, primarily religious, and remains incurably so. If he is told that mere "operational techniques" will see him through, whether these are put to work in society, or in the laboratory, or in industry, or in the arts, he may believe it for a while, and try to realize it; but like a child after the game is over and the fingers are uncrossed, he will return to the real world, unprepared and soon to be overwhelmed by it because he has been told that the real world does not exist.

Or perhaps you would prefer to call it merely another world, after the analogy of *an* actual world; not *the* other world and *the* actual world. For there must be a great many of these worlds, all actual, all to be participated in, all participating in us; yet I prefer the frank Platonism of *the* actual world, as Socrates himself preferred it when he told Ion that "poetry is one." And the impulse to reality which drives us through the engrossing image to the rational knowledge of our experience which, without that image, is mere process, must also be one. Once more the professed skeptic of thirty minutes ago reaches an immoderate deduction beyond any preparation that he has been able to ground it in.

For I should be chagrined could I feel that I have carried you, as well as myself, beyond known depths: are we not committed to the affirmation that actuality and poetry are respectively and even reciprocally one? If we are so committed, we must not affirm otherwise of humanity, which has been one from the beginning. And we cannot allow any novelty to our attempted insights.

Are we not saying something very old when we assert that we may know an actual world in the act of seeing the hovering fly? We are saying that our minds move through three necessities which, when in proper harmony and relation, achieve a dynamic and precarious unity of experience. Now that our oration is over I may say quite plainly that the three necessities—necessities at any rate for Western man— are the three liberal arts. And any one of them practiced to the exclusion of the others retires a portion of our experience into the shadows of the occult, the contingent, the uncontrolled. The grammarians of the modern world have allowed their specialization, the operational technique, to drive the two other arts to cover, whence they break forth in their own furies, the one the fury of irresponsible abstraction, the other the fury of irresponsible rhetoric. The philosopher serves the operational technique, whether in the laboratory or on the battlefield. The poet—and the poet is the rhetorician, the specialist in symbol—serves the operational technique because, being the simplest mind of his trinity, his instinct is to follow and to be near his fellow men.

In a last glance at the last scene of *The Idiot* let us imagine that Myshkin and Rogozhin do not appear. The body of Nastasya Filippovna lies indefinitely upon the narrow bed, the white toe exposed, the fly intermittently rising and falling over the corpse. The dead woman and the fly are a *locus* of the process of decomposition. But, of course, we cannot imagine it, unless like a modern positivist we can imagine ourselves out of our humanity; for to imagine the scene is to be there, and to be there, before the sheeted bed, is to have our own interests powerfully affected. The fiction that we are neither here nor there, but are only spectators who, by becoming, ourselves, objects of grammatical analysis, can arrive at some other actuality than that of process, is the great modern heresy: we can never be mere spectators, or if we can for a little time we shall probably, a few of us only, remain, until there is one man left, like a solitary carp in a pond, who has devoured all the others.

# A READING OF KEATS

## *1945*

IT IS proper that we celebrate the hundred and fiftieth anniversary of the birth of John Keats by testing our powers of reading him. For the perpetual task of criticism, every generation or two, is to understand again the poetry of the past. Poetry which cannot survive this renewal of understanding, and live again in the critical sensibility of posterity, must contain some radical flaw of interest; it is perhaps in this sense that time is the test of poetry. This view, commonly held today, presupposes the continuity of tradition which with occasional lapses has come down to us from the Greeks; but whether the best English poets shall survive the coming age is a question bearing less upon their value for us than upon our capacity to receive it. If Keats goes unread by the next generation, whose memory will not go back to the great historical era which now seems to be closing, I cannot think that the failure will be his. He will remain one of the great English poets for a later generation to rediscover.

This sounds like the prediction of Colvin in 1917; and I see no reason to argue generally with the Victorian estimate. Perhaps of Keats alone of the English romantics does this estimate still hold, possibly because the great claims were never made for him that were made for Wordsworth and Coleridge. If definitive criticism were possible, Bridges's *A Critical Introduction to Keats* (1894, revised 1914) and A. C. Bradley's "The Letters of Keats" (*Oxford Lectures on Poetry*, 1909) might be said to realize it; and to these should be added the fine textual study, Professor Ridley's *Keats' Craftsmanship* (1933), and Professor C. D. Thorpe's *The Mind of John Keats* (1926).[1] So, apart from the three full-length biographies by Houghton, Colvin, and Miss Lowell, there are four excellent critical studies of Keats, two from the late Victorian age, two from our own: there is probably less useless writing about Keats than about the other great English romantics. The reasons for this are obvious if a little hard to state: the bulk of Keats's work is comparatively slight; at his best (the odes, "Lamia," "The Eve of St. Agnes," and parts of "Hyperion") he has a masterful simplicity of purpose and control; in these poems, with the single exception of "Hyperion," the influences are so well assimilated that only the most trivial academic mind could suppose Keats's relation to the "history of ideas" to have more than the value of a few monographs. In this I take it "he is with Shakespeare." It has been easier for the critics to get at the essentials of Keats than of Wordsworth, Coleridge, and Shelley, who conceal more traps to catch scholars.

This is not to say that Keats was, in the sense of the phrase common a few years ago, a "pure poet." He was the great poet of his age, in the fullest sense; and even Matthew Arnold almost let himself see that he was. Arnold's essay remains one of the best "estimates" of Keats in the Victorian style (which goes back to Johnson) of combined moral and critical judgment; perhaps Arnold was the last great critic to use it effectively; for since its decay in the impressionism of Pater and in the dilettanteism of the "literary essay" of

---

[1] The value of Professor Thorpe's book is somewhat diminished by the instability of his critical terms; but as a rounded descriptive study it is excellent. I have not put Mr. Murry's *Keats and Shakespeare* (1926) in this list because I find its main argument incomprehensible; though the book is valuable for many brilliant insights.

the nineties and early nineteen-hundreds, we have been getting a new sort of criticism which was brought in by Eliot's *The Sacred Wood* (1920).

Arnold's essay still has a certain interest in the history of Keats's reputation, yet it must concern us now as perhaps the best evidence of Arnold's almost perverse use of critical standards. More than any other poet Keats pinned him upon the horns of his dilemma: "Natural magic" and/or "Moral interpretation." It has been said (by whom I do not remember) that the ambiguousness of Arnold's judgment of Keats was due to his humorless sense of responsibility for the poetry of his age: Keats was the greatest "natural magician" since Shakespeare; but what poetry then *needed* was moral interpretation, and Keats had been a harmful example. This is not the place to examine Arnold's critical dialectic (that has been admirably done by Mr. Trilling); yet it is not beside the point to remark Arnold's failure to see that in Keats's "principle of beauty in all things" lay a possible way out of his dilemma. Even the *Letters* (among the great letters of the world) give a clue to its significance, to say nothing of the structure of the odes. Arnold was not interested in structure unless it was a structure of action inviting moral interpretation. He saw Keats quite simply as a "sensuous" poet.

I have belabored this question more than either Arnold or it deserves (not more than they merit) because I think it is necessary before proceeding to Keats's poetry, to refer briefly to my own disabilities as a critic of Keats. They are not unlike Arnold's. It would be ludicrous to confess that I lack Arnold's general powers, or more particularly his capacity for awareness of what he did not like (it was this awareness that raised him above the level of the conventional Victorian moralist); but it is not beside the point to warn readers of this essay that my attitude towards Keats is reverent, yet distant without disinterestedness. Whether Keats is what we *need* I do not know; yet we neither want him nor use him. For the past fifteen years the direction of Anglo-American poetry has been rather towards Shelley than Keats, towards

"Godwin-perfectibility" and social consciousness than towards a dramatic-symbolic style. I hope I shall not sound like Margaret Fuller if I say that I am not indifferent to the utmost capacity of men for social and individual perfection; I simply do not think that poetry should be limited to exhorting men to these goods. My lack of sympathy with this school nevertheless does not qualify me as a critic of Keats, in spite of my conviction (which was Arnold's unhappy conviction) that Keats was in one of the great modes of poetry. It is perhaps a mode inaccessible to us today. I shall not try, because it is too difficult, to state directly why I think this obstacle exists; my understanding of it, such as it may be, will be implied in what I am about to say of "Ode to a Nightingale," in my opinion Keats's great poem in spite of its imperfect detail, greater than "Ode to Autumn," which because of its purity of tone and style Bridges ranks first among the odes; "Ode to Autumn" is a very nearly perfect piece of style but it has little to say. Because I believe that "Ode to a Nightingale" at least tries to say everything that poetry can say I am putting it at the center of this discussion.

## I I

THE testimony of the criticism of Keats which I have read (I cannot pause to summarize it here) is that he was a pictorial poet in the Spenserian tradition. I would add to this very general statement the observation: his progress from "Endymion" to the revised "Hyperion" is a direct line, at the end of which he achieved under Milton's influence a new kind of blank verse; but in it he could not control the heroic action. In a letter to Reynolds (September 21st, 1819), he said: "I have given up 'Hyperion'—there were too many Miltonic inversions in it . . ."; and in a letter to George Keats, written six days later: "I have but lately stood on my guard against Milton. Life to him would be death to me." I think the second of these explanations, general as it is, comes nearer to the truth: he could not write Miltonic verse without eventual frustration because he lacked a Miltonic subject; it would be "death" to him. For the framework of "Hyperion," of the more human, revised version no less than the first version, is pictorial, with declamatory summaries of action which Keats does not present. It is a succession of plastic scenes.

If this had been the only line of development from "Endymion," we should not, of course, have got the odes; and Keats would have remained a youthful experimenter of genius, considerably above Chatterton but not so impressive as Shelley. The other line runs in the order of time, from "Endymion" to the odes; but perhaps technically, as Professor Ridley has argued, the line is from the sonnets to the odes; that is to say, his experiments with the sonnet led him to modifications of the form which gave us the great stanzas of the Grecian Urn and the Nightingale. And within that narrow, lyrical, and potentially dramatic compass he had something ready to say that he could not have said in the other kinds of verse that he had tried. "The Eve of St. Agnes" is his masterpiece in the Spenserian tradition of *ut pictura, poesis,* and the originality is in the freshness of the language. Far more instructive for technical reasons (reasons which cannot be disconnected from the higher reasons) is the versification of "Lamia," based partly upon Dryden, but, as Professor Ridley shows, in no sense imitative. For example, "Lamia" has proportionately three times as many run-on lines as Dryden's "Fables" taken as a whole, thirty-three per cent being run on; there is a large number of tercets ending with alexandrines; but there are no feminine endings. The result of this adaptation of Dryden's verse is a movement of great speed and flexibility, firm yet supple; and altogether the most original contribution to narrative verse of the nineteenth century. But it should be remembered that "Lamia" is a narrative of a minor mythological incident which Keats picked up in Burton, not epic action: although Keats failed to sustain his blank verse because he could not fill it with action, he succeeded brilliantly with a new kind of verse in which the pictorial method supports the main effect, the simple action turning on a plot of recognition. For the moment we need not go into the symbolism; but it is significant that it was material which Keats found something like the perfect means to bring into form. Written in the summer of 1819 (Part I by mid-July), "Lamia" is the height of his achievement in the long poem. The important thing to remember is that Keats finished it at about the same time he abandoned "Hyperion."

I shall briefly anticipate the end that I am heading towards by setting down a few opinions which will both indicate its direction and gauge my understanding of Keats. "Lamia" is more closely related to the two great odes, the Nightingale and the Grecian Urn, than to "Hyperion," and the fact that he could successfully revise "The Eve of St. Agnes" at the time he was finishing "Lamia" is as much proof as criticism needs that it is not too far from the materials and methods of a poem which some critics would put with the other narratives, "Isabella" and the fragment "The Eve of St. Mark." Moreover, we must think of "Lamia" and "The Eve of St. Agnes" along with the great odes, as follows: "Ode to a Nightingale," "Ode on a Grecian Urn," "Ode to Psyche," "To Autumn," and "Ode on Melancholy." This cluster of poems is the center of Keats's great work, and they all deal with the same imaginative dilemma—or, if we wish to be biographical, the same conflict in Keats's experience. (I cannot agree with Bridges that there is anything in the sonnets as good as the best Shakespeare; I am convinced that they would not have won their great reputation apart from the other work; and I shall not discuss them here.)

The imaginative dilemma of Keats is, I assume, implicit in the poems, which are at its best statement: the most that criticism ought to attempt is perhaps a kind of circulatory description of its movements, from poem to poem. Bridges's astute remark that "Keats's art is primarily objective and pictorial, and whatever other qualities it has are as it were *added on to things as perceived*," contains critical insight of the first order. I have italicized *added on to things as perceived*, and I would double the italics of the last two words; they point directly to the imaginative limit of Keats's poetry, one horn of the dilemma out of which it does not move, in which it must, if it is to exceed the *ut pictura, poesis* formula, seek some conversion of that limit.

I should thus offer (for what it is worth) the very general analysis: Keats as a pictorial poet was necessarily presenting in a given poem a series of scenes, and even in the narratives the action does not flow from inside the characters, but is governed pictorially from the outside. He is thus a painting poet and would have earned Lessing's censure. But like every great artist he knew (in his own terms, which are none of our business) that his problem was to work within his limitations, and to transcend them. He was a poet of space whose problem was to find a way of conveying what happens in time; for it is time in which dramatic conflict takes place; and it is only by conversion into dramatic actuality that the parts of the verbal painting achieve relation and significance. "The form of thought in Keats," says Mr. Kenneth Burke, "is mystical, in terms of an eternal present" —and, I should add, in terms of the arrested action of painting.

### III

WHEN Keats adds to "things as perceived," what does he add? That, it seems to me, is the special problem of Keats. In the simplest language it is the problem of adding movement to a static picture, of putting into motion the "languor which lingers in the main design" (Bridges) of even the later work.

Of the eight stanzas of "Ode to a Nightingale" six are distinctly pictorial in method; a seventh, stanza three, in which Keats expresses his complaint of common life, develops as a meditation out of the second stanza, the picture of Provence. The only stanza which does not give us or in some way pertain to a definite scene is number seven; for though the method there is pictorial, the effect is allusive: the permanence of the nightingale's song is established in a rapid series of vignettes, ending with the famous "faëry lands forlorn." It is the only stanza, as some critic has remarked, which contains a statement contradictory of our sense of common reality.

Thou wast not born for death, immortal Bird,

he says to the nightingale; and we cannot agree. The assertion is out of form in an obvious sense; for the poem is an accumulation of pictorial situations; and the claim of immortality for the bird is dramatic and lyrical.

I am raising the question whether the metonymy which attributes to the literal nightingale the asserted immortality of the song is convincing enough to carry the whole imaginative insight of the poem. I think it is, given the limits of Keats's art, but I am still nagged by a difficulty that will not down. It seems to me that the ambivalence of the nightingale symbol contains almost the whole substance of the poem: the bird, as bird, shares the mortality of the world; as symbol, it purports to transcend it. And I feel that the pictorial technique has not been quite dramatic enough to give to the transcendence of the symbol life in some visibly presented experience. The far more implausible, even far-fetched, metaphor of the draughtsman's compasses, in Donne, comes out a little better because through a series of dialectical transformations, from the dying man to the Ptolemaic spheres, and then through the malleable gold to the compasses, there is a progression of connected analogies, given us step by step; and we acknowledge the identity of compasses and lovers as imaginatively possible. Keats merely *asserts:* song equals immortality; and I feel there is some disparity between the symbol and what it is expected to convey—not an inherent disparity, for such is not imaginatively conceivable; but a disparity such as we should get in the simple equation A = B, if we found that the assigned values of A and B were respectively 1 and 3.

This feature of Keats's art we shall find in "Ode on a Grecian Urn" but not in "Ode to Psyche." I confess that I do not know what to do about this anomalous poem, except to admire it. There appears to me to be very little genuine *sensation* in Keats (rather what Arnold and his contemporaries mistook for sensation), but there is more of it in "Ode to Psyche" than anywhere else in the great odes. Mr. T. S. Eliot puts it first among the odes, possibly because most of its detail is genuinely experienced and because it contains no developed attitude towards life. The other odes do; and it is an attitude less mature than that which Mr. Eliot finds in the *Letters*. With this part of his view of Keats one must agree. But it is a dangerous view, since it is very remotely possible that some letters from Shakespeare may turn up some day. But Mr. Eliot's preference for "Ode to Psyche" doubtless shares at bottom the common prejudice that romantic art tends not only to be pictorial but "off center" and lacking in that appearance of logical structure which we ordinarily associate with Donne and Dryden. I do not want to get into this classical-and-romantic affair, for the usual reason, and for a reason of my own, which is that it has a way of backfiring. Mr. Eliot has said that Coleridge and Wordsworth on one side are "as eighteenth century as anybody." So is Keats. The apostrophe to the nightingale, which I have been at some pains to try to understand, is quite "eighteenth century"; but it is not nearly so eighteenth century as the entire third stanza, which I shall now try to understand, assuming that what it says has a close connection with that literal part of the nightingale, the physical bird, which Keats seemed not to know what to do with (except to make it, in the last stanza, fly away). Here it is:

> Fade far away, dissolve, and quite forget
> What thou among the leaves hast never known,
> The weariness, the fever, and the fret
> Here where men sit and hear each other groan;

> Where palsy shakes a few, sad, last gray hairs,
>     Where youth grows pale, and spectre-thin, and dies;
>     Where but to think is to be full of sorrow
>        And leaden-eyed despairs,
>     Where beauty cannot keep her lustrous eyes,
>     Or new Love pine at them beyond tomorrow.[2]

Looked at from any point of view, this stanza is bad; the best that one ought to say of it perhaps is that there are worse things in Shelley and Wordsworth, and in Keats himself. (Even Colvin's habitual tone of eulogy is restrained when he comes to it.[3]) It is bad in the same way as the passages in Shelley's "Adonaïs" which exhibit the troops of mourners are bad. Keats here is relapsing into weakened eighteenth-century rhetoric; Blake could have put into the personifications imaginative power, and Pope genuine feeling, or at any rate an elegance and vigor which would have carried them.

There is not space enough in an essay to go into this matter as it needs to be gone into. What I wish to indicate, for the consideration of more thorough readers, is that stanza three may be of the utmost significance in any attempt to understand the structure of Keats's poetry. It gives us a "picture" of common reality, in which the life of man is all mutability and frustration. But here if anywhere in the poem the necessity to dramatize time, or the pressure of actuality, is paramount. *Keats has no language of his own for this realm of experience.* That is the capital point. He either falls into the poetic language of the preceding age, or, if he writes spontaneously, he commits his notorious errors of taste; in either case the language is not adequate to the feeling; or, to put it "cognitively," he lacks an ordered symbolism through which he may *know* the common and the ideal reality in a single imaginative act. One would like to linger upon the possible reasons for this. I suspect

---

[2] Quotations from the poems follow Garrod, *The Poetical Works of John Keats.* Oxford, 1939.

[3] Sidney Colvin, *John Keats* (New York, 1917), p. 419

that evidence from another source, which I shall point out later, will be more telling than anything, even this stanza, that we can find in the odes. The consciousness of change and decay, which can, and did in Keats, inform one of the great modes of poetry, is deeply involved with his special attitude towards sexual love. He never presents love directly and dramatically; it is in terms of Renaissance tapestry, as in "The Eve of St. Agnes," or in a fable of Italian violence, as in "Isabella"; or, most interesting of all, in terms of a little myth, Lamia the snake-woman, a symbol which permits Keats to objectify the mingled attraction and repulsion which his treatment of love requires. I sometimes think that for this reason "Lamia" is his best long poem: the symbol inherently contains the repulsive element, but keeps it at a distance, so that he does not have to face it in terms of common experience, his own, or as he was aware of it in his age. Is it saying too much to suppose that Keats's acceptance of the pictorial method is to a large extent connected with his unwillingness to deal with passion dramatically? (There is sensuous detail, but no sensation as direct experience, such as we find in Baudelaire.)

I need not labor a point which even the Victorian critics and biographers, almost without exception, remarked: Keats, both before and after his fatal illness (as other poets have been who were not ill at all) was filled with the compulsive image of the identity of death and the act of love (for example, "You must be mine to die upon the rack if I want you," he wrote to Fanny Brawne); and it is only an exaggeration of emphasis to say that death and love are interchangeable terms throughout his poetry. The "ecstasy" that the nightingale pours forth contains the Elizabethan pun on "die" with the wit omitted, and a new semi-mystical intensity of feeling added. And is it too much to say that Keats's constant tendency was to face the moment of love only in terms of an ecstasy so intense that he should not survive it? When Lamia vanishes Lycius "dies." And this affirmation of life through death is the element that Keats

"adds on to things as perceived." But life-in-death is presented pictorially, in space, as an eternal moment, not as a
moment of dramatic action in time, proceeding from previous action and looking towards its consequences.

The dialectical tension underlying "Ode to a Nightingale"
seems to me to be incapable of resolution, first in terms of
Keats's mind as we know it from other sources, and, secondly, in terms of the pictorial technique which dominates
the poetic method. This method, which seems to reflect a
compulsive necessity of Keats's experience, allows him to
present the thesis of his dilemma, the ideality of the nightingale symbol, but not the antithesis, the world of common
experience, which is the substance of stanza three. The
"resolution" is suspended in the intensity of the images setting forth the love-death identity and reaching a magnificent
climax in stanza six ("Now more than ever seems it rich to
die," etc.). But the climax contains a little less than the full
situation; it reaches us a little too simplified, as if Keats were
telling us that the best way to live is to die, or the best way
to die is to live intensely so that we may die intensely. There
may be concealed here one of the oldest syntheses of Christian thought, that we die only to live; but, if so, there has
been a marked shrinkage in range of that conception since
Donne wrote his "A Nocturnall upon S. Lucies Day."

Messrs. Brooks and Warren, in their excellent if somewhat confident analysis [4] of the Nightingale ode, argue with
much conviction that the dramatic frame of the poem, the
painful accession to the trance in the opening lines and
the return to immediate reality ("Do I wake or sleep?") at
the end, provides a sufficient form. I confess that I am not
sure. I am not certain of the meaning of what happens
inside the frame; but at times I am not certain that it is
necessary to understand it. There is no perfection in poetry.
All criticism must in the end be comparative (this does not
mean critical relativity); it must constantly refer to what

[4] Brooks and Warren, *Understanding Poetry*, pp. 409-415.

poetry has accomplished in order to estimate what it can accomplish, not what it ought to accomplish; we must heed Mr. Ransom's warning that perfect unity or integration in a work of art is a critical delusion. "Ode to a Nightingale" is by any standard one of the great poems of the world. Our philosophical difficulties with it are not the same as Keats's imaginative difficulties, which pertain to the order of experience and not of reason. The poem is an emblem of one limit of our experience: the impossibility of synthesizing, in the order of experience, the antinomy of the ideal and the real, and, although that antinomy strikes the human mind with a different force in different ages (Donne's dualism is not Keats's), it is sufficiently common to all men in all times to be understood.

If we glance at "Ode on a Grecian Urn," we shall see Keats trying to unify his pictorial effects by means of direct philosophical statement. "Do I wake or sleep?" at the end of the Nightingale ode asks the question: Which is reality, the symbolic nightingale or the common world? The famous Truth-Beauty synthesis at the end of the "Grecian Urn" contains the same question, but this time it is answered. As Mr. Kenneth Burke sees it, Truth is the practical scientific world and Beauty is the ideal world above change. The "frozen" figures on the urn, being both dead and alive, constitute a scene which is at once perceptible and fixed. "This transcendent scene," says Mr. Burke, "is the level at which the earthly laws of contradiction no longer prevail." [5] The one and the many, the eternal and the passing, the sculpturesque and the dramatic, become synthesized in a higher truth. Much of the little that I know about this poem I have learned from Mr. Burke and Mr. Cleanth Brooks, who have studied it more closely than any other critics; and what I am about to say will sound ungrateful. I suspect that the dialectical solution is Mr. Burke's rather than Keats's, and that Mr. Brooks's "irony" and "dramatic propriety" are like-

[5] Kenneth Burke, "Symbolic Action in a Poem by Keats," *Accent*, vol. 4, No. 1 (Autumn, 1943), p. 42.

wise largely his own.[6] Mr. Brooks rests his case for the Truth-Beauty paradox on an argument for its "dramatic propriety"; but this is just what I am not convinced of. I find myself agreeing with Mr. Middleton Murry (whom Mr. Brooks quotes), who admits that the statement is out of place "in the context of the poem itself." I would point to a particular feature, in the last six lines of stanza four, which I feel that neither Mr. Burke nor Mr. Brooks has taken into a certain important kind of consideration. Here Keats tells us that in the background of this world of eternal youth there is another, from which it came, and that this second world has thus been emptied and is indeed a dead world:

> What little town by river or sea-shore
>   Or mountain-built with peaceful citadel,
>     Is emptied of this folk, this pious morn?
> And, little town, thy streets for evermore
>   Will silent be; and not a soul to tell
>     Why thou art desolate, can e'er return.

Mr. Burke quite rightly sees in this passage the key to the symbolism of the entire poem. It is properly the "constatation" of the tensions of the imagery. What is the meaning of this perpetual youth on the urn? One of its meanings is that it is perpetually anti-youth and anti-life; it is in fact dead, and "can never return." Are we not faced again with the same paradox we had in the Nightingale ode, that the intensest life is achieved in death? Mr. Burke brings out with great skill the erotic equivalents of the life-death symbols; and for his analysis of the developing imagery throughout we owe him a great debt. Yet I feel that Mr. Burke's own dialectical skill leads him to consider the poem, when he is through with it, a philosophical discourse; but it is, if it is anything (and it is a great deal), what is ordinarily known as a work of art. Mr. Burke's elucidation of the Truth-Beauty proposition in the last stanza is the most convincing dialec-

---

[6] *The Well Wrought Urn* (New York, 1947), pp. 139-152.

tically that I have seen; but Keats did not write Mr. Burke's elucidation; and I feel that the entire last stanza, except the phrase "Cold Pastoral" (which probably ought to be somewhere else in the poem) is an illicit commentary added by the poet to a "meaning" which was symbolically complete at the end of the preceding stanza, number four. Or perhaps it may be said that Keats did to some extent write Mr. Burke's elucidation; that is why I feel that the final stanza (though magnificently written) is redundant and out of form.

To the degree that I am guilty with Mr. Burke of a prepossession which may blind me to the whole value of this poem (as his seems to limit his perception of possible defects) I am not qualified to criticize it. Here, towards the end of this essay, I glance back at the confession, which I made earlier, of the distance and detachment of my warmest admiration for Keats. It is now time that I tried to state the reasons for this a little more summarily, in a brief comparison of the two fine odes that we have been considering.

Both odes are constructed pictorially in spatial blocks, for the eye to take in serially. Though to my mind this method is better suited to the subject of the Grecian Urn, which is itself a plastic object, than to the Nightingale ode, I take the latter, in spite of the blemishes of detail (only some of which we have looked at), to be the finer poem. If there is not so much in it as in the Grecian Urn for the elucidation of verbal complexity, there is nowhere the radical violation of its set limits that one finds in the last stanza of the Grecian Urn:

> Thou shalt remain, in midst of other woes
> Than ours, a friend to man, to whom thou say'st,
> Beauty is truth, truth beauty,—that is all
> Ye know on earth, and all ye need to know.

It is here that the poem gets out of form, that the break in "point of view" occurs; and if it is a return to Samuel Johnson's dislike of "Lycidas" (I don't think it is) to ask how an urn can say anything, I shall have to suffer the consequences of that view. It is Keats himself, of course, who says it; but "Keats" is here not implicit in the structure of the poem, as he is in "Ode to a Nightingale"; what he says is what the mathematicians call an extrapolation, an intrusion of matter from another field of discourse, so that even if it be "true" philosophically it is not a visible function of what the poem says. With the "dead" mountain citadel in mind, could we not phrase the message of the urn equally well as follows: Truth is *not* beauty, since even art itself cannot do more with death than preserve it, and the beauty frozen on the urn is also dead, since it cannot move. This "pessimism" may be found as easily in the poem as Keats's comforting paradox. So I should return to the Nightingale ode for its superior *dramatic* credibility, even though the death-life antinomy is not more satisfactorily resolved than in the Grecian Urn. The fall of the "I" of "Ode to a Nightingale" into the trance-like meditation in the first stanza and the shocked coming to at the end *ground* the poem in imaginable action, so that the dialectics of the nightingale symbol do not press for resolution. So I confess a reserved agreement with Brooks and Warren.

The outlines of the conflicting claims of the ideal and the actual, in Keats's mind, I have touched upon; but now, with the two great odes in mind, I wish to give those hints a somewhat greater range and try, if possible, to point towards the *kind* of experience with which Keats was dealing when he came up short against the limit of his sensibility, the identity of love and death, or the compulsive image of erotic intensity realizing itself in "dying."

## I V

ONE of Keats's annotations to Burton's *Anatomy*, in the copy given him by Brown in 1819, in the great period, is as follows:

> Here is the old plague spot; the pestilence, the raw scrofula. I mean there is nothing disgraces me in my own

eyes so much as being one of a race of eyes nose and mouth beings in a planet call'd the earth who all from Plato to Wesley have always mingled goatish winnyish lustful love with the abstract adoration of the deity. I don't understand Greek—is the love of God and the Love of women express'd by the same word in Greek? I hope my little mind is wrong—if not I could . . . Has Plato separated these lovers? Ha! I see how they endeavour to divide—but there appears to be a horrid relationship.[7]

Keats had just read in Burton the chapter "Love-Melancholy" in which the two Aphrodites, Urania and Pandemos,[8] appear: there is no evidence that he ever knew more about them than this quotation indicates. Professor Thorpe valiantly tries to show us that Keats must have known from his literary environment something of Plato's doctrine of love, but there is no reason to believe that he ever felt the imaginative shock of reading *The Symposium*, and of experiencing first hand an intuition of a level of experience that the Western world, through Platonism and Christianity, had been trying for more than two millennia to reach. He apparently never knew that the two Aphrodites were merely the subject of Pausanias's speech, one of the preliminaries to Socrates's great dialectical synthesis. The curious thing about Keats's education is that it was almost entirely literary; he had presumably read very little philosophy and religion. He used the Greek myths, not for the complete (if pagan) religious experience in them, but to find a static and sculpturesque emblem of timeless experience—his own and the experience of his age; hence the pictorial method, and hence the necessity for that method.

In my reading of Keats I see his mind constantly reaching towards and recoiling from the experience, greatly extended,

[7] I am indebted to a note by Colvin (*op. cit.*, p. 549) for the hint which led me to this bitter confession. It appears in Forman, *The Complete Works of John Keats*, iii, p. 268.
[8] Modern readers will find the passage in the edition of Dell and Jordan-Smith, p. 620 (New York, 1927).

which is represented by the ambivalent Aphrodite. The conclusion of the sonnet "Bright Star! . . .":

> Still, still to hear her tender-taken breath,
> And so live ever—or else swoon to death . . .

is not Keats's best poetry, but it states very simply the conflict of emotion the symbolic limit of which I have tried to
see in terms of the double goddess. The immanence of the
Uranian in the Pandemic goddess was not beyond the range
of Keats's intellect, but it was at any rate, at the time of
his death, imaginatively beyond his reach. His goddess, in
so far as she is more than a decorative symbol in Keats, was
all Uranian; and to say in another way what I have already
said, his faulty taste (which is probably at its worst in one
of the lines in "Bright Star! . . .") lies in his inability to
come to terms with her Pandemic sister. His pictorial and
sculpturesque effects, which arrest time into space, tend to
remove from experience the dramatic agitation of Aphrodite
Pandemos, whose favors are granted and whose woes are
counted in the actuality of time. (There is, of course, a great
deal more in Keats than this obsessive symbol through which
I see him; and there is also less of the symbol, explicitly presented, than my discussion would indicate; there are only
eleven references to "Venus" in all Keats's poetry—he never
calls her Aphrodite—and in no instance is very much done
with her symbolically. She has only a fresh Botticellian surface; and one may observe that she is not mentioned in
"Ode to Psyche.")

This "horrid relationship" between the heavenly and
earthly Aphrodites had been in effect the great theme of St.
Augustine, and before him of Lucretius; and it was to inform
dramatically *The Divine Comedy.* It was perhaps the great
achievement of the seventeenth-century English poets to
have explored the relations of physical and spiritual love; of
this Keats seems oblivious; yet we must admit that an
awareness of the imaginative and spiritual achievements of
the past would not have ensured them to him, as our own

excessive awareness fails to ensure them to us. In Keats's mind there was, as I have said (why it should have had, even in so young a man, an exclusive dominance I do not know) —there was, to put it in the simplest language, a strong compulsion towards the realization of physical love, but he could not reconcile it with his idealization of the beloved. So we get what has been supposed to be a characteristically romantic attitude—that to *die* at the greatest intensity of love is to achieve that intensity without diminution. If this is the romantic attitude—and there is no reason to believe that Wordsworth's domestic pieties and evasions, or Shelley's rhetorical Godwinism and watered-down Platonism, ever achieved *as experience* a higher realization of the central human problem than Keats did—if this is romanticism, then romanticism (or romantic poetry) represents a decline in insight and in imaginative and moral power. In the interval between

> So must pure lovers soules descend
> T'affections, and to faculties,
> Which sense may reach and apprehend,
> Else a great Prince in prison lies . . .

and this:

> But Love has pitched his mansion in
> The place of excrement;
> For nothing can be sole or whole
> That has not been ren¯ . . .

—between Donne and Yeats there was evidently a shrinkage in the range and depth of Western man's experience, as that experience was expressed in works of the imagination, and not merely in the Goethean or Wordsworthian goodwill towards comprehensiveness or the inclusion of a little of everything. Keats seems to me to have been, in England at any rate, the master of the central experience of his age. His profound honesty, his dislike of system and opinion as substitutes for what the imagination is actually able to control, and his perfect artistic courage, will keep him not only among the masters of English poetry but among the few heroes of literature. To adapt to Keats a remark of Eliot's about Arnold, I should say that he did not know, because he lacked the maturity to know, the boredom; he knew a little of the horror; but he knew much of the glory, of human life.

# HARDY'S PHILOSOPHIC
# METAPHORS

## *1940*

AFTER Thomas Hardy had become a great literary figure
on the British model—that is to say, a personage to whom
one makes pilgrimages—criticism of his works languished:
once the battle over the obscenity of Jude and the pessimism of his "philosophy" had been won, critics had very little
to say, except that they admired him. So far as I know, only
two critical works on Hardy exist: Lionel Johnson's fine study
of the novels, *The Art of Thomas Hardy*, which, first published in 1894, appeared before Hardy was known as a poet;
and Lascelles Abercrombie's *Thomas Hardy*, a book of considerable value for the criticism of the novels but of not
much use for the poetry. One must add to these works the
excellent essay, "The Poetry of Thomas Hardy," by J. E.
Barton, which appears as an appendix to the John Lane edition of Johnson's study (1923). The centennial biography,
*Hardy of Wessex*, by C. J. Weber, no doubt adds to our
store of facts about Hardy; yet Mr. Weber's critical inepti-
tude contributes little to our understanding of either the
poetry or the novels.

For two reasons I have wished to make this comment upon
the critics of Hardy's poetry: they have given us very little
to start with, and their assertion of Hardy's greatness as a

poet is worse than nothing to start with. I do not intend in this commentary to deny the "greatness" of Hardy's poetry, nor to deny meaning to the pious enthusiasm of two generations of devoted readers, among whom intermittently I count myself. But the enthusiasm is largely sentimental; it implies an equivocal judgment of both the poetry and the man. It is sentimental because it does not distinguish man from poet or tell us upon what terms we may talk about them together. We have here in the case of Hardy—though for no doubt quite different reasons—the figure of the poet-sage not unlike that of Mr. Robert Frost, whose admirers will not permit the critics to dissociate the poetry from the wise man who wrote it. When without the admirers' permission Mr. R. P. Blackmur assumed that his task was to discuss Mr. Frost's language, he suffered the fanatical obloquy of a popular spellbinder, Mr. Bernard DeVoto, who promptly called Mr. Blackmur a fool.

Now very much the same sort of thing went on towards the end of Thomas Hardy's life, and one must strongly suspect, from all the evidence, that he liked it, and that he liked it because, like most critically naïve minds, he could accept the personal tribute as tribute to the power of his message, which was the message of a "philosopher." Hardy was a great poet, but I arrive at that conclusion after disposing of a prejudice against the personal qualities that have led his admirers to believe him a great man. I see him as a somewhat complacent and tiresome old gentleman, mellow and wise; a man who in his youth had set about conquering a career; who married a woman his inferior but above him socially, and could never forget the social difference—a fact that forbids us to forget it; who permitted his literary reputation to lead him into the tow of society hostesses who could have seen in him only his fame and from whom, as he frequently confessed, he got nothing. Yet he continued until late in life to appear as the literary lion. Why did he do it? It is useless to pretend that Thomas Hardy's social sense was distinguished (a distinction that has nothing to do with "class") or that he was not lacking in a certain knowledge of the world that would have been valuable even to the historian of a yeoman society: in so far as historical and biographical criticism will illuminate Hardy's poetry, it is important to keep his defects steadily in mind, for he never overcame them. Shakespeare's origins were humbler than Hardy's, yet they are irrelevant in the criticism of Shakespeare, because the confusion of feeling that one finds in Hardy cannot be found in Shakespeare. Hardy's background and education, like other backgrounds and other educations for poetry, will give us a clue to the defects of the work, but not to its merits, and it is with the merits that criticism must be specifically occupied. Literature can be written from any background, and Hardy wrote literature.

Mr. Weber quotes from Hardy's famous description of Clym Yeobright the following passage, and applies it to Hardy's own young manhood:

> Mentally he was in a provincial future, that is, he was in many points abreast with the central town thinkers of his date. Much of this development he may have owed to his studious life in Paris, where he had become acquainted with ethical systems popular at the time. In consequence of this relatively advanced position, Yeobright might have been called unfortunate. The rural world was not ripe for him.

From this and other passages in the novels, in which Hardy presents himself in the disguise of certain characters, we get a portrait of the young Hardy against the background from which he sprang. Like Yeobright he was a young man "educated" out of the folk culture of his region: he had read Darwin, Huxley, Hume, Gibbon—the Victorian agnostics and their naturalistic forerunners of the eighteenth century. He began to see the world through "ethical systems popular at the time"; more than that, he began to see the people of Dorset in terms of the metaphysical bias of these systems;

so that when he came back to Dorset from his studies in London he must have felt that his "advanced position" had cut him off from his people.

Yet there can be no doubt that, if this situation actually confronted Hardy at the outset of his literary career, it offered him tremendous advantages. He had been possessed from birth of an immense, almost instinctive knowledge of the life of a people rooted in ancient folk-traditions and fixed, also, in the objective patterns of nature and of the occupations close to nature. This knowledge of a provincial scene, where "life had bared its bones" to him, must have toughened his skepticism against the cruder aspects of Victorian thought, liberalism, optimism, and the doctrine of progress, and he could concentrate with a sort of classical purity upon the permanent human experiences.

Yet he did have a philosophical view of the significance of the human situation. As William R. Rutland indicates in his *Thomas Hardy* (the best general book on the subject), Hardy maintained with great consistency, from the beginning of his literary career, a philosophical attitude. The attitude did not change. Mr. Rutland makes an astute analysis of it:

> It is an interesting paradox that Hardy should have placed so high a value upon intellectual reason, while his own mental life was almost entirely governed by emotion . . . he criticized J. H. Newman for failing to provide logical support for his beliefs. The outlook upon life of his mature manhood was almost wholly due to emotional reactions against suffering and injustice; but he sought for intellectual explanations of the universe in the writing of the philosophers. He went on reading philosophy till he was old, but he never advanced beyond what had been in the forefront of thought during his early manhood. When, in 1915, he read that no modern philosopher subscribes to Herbert Spencer's doctrine of "the Unknowable" (which had greatly influenced him) he declared himself "utterly bewildered."

How much this philosophical reading did to make the
young Hardy, like Clym Yeobright, an outsider in his own
region, nobody could estimate accurately; but that it did
affect him in this manner I believe no one will deny. To say
that he had reached an "advanced position" is only another
way of saying that he had very early come to be both inside
and outside his background, which was to be the material
of his art: an ambivalent point of view that, in its infinite
variations from any formula that we may state for it, is at
the center of the ironic consciousness. While Hardy had a
direct "emotional reaction" to his Wessex people, who were
the human substance of the only world he really knew, he
nevertheless tried to philosophize about them in the terms of
Victorian materialism.

This, I think, was his intellectual situation, and Mr. Rutland has given us a clue to its meaning that ought to receive
at some future time a more detailed analysis than I can give
it here. In setting forth the experiences of people deeply
involved in the cycle of the earth and "conditioned" in
their emotional relations by close familiarity with the processes of nature, he had constantly before him a kind of
"naturalism" that only an astute philosophical mind could
have kept, in that period, distinct from a naturalism of a
wholly different order: the philosophic naturalism of Huxley
and Spencer which, according to Mr. Rutland, Hardy tended
to look upon as "explanations" of the world, not as theories.
When he was shocked in 1915 by the decline of Spencer's
reputation, he doubtless felt that a final conclusion had been
upset; his outlook was not philosophical but brooding and
ruminative; and I believe that here, again, we get the image
of Clym Yeobright, the young man ill-prepared to digest the
learning of the great world, the provincial amateur who sees
farther than his neighbors but who, if he had seen still
farther, might not have accepted, *in an act of faith,* the
Darwinian naturalism of his time. As late as 1922 he wrote
in the "Apology" to *Late Lyrics and Earlier* that "when belief in witches of Endor is displacing the Darwinian theory

and 'the truth that shall make you free,' men's minds appear, as above noted, to be moving backwards rather than on." The witches of Endor had doubtless presided over the irrational passions of the War; but the going backwards instead of forwards indicates, I believe, a somewhat greater belief in one of the leading Victorian ideas, Progress, than is usually attributed to Hardy.

Perhaps Hardy's intense awareness of the folk-realism of his people modified the liberal optimism of his time, and checked his assent to the enthusiasms of his age at a particular stage, which he described as "evolutionary meliorism." Nevertheless, the reader of Hardy's novels gets a total impression in which this doctrine of "meliorism" is occasionally stated but in which it plays little part in terms of the characters and their plots. It has often been said that Hardy's two leading ideas, Necessity and Chance, Fate and "Crass Casualty," continue the Greek tradition; but it seems more likely that his Necessity is only Victorian Mechanism, and that Chance represents the occasional intercession into the mechanical routine of the universe, of Spencer's Unknowable.

It is a curious feature of Hardy's treatment of the Dorchester peasantry that they are not permitted to have religious experiences: their religious emotions are thoroughly "psychologized" and naturalistic. It would seem, then, that Hardy, like Clym, had reached an "advanced position" which forbade him to take seriously the religious life of his people. The peculiar compound of pagan superstition and Christianity which issued in a simple miraculism (as opposed to Hardy's mechanism of fate interrupted by blind chance) he tended from the first to look at from the outside, where it seemed quaint and picturesque. This, of course, is not quite the whole story of Hardy's profound insight into human character, or of his mastery of dramatic form which he achieved in spite of technical limitations and of a highfalutin' prose style of which the best that can be said is that

it has an occasional descriptive grandeur and a frequent
bathos. (He once said that while poetry requires technique,
prose writes itself—perhaps a British as well as a personal
blindness.) I have offered this brief simplification of Hardy's
intellectual "position" not as an explanation of his work, but
merely as a pointer towards a certain kind of meaning that
I have seen in his poetry.

## II

ONE of Hardy's most powerful poems is "Nature's Questioning." It is written in a four-line stanza that seems characteristically to be derived from a hymn meter in the first two
lines, but instead of completing the 4—3—4—3 stanza that
the first two lines have led us to expect, he boldly finishes it
off, 3—6, thus:

> When I look forth at dawning, pool,
>> Field, flock, and lonely tree,
>> All seem to gaze at me
> Like chastened children sitting silent in school;

> Their faces dulled, constrained, and worn,
>> As though the master's ways
>> Through the long teaching days
> Had cowed them till their early zest was overborne.

The Alexandrines in these stanzas are prosodically among
the most successful in English: the sense overlaps the caesura,
imparting to the structure a firmness that keeps the line
from breaking down into two trimeters. The poem proceeds,
after two stanzas setting forth cosmic questions from nature:

> Or come we of an Automaton
>> Unconscious of our pains? . . .
>> Or are we live remains
> Of Godhead dying downwards, brain and eye now gone?

The two last lines are often cited as Hardy's most brilliant,
and I think there can be no doubt of their magnificence. The

phrase *now gone* could not be better: one is reminded of Henry James's tact concerning the presentation of super-natural beings in fiction, that "weak specifications" limit their credibility. *Now gone* is just specific enough, its col-loquial tone bringing the idea of God within the range of familiarity without the risks of a too concrete image: brain and eye are not images, but rather objects denoted. The rhythm of the line seems to me to be masterly. The pre-vailing falling rhythm is suddenly shifted, from "brain" to the end of the line, to a counter, mounting rhythm; moreover, the trimeter line latent in the hexameter becomes explicit —"Of Godhead dying downwards"—and the shock of *down-wards* has the prolonged effect of the feminine ending; when the hexameter is resumed, *brain* strikes with tremendous force, with a secondary stress on *eye;* and *now gone* reads to my ear almost as a spondee. In this last feature it seems to me that the final proof of the technical mastery appears (conscious in Hardy, or not). The rhythmic conflict in the line is never quite resolved. There has been a regular alterna-tion of stressed and unstressed syllables, so that when we reach *now* we are under a strong compulsion to pass it over lightly; yet we cannot do so; the quantity of the syllable, reinforced by its rhetoric, stops us. Could we pass it lightly, *now gone* as an iambus would restore the prevailing pattern of mounting rhythm; as a spondee it suspends the conflict, the particular effect of meaning and rhythm being a kind of kinesthetic sensation that we soon discover that we have been attributing to the agony of the dying Godhead.

I do not apologize for laboring this point. Great passages of poetry are rare; because they are exceptionally rare in Hardy we must exert ourselves to the utmost to understand their value. There is nothing else in "Nature's Questioning" to reward our close attention—if we are looking for poetry; but there is a great deal that will illuminate our understand-ing of Hardy's poetry. The two last stanzas:

> Or is it that some high Plan betides,
>    As yet not understood,
>    Of Evil stormed by Good,
> We the Forlorn Hope over which Achievement strides?
>
> Thus things around No answerer I . . .
>    Meanwhile the winds, and rains,
>    And Earth's old glooms and pains
> Are still the same, and Life and Death are neighbors nigh.

Now this poem as a whole fairly represents a use of metaphor practiced by certain Victorian poets. The inanimate "things around" that have asked the questions appear in the first stanza as pool, field, flock, and a tree whose sole quality is its loneliness; these objects quickly become school children, before they have been sufficiently particularized to be themselves. The transformation of the natural objects into persons is initiated with some degree of tact in terms of simile—"Like chastened children"—that we can accept because not too much is claimed for it at that stage. But in the second stanza what appeared to be simile becomes completed metaphor. We have here, in the terms of Mr. I. A. Richards, an instance of metaphor in which the "vehicle" replaces the "tenor": the natural objects (tenor) are so weakly perceived that the children (vehicle), who appear as the conveyance of their significance, cancel out the natural objects altogether; so that, as the poem proceeds to the fourth stanza, we get a group of inanimate objects as school children asking this question:

> Has some vast Imbecility,
>    Mighty to build and blend,
>    But impotent to tend,
> Framed us in jest, and left us now to hazardry?

Now Hardy is saying that the children are Nature, and would like to say, since he is a nineteenth-century monist, that they are mechanically determined, as Nature is; both

human and nonhuman nature suffer the neglect of the
absentee God of Deism, who is

> Mighty to build and blend,
> But impotent to tend . . .

This God is the schoolmaster of line two, stanza two;
here again the metaphorical vehicle replaces the tenor; and
in view of the deistic character of this God, the figure of
the "master," who is the personal, anthropomorphic representation of the Unknowable, contradicts his logical significance: to render this God dramatically, Hardy has made
him the God of theism, a personal, if not the Christian, God,
but if he is the Automaton of stanza five, he is not equipped
to teach a class; he cannot even be present if he is "im-
potent to tend."

Throughout this poem (and I should risk the guess, in
most of the "philosophical" poems of Hardy) the margin of
intelligible meaning achieved by the union of the tenor and
the vehicle is very narrow. Even in the magnificent image of
the "Godhead dying downwards" we get a certain degree of
contradiction between tenor and vehicle: in order to say
that God has left the universe to chance after setting it in
motion, Hardy can merely present us with the theistic God
as blind and imbecile.

So generally of Hardy it may perhaps be said that his
"philosophy" tends to be a little beyond the range of his
feeling: his abstractions are thus somewhat irresponsible,
since he rarely shows us the experience that ought to justify
them, that would give them substance, visibility, and meaning. The visible embodiment of the meaning of "Nature's
Questioning" ought doubtless to be "pool, field, flock, and
lonely tree," which are not experienced objects of nature,
but only universals of so thinly perceived quality that Hardy
apparently had no trouble at all in absorbing them into the
analogy of the school children; and likewise the schoolmaster is so thinly particularized that the next analogical
development, master into God, is easy and unconvincing.

It is likely that other critics will from time to time examine other examples of Hardy's verse; it will probably be many years before a comprehensive study of all his poetry can appear. I have a strong impression that the ballads, songs, and occasional lyrics, as well as the versified tales and the little ironic incidents of the *Satires of Circumstance,* exhibit the greatest freedom of sensibility of which Hardy, the poet, was capable: in the vast number of these slighter pieces Hardy is at his least philosophical; he is closer to the immediate subject, he is free to observe directly and to record the direct impression. But when he begins to think, when he begins to say what the impression, the observation, the incident means, he can only bring in his ill-digested philosophy—a *mélange* of Schopenhauer, Darwin, and Spencer, against a cosmological background of eighteenth-century Deism that he could not project imaginatively into his immediate experience.

Is this not the common situation of the Victorian poets and, with some differences, our predicament today? Our chief difference seems to consist in a greater awareness of the problem—not in its solution. Hardy's philosophical limitations permitted him to accept as "truth" Spencer's *Synthetic Philosophy,* with the result that he held to the mechanistic theories of his time with greater single-mindedness than Tennyson or Browning ever achieved. This single-mindedness probably kept him immune to the eclectic miscellany of easy speculations and solutions to which his more sensitive contemporaries succumbed. There can be no doubt that the poetic language of Hardy, particularly in poems like "God's Funeral" and "The Convergence of the Twain," achieves a weight and solidity that only Arnold of the Victorians—and then only in his best moments—could rival: perhaps his lack of a university training in literature permitted him to seize the language afresh, so that even his heavily Latinized vocabulary is capable of effects that a better educated poet in his age would have missed. It is as dangerous as it is meaningless to wish that a great poet might have either corrected, or had the literary tact to avoid the exposure of, his deficiencies. Had he been "better educated" he might have been like Browning or Swinburne—both men his inferiors; had he been worse educated, it is not inconceivable that he should have been even more like James Thomson (B.V.) than he was; but fortunately he was Thomas Hardy.

# EMILY DICKINSON

## *1932*

GREAT poetry needs no special features of difficulty to make it mysterious. When it has them, the reputation of the poet is likely to remain uncertain. This is still true of Donne, and it is true of Emily Dickinson, whose verse appeared in an age unfavorable to the use of intelligence in poetry. Her poetry is not like any other poetry of her time; it is not like any of the innumerable kinds of verse written today. In still another respect it is far removed from us. It is a poetry of ideas, and it demands of the reader a point of view—not an opinion of the New Deal or of the League of Nations, but an ingrained philosophy that is fundamental, a settled attitude that is almost extinct in this eclectic age. Yet it is not the sort of poetry of ideas which, like Pope's, requires a point of view only. It requires also, for the deepest understanding, which must go beneath the verbal excitement of the style, a highly developed sense of the specific quality of poetry—a quality that most persons accept as the accidental feature of something else that the poet thinks he has to say. This is one reason why Miss Dickinson's poetry has not been widely read.

There is another reason, and it is a part of the problem peculiar to a poetry that comes out of fundamental ideas.

We lack a tradition of criticism. There were no points of critical reference passed on to us from a preceding generation. I am not upholding here the so-called dead-hand of tradition, but rather a rational insight into the meaning of the present in terms of some imaginable past implicit in our own lives: we need a body of ideas that can bear upon the course of the spirit and yet remain coherent as a rational instrument. We ignore the present, which is momently translated into the past, and derive our standards from imaginative constructions of the future. The hard contingency of fact invariably breaks these standards down, leaving us the intellectual chaos which is the sore distress of American criticism. Marxian criticism has become the latest disguise of this heresy.

Still another difficulty stands between us and Miss Dickinson. It is the failure of the scholars to feel more than biographical curiosity about her. We have scholarship, but that is no substitute for a critical tradition. Miss Dickinson's value to the research scholar, who likes historical difficulty for its own sake, is slight; she is too near to possess the remoteness of literature. Perhaps her appropriate setting would be the age of Cowley or of Donne. Yet in her own historical setting she is, nevertheless, remarkable and special.

Although the intellectual climate into which she was born, in 1830, had, as all times have, the features of a transition, the period was also a major crisis culminating in the war between the States. After that war, in New England as well as in the South, spiritual crises were definitely minor until the First World War.

Yet, a generation before the war of 1861-65, the transformation of New England had begun. When Samuel Slater in 1790 thwarted the British embargo on mill-machinery by committing to memory the whole design of a cotton spinner and bringing it to Massachusetts, he planted the seed of the "Western spirit." By 1825 its growth in the East was rank enough to begin choking out the ideas and habits of living that New England along with Virginia had kept in unconscious allegiance to Europe To the casual observer, perhaps, the New England character of 1830 was largely an eighteenth-century character. But theocracy was on the decline, and industrialism was rising—as Emerson, in an unusually lucid moment, put it, "Things are in the saddle." The energy that had built the meeting-house ran the factory.

Now the idea that moved the theocratic state is the most interesting historically of all American ideas. It was, of course, powerful in seventeenth-century England, but in America, where the long arm of Laud could not reach, it acquired an unchecked social and political influence. The important thing to remember about the puritan theocracy is that it permeated, as it could never have done in England, a whole society. It gave final, definite meaning to life, the life of pious and impious, of learned and vulgar alike. It gave —and this is its significance for Emily Dickinson, and in only slightly lesser degree for Melville and Hawthorne—it gave an heroic proportion and a tragic mode to the experience of the individual. The history of the New England theocracy, from Apostle Eliot to Cotton Mather, is rich in gigantic intellects that broke down—or so it must appear to an outsider —in a kind of moral decadence and depravity. Socially we may not like the New England idea. Yet it had an immense, incalculable value for literature: it dramatized the human soul.

But by 1850 the great fortunes had been made (in the rum, slave, and milling industries), and New England became a museum. The whatnots groaned under the load of knickknacks, the fine china dogs and cats, the pieces of Oriental jade, the chips off the leaning tower at Pisa. There were the rare books and the cosmopolitan learning. It was all equally displayed as the evidence of a superior culture. The Gilded Age had already begun. But culture, in the true sense, was disappearing. Where the old order, formidable as it was, had held all this personal experience, this eclectic excitement, in a comprehensible whole, the new order tended to flatten it out in a common experience that was not quite in common;

it exalted more and more the personal and the unique in
the interior sense. Where the old-fashioned puritans got
together on a rigid doctrine, and could thus be individualists
in manners, the nineteenth-century New Englander, lacking
a genuine religious center, began to be a social conformist.
The common idea of the Redemption, for example, was replaced by the conformist idea of respectability among neighbors whose spiritual disorder, not very evident at the surface,
was becoming acute. A great idea was breaking up, and
society was moving towards external uniformity, which is
usually the measure of the spiritual sterility inside.

At this juncture Emerson came upon the scene: the Lucifer
of Concord, he had better be called hereafter, for he was the
light-bearer who could see nothing but light, and was fear-
fully blind. He looked around and saw the uniformity of
life, and called it the routine of tradition, the tyranny of the
theological idea. The death of Priam put an end to the hope
of Troy, but it was a slight feat of arms for the doughty
Pyrrhus; Priam was an old gentleman and almost dead. So
was theocracy; and Emerson killed it. In this way he ac-
celerated a tendency that he disliked. It was a great intellectual mistake. By it Emerson unwittingly became the
prophet of a piratical industrialism, a consequence of his
own transcendental individualism that he could not foresee. He was hoist with his own petard.

He discredited more than any other man the puritan
drama of the soul. The age that followed, from 1865 on,
expired in a genteel secularism, a mildly didactic order of
feeling whose ornaments were Lowell, Longfellow, and
Holmes. "After Emerson had done his work," says Mr.
Robert Penn Warren, "any tragic possibilities in that culture were dissipated." Hawthorne alone in his time kept
pure, in the primitive terms, the primitive vision; he brings
the puritan tragedy to its climax. Man, measured by a great
idea outside himself, is found wanting. But for Emerson
man is greater than any idea and, being himself the Over-
Soul, is innately perfect; there is no struggle because—I state

the Emersonian doctrine, which is very slippery, in its extreme terms—because there is no possibility of error. There
is no drama in human character because there is no tragic
fault. It is not surprising, then, that after Emerson New
England literature tastes like a sip of cambric tea. Its center
of vision has disappeared. There is Hawthorne looking back,
there is Emerson looking not too clearly at anything ahead:
Emily Dickinson, who has in her something of both, comes
in somewhere between.

With the exception of Poe there is no other American poet
whose work so steadily emerges, under pressure of certain
disintegrating obsessions, from the framework of moral character. There is none of whom it is truer to say that the poet
*is* the poetry. Perhaps this explains the zeal of her admirers
for her biography; it explains, in part at least, the gratuitous
mystery that Mrs. Bianchi, a niece of the poet and her official
biographer, has made of her life. The devoted controversy
that Miss Josephine Pollitt and Miss Genevieve Taggard
started a few years ago with their excellent books shows the
extent to which the critics feel the intimate connection of
her life and work. Admiration and affection are pleased to
linger over the tokens of a great life; but the solution to the
Dickinson enigma is peculiarly superior to fact.

The meaning of the identity—which we merely feel—of
character and poetry would be exceedingly obscure, even if
we could draw up a kind of Binet correlation between the
two sets of "facts." Miss Dickinson was a recluse; but her
poetry is rich with a profound and varied experience. Where
did she get it? Now some of the biographers, nervous in the
presence of this discrepancy, are eager to find her a love
affair, and I think this search is due to a modern prejudice:
we believe that no virgin can know enough to write poetry.
We shall never learn where she got the rich quality of her
mind. The moral image that we have of Miss Dickinson
stands out in every poem: it is that of a dominating spinster
whose very sweetness must have been formidable. Yet her
poetry constantly moves within an absolute order of truths

that overwhelmed her simply because to her they were unalterably fixed. It is dangerous to assume that her "life," which to the biographers means the thwarted love affair she is supposed to have had, gave to her poetry a decisive direction. It is even more dangerous to suppose that it made her a poet.

Poets are mysterious, but a poet when all is said is not much more mysterious than a banker. The critics remain spellbound by the technical license of her verse and by the puzzle of her personal life. Personality is a legitimate interest because it is an incurable interest, but legitimate as a personal interest only; it will never give up the key to anyone's verse. Used to that end, the interest is false. "It is apparent," writes Mr. Conrad Aiken, "that Miss Dickinson became a hermit by deliberate and conscious choice"—a sensible remark that we cannot repeat too often. If it were necessary to explain her seclusion with disappointment in love, there would remain the discrepancy between what the seclusion produced and the seclusion looked at as a cause. The effect, which is her poetry, would imply the whole complex of anterior fact, which was the social and religious structure of New England.

The problem to be kept in mind is thus the meaning of her "deliberate and conscious" decision to withdraw from life to her upstairs room. This simple fact is not very important. But that it must have been her sole way of acting out her part in the history of her culture, which made, with the variations of circumstance, a single demand upon all its representatives—this is of the greatest consequence. All pity for Miss Dickinson's "starved life" is misdirected. Her life was one of the richest and deepest ever lived on this continent.

When she went upstairs and closed the door, she mastered life by rejecting it. Others in their way had done it before; still others did it later. If we suppose—which is to suppose the improbable—that the love-affair precipitated the seclusion, it was only a pretext; she would have found another. Mastery of the world by rejecting the world was the doctrine, even if it was not always the practice, of Jonathan Edwards and Cotton Mather. It is the meaning of fate in Hawthorne: his people are fated to withdraw from the world and to be destroyed. And it is one of the great themes of Henry James.

There is a moral emphasis that connects Hawthorne, James, and Miss Dickinson, and I think it is instructive. Between Hawthorne and James lies an epoch. The temptation to sin, in Hawthorne, is, in James, transformed into the temptation not to do the "decent thing." A whole world-scheme, a complete cosmic background, has shrunk to the dimensions of the individual conscience. This epoch between Hawthorne and James lies in Emerson. James found himself in the post-Emersonian world, and he could not, without violating the detachment proper to an artist, undo Emerson's work; he had that kind of intelligence which refuses to break its head against history. There was left to him only the value, the historic rôle, of rejection. He could merely escape from the physical presence of that world which, for convenience, we may call Emerson's world: he could only take his Americans to Europe upon the vain quest of something that they had lost at home. His characters, fleeing the wreckage of the puritan culture, preserved only their honor. Honor became a sort of forlorn hope struggling against the forces of "pure fact" that had got loose in the middle of the century. Honor alone is a poor weapon against nature, being too personal, finical, and proud, and James achieved a victory by refusing to engage the whole force of the enemy.

In Emily Dickinson the conflict takes place on a vaster field. The enemy to all those New Englanders was Nature, and Miss Dickinson saw into the character of this enemy more deeply than any of the others. The general symbol of Nature, for her, is Death, and her weapon against Death is the entire powerful dumb-show of the puritan theology led by Redemption and Immortality. Morally speaking, the problem for James and Miss Dickinson is similar. But her advantages were greater than his. The advantages lay in the availability to her of the puritan ideas on the theological plane.

These ideas, in her poetry, are momently assailed by the disintegrating force of Nature (appearing as Death) which, while constantly breaking them down, constantly redefines and strengthens them. The values are purified by the triumphant withdrawal from Nature, by their power to recover from Nature. The poet attains to a mastery over experience by facing its utmost implications. There is the clash of powerful opposites, and in all great poetry—for Emily Dickinson is a great poet—it issues in a tension between abstraction and sensation in which the two elements may be, of course, distinguished logically, but not really. We are shown our roots in Nature by examining our differences with Nature; we are renewed by Nature without being delivered into her hands. When it is possible for a poet to do this for us with the greatest imaginative comprehension, a possibility that the poet cannot himself create, we have the perfect literary situation. Only a few times in the history of English poetry has this situation come about, notably, the period between about 1580 and the Restoration. There was a similar age in New England from which emerged two talents of the first order —Hawthorne and Emily Dickinson.

There is an epoch between James and Miss Dickinson. But between her and Hawthorne there exists a difference of intellectual quality. She lacks almost radically the power to seize upon and understand abstractions for their own sake; she does not separate them from the sensuous illuminations that she is so marvelously adept at; like Donne, she *perceives abstraction* and *thinks sensation.* But Hawthorne was a master of ideas, within a limited range; this narrowness confined him to his own kind of life, his own society, and out of it grew his typical forms of experience, his steady, almost obsessed vision of man; it explains his depth and

intensity. Yet he is always conscious of the abstract, doc-
trinal aspect of his mind, and when his vision of action and
emotion is weak, his work becomes didactic. Now Miss
Dickinson's poetry often runs into quasi-homiletic forms, but
it is never didactic. Her very ignorance, her lack of formal
intellectual training, preserved her from the risk that im-
periled Hawthorne. She cannot reason at all. She can only
*see*. It is impossible to imagine what she might have done
with drama or fiction; for, not approaching the puritan
temper and through it the puritan myth, through human
action, she is able to grasp the terms of the myth directly
and by a feat that amounts almost to anthropomorphism,
to give them a luminous tension, a kind of drama, among
themselves.

One of the perfect poems in English is "The Chariot,"
and it illustrates better than anything else she wrote the
special quality of her mind. I think it will illuminate the
tendency of this discussion:

> Because I could not stop for death,
> He kindly stopped for me;
> The carriage held but just ourselves
> And immortality.
>
> We slowly drove, he knew no haste,
> And I had put away
> My labor, and my leisure too,
> For his civility.
>
> We passed the school where children played,
> Their lessons scarcely done;
> We passed the fields of gazing grain,
> We passed the setting sun.
>
> We paused before a house that seemed
> A swelling of the ground;
> The roof was scarcely visible,
> The cornice but a mound.

Since then 'tis centuries; but each
Feels shorter than the day
I first surmised the horses' heads
Were toward eternity.

If the word great means anything in poetry, this poem is
one of the greatest in the English language. The rhythm
charges with movement the pattern of suspended action back
of the poem. Every image is precise and, moreover, not
merely beautiful, but fused with the central idea. Every
image extends and intensifies every other. The third stanza
especially shows Miss Dickinson's power to fuse, into a
single order of perception, a heterogeneous series: the children, the grain, and the setting sun (time) have the same
degree of credibility; the first subtly preparing for the last.
The sharp *gazing* before *grain* instills into nature a cold
vitality of which the qualitative richness has infinite depth.
The content of death in the poem eludes explicit definition.
He is a gentleman taking a lady out for a drive. But note the
restraint that keeps the poet from carrying this so far that it
becomes ludicrous and incredible; and note the subtly inter-
fused erotic motive, which the idea of death has presented
to most romantic poets, love being a symbol interchangeable
with death. The terror of death is objectified through this
figure of the genteel driver, who is made ironically to serve
the end of Immortality. This is the heart of the poem: she
has presented a typical Christian theme in its final irresolu-
tion, without making any final statements about it. There is
no solution to the problem; there can be only a presentation
of it in the full context of intellect and feeling. A construction
of the human will, elaborated with all the abstracting powers
of the mind, is put to the concrete test of experience: the
idea of immortality is confronted with the fact of physical
disintegration. We are not told what to think; we are told
to look at the situation.

The framework of the poem is, in fact, the two abstractions, mortality and eternity, which are made to associate in

equality with the images: she sees the ideas, and thinks the perceptions. She did, of course, nothing of the sort; but we must use the logical distinctions, even to the extent of paradox, if we are to form any notion of this rare quality of mind. She could not in the proper sense think at all, and unless we prefer the feeble poetry of moral ideas that flourished in New England in the eighties, we must conclude that her intellectual deficiency contributed at least negatively to her great distinction. Miss Dickinson is probably the only Anglo-American poet of her century whose work exhibits the perfect literary situation—in which is possible the fusion of sensibility and thought. Unlike her contemporaries, she never succumbed to her ideas, to easy solutions, to her private desires.

Philosophers must deal with ideas, but the trouble with most nineteenth-century poets is too much philosophy; they are nearer to being philosophers than poets, without being in the true sense either. Tennyson is a good example of this; so is Arnold in his weak moments. There have been poets like Milton and Donne, who were not spoiled for their true business by leaning on a rational system of ideas, who understood the poetic use of ideas. Tennyson tried to mix a little Huxley and a little Broad Church, without understanding either Broad Church or Huxley; the result was fatal, and what is worse, it was shallow. Miss Dickinson's ideas were deeply imbedded in her character, not taken from the latest tract. A conscious cultivation of ideas in poetry is always dangerous, and even Milton escaped ruin only by having an instinct for what in the deepest sense he understood. Even at that there is a remote quality in Milton's approach to his material, in his treatment of it; in the nineteenth century, in an imperfect literary situation where literature was confused with documentation, he might have been a pseudo-philosopher-poet. It is difficult to conceive Emily Dickinson and John Donne succumbing to rumination about "problems"; they would not have written at all.

Neither the feeling nor the style of Miss Dickinson belongs

to the seventeenth century; yet between her and Donne there are remarkable ties. Their religious ideas, their abstractions, are momently toppling from the rational plane to the level of perception. The ideas, in fact, are no longer the impersonal religious symbols created anew in the heat of emotion, that we find in poets like Herbert and Vaughan. They have become, for Donne, the terms of personality; they are mingled with the miscellany of sensation. In Miss Dickinson, as in Donne, we may detect a singularly morbid concern, not for religious truth, but for personal revelation. The modern word is self-exploitation. It is egoism grown irresponsible in religion and decadent in morals. In religion it is blasphemy; in society it means usually that culture is not self-contained and sufficient, that the spiritual community is breaking up. This is, along with some other features that do not concern us here, the perfect literary situation.

## I I

PERSONAL revelation of the kind that Donne and Miss Dickinson strove for, in the effort to understand their relation to the world, is a feature of all great poetry; it is probably the hidden motive for writing. It is the effort of the individual to live apart from a cultural tradition that no longer sustains him. But this culture, which I now wish to discuss a little, is indispensable: there is a great deal of shallow nonsense in modern criticism which holds that poetry —and this is a half-truth that is worse than false—is essentially revolutionary. It is only indirectly revolutionary: the intellectual and religious background of an age no longer contains the whole spirit, and the poet proceeds to examine that background in terms of immediate experience. But the background is necessary; otherwise all the arts (not only poetry) would have to rise in a vacuum. Poetry does not dispense with tradition; it probes the deficiencies of a tradition. But it must have a tradition to probe. It is too bad that Arnold did not explain his doctrine, that poetry is a criticism of life, from the viewpoint of its background: we should have been spared an era of academic misconception, in which criticism of life meant a diluted pragmatism, the criterion of which was respectability. The poet in the true sense "criticizes" his tradition, either as such, or indirectly by comparing it with something that is about to replace it; he does what the root-meaning of the verb implies—he *discerns* its real elements and thus establishes its value, by putting it to the test of experience.

What is the nature of a poet's culture? Or, to put the question properly, what is the meaning of culture for poetry? All the great poets become the material of what we popularly call culture; we study them to acquire it. It is clear that Addison was more cultivated than Shakespeare; nevertheless Shakespeare is a finer source of culture than Addison. What is the meaning of this? Plainly it is that learning has never had anything to do with culture except instrumentally: the poet must be exactly literate enough to write down fully and precisely what he has to say, but no more The source of a poet's true culture lies back of the paraphernalia of culture, and not all the historical activity of an enlightened age can create it.

A culture cannot be consciously created. It is an available source of ideas that are imbedded in a complete and homogeneous society. The poet finds himself balanced upon the moment when such a world is about to fall, when it threatens to run out into looser and less self-sufficient impulses. This world order is assimilated, in Miss Dickinson, as medievalism was in Shakespeare, to the poetic vision; it is brought down from abstraction to personal sensibility.

In this connection it may be said that the prior conditions for great poetry, given a great talent, may be reduced to two: the thoroughness of the poet's discipline in an objective system of truth, and his lack of consciousness of such a discipline. For this discipline is a number of fundamental ideas the origin of which the poet does not know; they give form and stability to his fresh perceptions of the world; and he cannot shake them off. This is his culture, and like Tennyson's God it is nearer than hands and feet. With reasonable certainty we unearth the elements of Shakespeare's culture, and yet it is equally certain—so innocent was he of his own resources—that he would not know what our discussion is about. He appeared at the collapse of the medieval system as a rigid pattern of life, but that pattern remained in Shakespeare what Shelley called a "fixed point of reference" for his sensibility. Miss Dickinson, as we have seen, was born into the equilibrium of an old and a new order. Puritanism could not be to her what it had been to the generation of Cotton Mather—a body of absolute truths; it was an unconscious discipline timed to the pulse of her life.

The perfect literary situation: it produces, because it is rare, a special and perhaps the most distinguished kind of poet. I am not trying to invent a new critical category. Such poets are never very much alike on the surface; they show us all the varieties of poetic feeling; and like other poets they resist all classification but that of temporary convenience. But, I believe, Miss Dickinson and John Donne would have this in common: their sense of the natural world is not blunted by a too rigid system of ideas; yet the ideas, the abstractions, their education or their intellectual heritage, are not so weak as to let their immersion in nature, or their purely personal quality, get out of control. The two poles of the mind are not separately visible; we infer them from the lucid tension that may be most readily illustrated by polar activity. There is no thought as such at all; nor is there feeling; there is that unique focus of experience which is at once neither and both.

Like Miss Dickinson, Shakespeare is without opinions; his peculiar merit is also deeply involved in his failure to think about anything; his meaning is not in the content of his expression; it is in the tension of the dramatic relations of his characters. This kind of poetry is at the opposite of intellectualism. (Miss Dickinson is obscure and difficult, but that is not intellectualism.) To T. W. Higginson, the editor of *The Atlantic Monthly*, who tried to advise her, she wrote that she had no education. In any sense that Higginson could understand, it was quite true. His kind of education was the conscious cultivation of abstractions. She did not reason about the world she saw; she merely saw it. The "ideas" implicit in the world within her rose up concentrated in her immediate perception.

That kind of world at present has for us something of the fascination of a buried city. There is none like it. When such worlds exist, when such cultures flourish, they support not only the poet but all members of society. For, from these, the poet differs only in his gift for exhibiting the structure, the internal lineaments, of his culture by threatening to tear them apart: a process that concentrates the symbolic emotions of society while it seems to attack them. The poet may hate his age; he may be an outcast like Villon; but this world is always there as the background to what he has to say. It is the lens through which he brings nature to focus and control—the clarifying medium that concentrates his personal feeling. It is ready-made; he cannot make it; with it, his poetry has a spontaneity and a certainty of direction that, without it, it would lack. No poet could have invented the ideas of "The Chariot"; only a great poet could have found their imaginative equivalents. Miss Dickinson was a deep mind writing from a deep culture, and when she came to poetry, she came infallibly.

Infallibly, at her best; for no poet has ever been perfect, nor is Emily Dickinson. Her precision of statement is due to the directness with which the abstract framework of her thought acts upon its unorganized material. The two elements of her style, considered as point of view, are immortality, or the idea of permanence, and the physical process of death or decay. Her diction has two corresponding features: words of Latin or Greek origin and, sharply opposed to these, the concrete Saxon element. It is this verbal conflict that gives to her verse its high tension; it is not a device deliberately seized upon, but a feeling for language that senses out the two fundamental components of

English and their metaphysical relation: the Latin for ideas
and the Saxon for perceptions—the peculiar virtue of English as a poetic language.

Like most poets Miss Dickinson often writes out of habit;
the style that emerged from some deep exploration of an
idea is carried on as verbal habit when she has nothing to
say. She indulges herself:

> There's something quieter than sleep
> Within this inner room!
> It wears a sprig upon its breast,
> And will not tell its name.
>
> Some touch it and some kiss it,
> Some chafe its idle hand;
> It has a simple gravity
> I do not understand!
>
> While simple hearted neighbors
> Chat of the "early dead,"
> We, prone to periphrasis,
> Remark that birds have fled!

It is only a pert remark; at best a superior kind of punning
—one of the worst specimens of her occasional interest in
herself. But she never had the slightest interest in the public.
Were four poems or five published in her lifetime? She never
felt the temptation to round off a poem for public exhibition.
Higginson's kindly offer to make her verse "correct" was an
invitation to throw her work into the public ring—the ring
of Lowell and Longfellow. He could not see that he was
tampering with one of the rarest literary integrities of all
time. Here was a poet who had no use for the supports of
authorship—flattery and fame; she never needed money.

She had all the elements of a culture that has broken
up, a culture that on the religious side takes its place in the
museum of spiritual antiquities. Puritanism, as a unified
version of the world, is dead; only a remnant of it in trade
may be said to survive. In the history of puritanism she

comes between Hawthorne and Emerson. She has Hawthorne's matter, which a too irresponsible personality tends to dilute into a form like Emerson's; she is often betrayed by words. But she is not the poet of personal sentiment; she has more to say than she can put down in any one poem. Like Hardy and Whitman she must be read entire; like Shakespeare she never gives up her meaning in a single line.

She is therefore a perfect subject for the kind of criticism which is chiefly concerned with general ideas. She exhibits one of the permanent relations between personality and objective truth, and she deserves the special attention of our time, which lacks that kind of truth.

She has Hawthorne's intellectual toughness, a hard, definite sense of the physical world. The highest flights to God, the most extravagant metaphors of the strange and the remote, come back to a point of casuistry, to a moral dilemma of the experienced world. There is, in spite of the homiletic vein of utterance, no abstract speculation, nor is there a message to society; she speaks wholly to the individual experience. She offers to the unimaginative no riot of vicarious sensation; she has no useful maxims for men of action. Up to this point her resemblance to Emerson is slight: poetry is a sufficient form of utterance, and her devotion to it is pure. But in Emily Dickinson the puritan world is no longer self-contained; it is no longer complete; her sensibility exceeds its dimensions. She has trimmed down its supernatural proportions; it has become a morality; instead of the tragedy of the spirit there is a commentary upon it. Her poetry is a magnificent personal confession, blasphemous and, in its self-revelation, its honesty, almost obscene. It comes out of an intellectual life towards which it feels no moral responsibility. Cotton Mather would have burnt her for a witch.

# YEATS'S ROMANTICISM

*Notes and Suggestions*

## 1942

THE profundity of Yeats's vision of the modern world and the width of its perspective have kept me until this occasion [1] from writing anything about the poetry of our time which I most admire. The responsibility enjoins the final effort of understanding—an effort that even now I have not been able to make. The lesser poets invite the pride of the critic to its own affirmation; the greater poets—and Yeats is among them —ask us to understand not only their minds but our own; they ask us in fact to have minds of a related caliber to theirs. And criticism must necessarily remain in the presence of the great poets a business for the ant-hill: the smaller minds pooling their efforts. For the power of a Yeats will be given to the study of other poets only incidentally, for shock and technique and for the test of its own reach: this kind of power has its own task to perform.

Ours is the smaller task. The magnitude of Yeats is already visible in the failure of the partial, though frequently valuable, insights that the critics have given us in the past twenty years. There is enough in Yeats for countless studies from many points of view, yet I suspect that we shall languish far

[1] This paper was written for the special Yeats number of *The Southern Review* (Winter, 1942, vol. 7, no. 3).

this side of the complete version of Yeats until we cease to look into him for qualities that neither Yeats nor any other poet can give us; until we cease to censure him for possessing "attitudes" and "beliefs" which we do not share. Mr. Edmund Wilson's essay on Yeats in the influential study of symbolism *Axel's Castle* asks the poet for a political and economic philosophy; or if this is unfair to Mr. Wilson, perhaps it could be fairly said that Mr. Wilson, when he was writing the essay, was looking for a political and economic philosophy, and inevitably saw in Yeats and the other heirs of symbolism an evasion of the reality that he, Mr. Wilson, was looking for. (If you are looking for pins you do not want needles, though both will prick you.) Mr. Louis MacNeice's book-length study of Yeats says shrewd things about the poetry, but on the whole we get the impression that Yeats had bad luck in not belonging to the younger group of English poets, who had a monopoly on "reality." (The word is Mr. MacNeice's.) Those were the days when not to be a communist was to be fascist, which is what Mr. MacNeice makes Yeats out to be. (Yeats liked the ancient "nobility," of which for Mr. MacNeice, Wall Street and the City offer examples.)

I cite these two writers on Yeats because in them we get summed up the case for Yeats's romanticism, the view that he was an escapist retiring from problems, forces, and theories "relevant" to the modern world. While it is true that Yeats, like every poet in English since the end of the eighteenth century, began with a romantic use of language in the early poems, he ended up very differently, and he is no more to be fixed as a romantic than Shakespeare as a Senecan because he wrote passages of Senecan rhetoric. If one of the historic marks of romanticism is the division between sensibility and intellect, Yeats's career may be seen as unromantic (I do not know the opposite term) because he closed the gap. His critics would then be the romantics. I do not think that these squabbles are profitable. It is still true that Yeats had a more inclusive mind than any of his critics has had.

## I I

TWO years before Yeats died he wrote to Dorothy Wellesley: "At this moment all the specialists are about to run together in our new Alexandria, thought is about to be unified as its own free act, and the shadow in Germany and elsewhere is an attempted unity by force. In my life I have never felt so acutely the presence of a spiritual virtue and that is accompanied by intensified desire."

Scattered throughout Yeats's prose there are similar passages, but this one is only from a letter, and it lacks the imaginative reach and synthesis of the great passages towards the end of A Vision, where I recall particularly the fine paragraph on early Byzantium and Section III of "Dove or Swan" in which Yeats describes the annunciation to Leda which brought in the classical civilization, as the annunciation to the Virgin brought in the Christian. Of Byzantium he says:

"I think that in early Byzantium, maybe never before or since in recorded history, religious, aesthetic, and practical life were one, that architect and artificers—though not, it may be, poets, for language had been the instrument of controversy and must have gone abstract—spoke to the multitude and the few alike. The painter, the mosaic worker, the worker in gold and silver, the illuminator of sacred books, were almost impersonal, almost perhaps without the consciousness of individual design, absorbed in their subject-matter and that the vision of a whole people."

Mr. Cleanth Brooks has shown that the great sonnet "Leda" is no pretty picture out of mythology, that it gets its power from the powerful forces of the imagination behind it. Section III of "Dove or Swan" begins:

"I imagine the annunciation which founded Greece as made to Leda, remembering that they showed in a Spartan temple, strung up to the roof as a holy relic, an unhatched

egg of hers; and that from one of her eggs came Love and
from the other War. But all things are from antithesis, and
when in my ignorance I try to imagine what older civilization
that annunciation rejected I can but see bird and woman
blotting out some corner of the Babylonian mathematical
starlight."

In these three passages I believe that we get the main
threads of Yeats's thought expressed in language which refers
to the famous "system" but which is nevertheless sufficiently
clear to persons who have not mastered the system or who
even know nothing of it. Study of the Great Wheel with its
gyres and cones might give us extensive references for certain ideas in the passage from the letter. We should learn
that we are now in the twenty-third phase of our historical
cycle, in which thought is abstract and unity of life must be
imposed by force, and that culture is Alexandrian. The picture of a perfect culture that he gives us in Byzantium (which
in the poem of that name becomes something more than
mere historical insight) where men enjoy full unity of being
has too many features in common with familiar Western
ideas to be seen as an eccentric piece of utopianism. Byzantium is a new pastoral symbol and will be taken as that by
anybody who sees more in the pastoral tradition than ideal
shepherds and abstract sheep. The annunciation to Leda
offers historical and philosophical difficulties; yet in spite
of Yeats's frequently expressed belief that he had found a
new historical vision, the conception is not historical in any
sense that we understand today. It is a symbol established in
analogical terms; that is, our literal grasp of it depends upon
prior knowledge of the Annunciation to the Virgin. The
"Babylonian mathematical starlight" is self-evidently clear
without Yeats's scattered glosses on it: it is darkness and
abstraction, quantitative relations without imagination; and
I doubt that Yeats's definitions make it much clearer than
that. If Leda rejected it, we only learn from Yeats's "system"
that the coming of Christ brought it back in: for an entire
cultural cycle can be predominantly antithetical or predomi-

nantly primary, at the same time that it goes through the twenty-eight phases from primary to antithetical back to primary again.

In the letter to Dorothy Wellesley occurs a sentence which sounds ·casual, even literally confessional; there is no harm done if we take it at that level; there is merely a loss of insight such as we get in Mr. MacNeice's *The Poetry of W. B. Yeats*, in which Yeats's myth is dismissed as "arid" and "unsound." In the midst of the "attempted unity by force," he writes: "In my own life I have never felt so acutely the presence of a spiritual virtue and that is accompanied by intensified desire." The literal student of *A Vision*, coming upon statements like this, may well wonder what has become of the determinism of the system, which, with an almost perverse ingenuity, seems to fix the individual in a system of co-ordinates from which he cannot escape. Mr. Cleanth Brooks believes that some measure of free will lies in Yeats's conception of the False Mask, which some unpredictable force in the individual may lead him to choose instead of the True Mask. I believe this is only part of the explanation.

Does not the true explanation lie in there being *no* explanation in terms of the system? Even if we see Yeats as he saw himself, a man of Phase 17 living in Phase 23 of our civilization, the discrepancy merely introduces a complication which the system can easily take account of. Mr. MacNeice at this point enlightens us almost in spite of himself: "Freedom for Yeats, as for Engels, was a recognition of necessity—but not of economic necessity, which he considered a vulgarism." Yes; and he would have considered psychological necessity, or any inner determinism no less than an outer, economic determinism, a vulgarism also. But in the phrase the "recognition of necessity" we get a clue to Yeats's own relation to his system and to what seems to me the right way to estimate its value. He only wanted what all men want, a world larger than himself to live in; for the modern world as he saw it was, in human terms, too small for the human spirit, though quantitatively large if looked at with the scientist. If we say, then, that he wanted a *dramatic* recognition of necessity, we shall have to look at the system not as arid or unsound or eccentric, which it well may be in itself, but through Yeats's eyes, which are the eyes of his poetry.

If we begin with the poetry we shall quickly see that there is some source of power or illumination which is also in us, waiting to be aroused; and that this is true of even the greater number of the fine poems in which the imagery appears upon later study to lean upon the eccentric system. I would say, then, that even the terms of the system, when they appear in the richer texture of the poems, share a certain large margin of significance with a wider context than they have in the system itself. May we say that Yeats's *A Vision*, however private and almost childishly eclectic it may seem, has somewhat the same relation to a central tradition as the far more rigid structure of *The Divine Comedy* has to the Christian myth? I dare say that Mr. Eliot would not chide Dante for accepting a "lower mythology." Perhaps the central tradition in Dante and Yeats lies in a force that criticism cannot specifically isolate, the force that moved both poets to the dramatic recognition of necessity; yet the visible structure of the necessity itself is perhaps not the source of that power. I do not say that Yeats is comparable in stature to Dante; only that both poets strove for a visible structure of action which is indeed necessary to what they said, but which does not explain what they said. I believe that Mr. Eliot should undertake to explain why Arnold's Higher Mythology produced poetry less interesting than Yeats's Lower Mythology, which becomes in Yeats's verse the vehicle of insights and imaginative syntheses as profound as those which Arnold talked about but never, as a poet, fully achieved. Myths differ in range and intensity, but not I take it as high and low; for they are in the end what poets can make of them.

If Yeats could feel in the midst of the Alexandrian rigidity and disorder the "presence of a spiritual virtue," was he denying the inclusiveness of the system; or could he have seen his senile vigor and insight in terms of the system? Possibly the latter; but it makes little difference.

## III

*A Vision* has been described by more than one critic as a philosophy; I speak of it here as a "system"; but I doubt that it is a system of philosophy. What kind of system is it? Yeats frequently stated his own purpose, but even that is a little obscure: to put myth back into philosophy. This phrase may roughly describe the result, but it could not stand for the process; it attributes to the early philosophers a deliberation of which they would have been incapable. The language of Plotinus, whose *Enneads* Yeats read late in life, is compounded of primitive symbolism, the esoteric fragments of classical myth, and the terms of Greek technical metaphysics; but there is no calculated intention of instilling myth into philosophy.

In what sense is *A Vision* a myth? There are fragments of many myths brought in to give dramatic and sensuous body to the framework, which attains to the limit of visualization that a complex geometrical picture can provide.

A broad view of this picture, with its gyres and cones, to say nothing of the Daimons and the Principles whose relation to the Faculties defies my understanding, gleans at least two remarkable features. I merely note them:

(1) ". . . the subjective cone is called that of the *antithetical tincture* because it is achieved and defended by continual conflict with its opposite; the objective cone is called that of the *primary tincture* because whereas subjectivity—in Empedocles 'Discord' as I think—tends to separate man from man, objectivity brings us back to the mass where we began." From this simple definition—verbally simple, but very obscure—we get the first picture of the intersecting cones; and from this the whole structure is elaborated.

It is clear visually with the aid of the diagrams; but when Yeats complicates it with his Principles and Daimons, and extends the symbol of the gyres to cover historical eras, visualization breaks down. It is an extended metaphor which increasingly tends to dissolve in the particulars which it tries to bring together into unity.

When we come to the magnificent passages on history in "Dove or Swan" all the intricacies of the geometrical metaphor disappear; and the simple figure of historical cycles, which Yeats evidently supposed came out of his gyres, is sufficient to sustain his meaning. Again Yeats's "system" overlaps a body of insight common to us all.

I would suggest, then, for the study of the relation of Yeats's "system" to his vision of man, both historical and individual, this formula: As the system broadens out and merges with the traditional insights of our culture, it tends to disappear in its specific, technical aspects. What disappears is not a philosophy, but only a vast metaphorical structure. In the great elegy, "In Memory of Major Robert Gregory," we get this couplet:

> But as the outrageous stars incline
> By opposition, square, and trine—

which is the only astrological figure in the poem. Yet it must not be assumed that Yeats on this occasion turned off the system; it must be there. Why does it not overtly appear? It has been absorbed into the concrete substance of the poem; the material to be symbolized replaces the symbol, and contains its own meaning. I would select this poem out of all others of our time as the most completely expressed: it has a perfect articulation and lucidity which cannot be found in any other modern poem in English.

(2) In his early poems Yeats is concerned with the myths of ancient Ireland. We may find unreadable today a poem like "The Wanderings of Oisin" or plays like "Deidre" or "The Land of Heart's Desire." The later poems are less dependent upon fable and fully developed mythical plots for their structures. And yet Yeats entered his later poetic phase at about the same time he began to be interested in his sys-

tem, in putting myth back into philosophy. Did this mean that he was taking myth out of his poetry?

Thus the second remarkable feature of the system, as I see it, is that it is not a mythology at all, but rather an extended metaphor, as I have already pointed out, which permits him to establish relations between the tag-ends of myths eclectically gathered from all over the world. For example, there is nothing in the geometrical structure of the system which inherently provides for the annunciation to Leda; it is an arbitrary association of two fields of imagery; but once it is established, it is not hard to pass on through analogy to the Annunciation to the Virgin.

## I V

THUS it is difficult for me to follow those critics who accept Yeats's various utterances that he was concerned with a certain relation of philosophy to myth. Any statement about "life" must have philosophical implications, just as any genuine philosophical statement must have, because of the nature of language, mythical implications. Yeats's doctrine of the conflict of opposites says nothing about the fundamental nature of reality; it is rather a dramatic framework through which is made visible the perpetual oscillation of man between extreme introspection and extreme loss of the self in the world of action. The intricacies of Yeats's system provide for many of the permutations of this relation; but it cannot foresee them all; and we are constantly brought back to the individual man, not as a symbolic counter, but as a personality rich and unpredictable. Yeats's preference for the nobleman, the peasant, and the craftsman does not betray, as Mr. MacNeice's somewhat provincial contention holds, the "budding fascist"; it is a "version of pastoral" which permits Yeats to see his characters acting above the ordinary dignity of men, in a concrete relation to life undiluted by calculation and abstraction. I can only repeat here that the "system" is perpetually absorbed into action. If Yeats were only an allegorist, the meaning of his poetry could be ascertained by getting hold of the right key. The poetry would serve to illustrate the "system," as the poetry of the Prophetic Books fleshes out the homemade system of Blake.

## V

MR. ELIOT'S view, that Yeats got off the central tradition into a "minor mythology," and Mr. Blackmur's view, that he took "magic" (as opposed to religion) as far as any poet could, seem to me to be related versions of the same fallacy. Which is: that there must be a direct and effective correlation between the previously established truth of the poet's ideas and the value of the poetry. (I am oversimplifying Blackmur's view, but not Eliot's.) In this difficulty it is always useful to ask: *Where* are the poet's ideas? Good sense in this matter ought to tell us that while the ideas doubtless exist in some form outside the poetry, as they exist for Yeats in the letters, the essays, and *A Vision*, we must nevertheless test them in the poems themselves, and not "refute" a poem in which the gyres supply certain images by showing that gyres are amateur philosophy.

> Turning and turning in the widening gyre
> The falcon cannot hear the falconer. . . .

—the opening lines of "The Second Coming": and they make enough sense apart from our knowledge of the system; the gyre here can be visualized as the circling flight of the bird constantly widening until it has lost contact with the point, the center, to which it ought to be able to return. As a symbol of disunity it is no more esoteric than Eliot's "Gull against the wind," at the end of "Gerontion," which is a casual, not traditional or systematic, symbol of disunity. Both Mr. Blackmur and Mr. Brooks—Mr. Brooks more than Mr. Blackmur—show us the systematic implications of the symbols of the poem "Byzantium." The presence of the system at its most formidable cannot be denied to this poem. I should like to see, nevertheless, an analysis of it in which no special knowledge is used. I should like to see it examined with the ordinary critical equipment of the educated critic; I should be surprised if the result were very different from Mr. Brooks's reading of the poem. The symbols are "made good" in the poem; they are drawn into a wider convention (Mr. Blackmur calls it the "heaven of man's mind") than they would imply if taken separately.

I conclude these notes with the remark: the study of Yeats in the coming generation is likely to overdo the scholarly procedure, and the result will be the occultation of a poetry which I believe is nearer the center of our main traditions of sensibility and thought than the poetry of Eliot or of Pound. Yeats's special qualities will instigate special studies of great ingenuity, but the more direct and more difficult problem of the poetry itself will probably be delayed. This is only to say that Yeats's romanticism will be created by his critics.

# HART CRANE

## 1932-1937

THE career of Hart Crane will be written by future critics as a chapter in the neo-symbolist movement.[1] An historical view of his poetry at this time would be misleading and incomplete. Like most poets of his age in America, Crane discovered Rimbaud through Eliot and the Imagists; it is certain that long before he had done any of his best work he had come to believe himself the spiritual heir of the French poet. He had an instinctive mastery of the fused metaphor of symbolism, but it is not likely that he ever knew more of the symbolist poets than he had got out of Pound's *Pavannes and Divisions*. Whether Crane's style is symbolistic, or should, in many instances, like the first six or seven stanzas of "The River," be called Elizabethan, is a question that need not concern us now.

Between "The Bridge" and "Une Saison d'Enfer" there is little essential affinity. Rimbaud achieved "disorder" out of implicit order, after a deliberate cultivation of "derangement," but in our age the disintegration of our intellectual systems is accomplished. With Crane the disorder is original

---

[1] This essay is composed of two papers written several years apart, the one in 1932, a few months after Crane's death, the other in 1937 as a review of Philip Horton's *Hart Crane: The Life of an American Poet.*

and fundamental. That is the special quality of his mind that belongs peculiarly to our own time. His aesthetic problem, however, was more general; it was the historic problem of romanticism.

Harold Hart Crane, one of the great masters of the romantic movement, was born in Garrettsville, Ohio, on July 21, 1899. His birthplace is a small town near Cleveland, in the old Western Reserve, a region which, as distinguished from the lower portions of the state, where people from the Southern up-country settled, was populated largely by New England stock. He seems to have known little of his ancestry, but he frequently said that his maternal forbears had given Hartford, Connecticut, its name, and that they went "back to Stratford-on-Avon"—a fiction surely, but one that gave him distinct pleasure. His formal education was slight. After the third year at high school, when he was fifteen, it ended, and he worked in his father's candy factory in Cleveland, where the family had removed in his childhood. He repeatedly told me that money had been set aside for his education at college, but that it had been used for other purposes. With the instinct of genius he read the great poets, but he never acquired an objective mastery of any literature, or even of the history of his country—a defect of considerable interest in a poet whose most ambitious work is an American epic.

In any ordinary sense Crane was not an educated man; in many respects he was an ignorant man. There is already a Crane legend, like the Poe legend—it should be fostered because it will help to make his poetry generally known—and the scholars will decide it was a pity that so great a talent lacked early advantages. It is probable that he was incapable of the formal discipline of a classical education, and probable, too, that the eclectic education of his time would have scattered and killed his talent. His poetry not only has defects of the surface, it has a defect of vision; but its great and peculiar value cannot be separated from its limitations. Its qualities are bound up with a special focus of the intellect and sensibility, and it would be folly to wish that his mind had been better trained or differently organized.

The story of his suicide is well known. The information that I have seems authentic, but it is incomplete and subject to excessive interpretation. Toward the end of April, 1932, he embarked on the S.S. *Orizaba* bound from Vera Cruz to New York. On the night of April 26 he got into a brawl with some sailors; he was severely beaten and robbed. At noon the next day, the ship being in the Caribbean a few hours out of Havana, he rushed from his stateroom clad in pajamas and overcoat, walked through the smoking-room out onto the deck, and then the length of the ship to the stern. There without hesitation he made a perfect dive into the sea. It is said that a life-preserver was thrown to him; he either did not see it or did not want it. By the time the ship had turned back he had disappeared. Whether he forced himself down —for a moment he was seen swimming—or was seized by a shark, as the captain believed, cannot be known. After a search of thirty-five minutes his body was not found, and the *Orizaba* put back into her course.

In the summer of 1930 he had written to me that he feared his most ambitious work, *The Bridge*, was not quite perfectly "realized," that probably his soundest work was in the shorter pieces of *White Buildings*, but that his mind, being once committed to the larger undertaking, could never return to the lyrical and more limited form. He had an extraordinary insight into the foundations of his work, and I think this judgment of it will not be refuted.

From 1922 to 1928—after that year I saw him and heard from him irregularly until his death—I could observe the development of his style from poem to poem; and his letters —written always in a pure and lucid prose—provide a valuable commentary on his career. This is not the place to bring all this material together for judgment. As I look back upon his work and its relation to the life he lived, a general statement about it comes to my mind that may throw some light on the dissatisfaction that he felt with his career. It will be

a judgment upon the life and works of a man whom I knew
*affectionately for ten years as a friend.

Suicide was the sole act of will left to him short of a profound alteration of his character. I think the evidence of this
is the locked-in sensibility, the insulated egoism, of his poetry
—a subject that I shall return to. The background of his death
was dramatically perfect: a large portion of his finest imagery
was of the sea, chiefly the Caribbean:

> O minstrel galleons of Carib fire,
> Bequeath us to no earthly shore until
> Is answered in the vortex of our grave
> The seal's wide spindrift gaze towards paradise.

His verse is full of splendid images of this order, a rich symbolism for an implicit pantheism that, whatever may be its
intrinsic merit, he had the courage to vindicate with death
in the end.

His pantheism was not passive and contemplative; it rose
out of the collision between his own locked-in sensibility
and the ordinary forms of experience. Every poem is a thrust
of that sensibility into the world: his defect lay in his inability to face out the moral criticism implied in the failure
to impose his will upon experience.

*The Bridge* is presumably an epic. How early he had
conceived the idea of the poem and the leading symbolism,
it is difficult to know; certainly as early as February, 1923.
Up to that time, with the exception of "For the Marriage of
Faustus and Helen" (1922), he had written only short poems,
but most of them, "Praise for an Urn," "Black Tambourine,"
"Paraphrase," and "Emblems of Conduct," [2] are among his
finest work. It is a mistake then to suppose that all of *White
Buildings* is early experimental writing; a large portion of
that volume, and perhaps the least successful part of it, is
made up of poems written after *The Bridge* was begun.

[2] It is now known that this poem is an elaboration of a "sonnet" entitled
"Conduct" by Samuel Greenberg. See *Poems* by Samuel Greenberg, edited by
Harold Holden and Jack McManis (New York, 1947).

"Praise for an Urn" was written in the spring of 1922—one
of the finest elegies by an American poet—and although his
later development gave us a poetry that the period would
be much the less rich for not having, he never again had
such perfect mastery of his subject—because he never again
quite knew what his subject was.

Readers familiar with "For the Marriage of Faustus and
Helen" admire it by passages, but the form of the poem, in
its framework of symbol, is an abstraction empty of any
knowable experience. The originality of the poem is in its
rhythms, but it has the conventional diction that a young
poet picks up in his first reading. Crane, I believe, felt that
this was so; and he became so dissatisfied, not only with the
style of the poem, which is heavily influenced by Eliot and
Laforgue, but with the "literary" character of the symbolism,
that he set about the greater task of writing *The Bridge*.
He had looked upon his "Faustus and Helen" as an answer
to the pessimism of the school of Eliot, and *The Bridge*
was to be an even more complete answer.

There was a fundamental mistake in Crane's diagnosis of
Eliot's problem. Eliot's "pessimism" grows out of an awareness of the decay of the individual consciousness and its
fixed relations to the world; but Crane thought that it was
due to something like pure "orneryness," an unwillingness "to
share with us the breath released," the breath being a new
kind of freedom that he identified emotionally with the age
of the machine. This vagueness of purpose, in spite of the
apparently concrete character of the Brooklyn Bridge, which
became the symbol of his epic, he never succeeded in correcting. The "bridge" stands for no well-defined experience; it
differs from the Helen and Faust symbols only in its un-
literary origin. I think Crane was deceived by this difference,
and by the fact that Brooklyn Bridge is "modern" and a fine
piece of "mechanics." His more ambitious later project permitted him no greater mastery of formal structure than the
more literary symbolism of his youth.

The fifteen parts of *The Bridge* taken as one poem suffer

from the lack of a coherent structure, whether symbolic or narrative: the coherence of the work consists in the personal quality of the writing—in mood, feeling, and tone. In the best passages Crane has perfect mastery over the quality of his style; but the style lacks an objective pattern of ideas elaborate enough to carry it through an epic or heroic work. The single symbolic image, in which the whole poem centers, is at one moment the actual Brooklyn Bridge; at another, it is any bridge or "connection"; at still another, it is a philosophical pun and becomes the basis of a series of analogies.

In "Cape Hatteras," the aëroplane and Walt Whitman are analogous "bridges" to some transcendental truth. Because the idea is variously metaphor, symbol, and analogy, it tends to make the poem static. The poet takes it up, only to be forced to put it down again *when the poetic image of the moment is exhausted.* The idea does not, in short, fill the poet's mind; it is the starting point for a series of short flights, or inventions connected only in analogy—which explains the merely personal passages, which are obscure, and the lapses into sentimentality. For poetic sentimentality is emotion undisciplined by the structure of events or ideas of which it is ostensibly a part. The idea is not objective and articulate in itself; it lags after the poet's vision; it appears and disappears; and in the intervals Crane improvises, often beautifully, as in the flight of the aëroplane, sometimes badly, as in the passage on Whitman in the same poem.

In the great epic and philosophical works of the past, notably *The Divine Comedy*, the intellectual groundwork is not only simple philosophically; we not only know that the subject is personal salvation, just as we know that Crane's is the greatness of America: we are given also the complete articulation of the idea down to the slightest detail, and we are given it objectively apart from anything that the poet is going to say about it. When the poet extends his perception, there is a further extension of the groundwork ready to meet it and discipline it, and to compel the sensibility of the poet to stick to the subject. It is a game of chess; neither side can move without consulting the other. Crane's difficulty is that of modern poets generally: they play the game with half of the men, the men of sensibility, and because sensibility can make any move, the significance of all moves is obscure.

If we subtract from Crane's idea its periphery of sensation, we have left only the dead abstraction, the Greatness of America, which is capable of elucidation neither on the logical plane nor in terms of a generally known idea of America.

The theme of *The Bridge* is, in fact, an emotional over-simplification of a subject-matter that Crane did not, on the plane of narrative and idea, simplify at all. The poem is emotionally homogeneous and simple—it contains a single purpose; but because it is not structurally clarified it is emotionally confused. America stands for a passage into new truths. Is this the meaning of American history? The poet has every right to answer yes, and this he has done. But just what in America or about America stands for this? Which American history? The historical plot of the poem, which is the groundwork on which the symbolic bridge stands, is arbitrary and broken, where the poet would have gained an overwhelming advantage by choosing a single period or episode, a concrete event with all its dramatic causes, and by following it up minutely, and being bound to it. In short, he would have gained an advantage could he have found a subject to stick to.

Does American culture afford such a subject? It probably does not. After the seventeenth century the sophisticated history of the scholars came into fashion; our popular, legendary chronicles come down only from the remoter European past. It was a sound impulse on Crane's part to look for an American myth, some simple version of our past that lies near the center of the American consciousness; an heroic tale with just enough symbolism to give his mind both direction and play. The soundness of his purpose is witnessed also by the kind of history in the poem: it is inaccurate, and it will not at all satisfy the sticklers for historical fact. It is the history

of the motion picture, of naïve patriotism. This is sound; for
it ignores the scientific ideal of historical truth-in-itself, and
looks for a cultural truth which might win the spontaneous
allegiance of the people. It is on such simple integers of
truth, not truth of fact but of religious necessity, that men
unite. The American mind was formed by the eighteenth-
century Enlightenment, which broke down the European
"truths" and gave us a temper deeply hostile to the making
of new religious truths of our own.

The impulse in The Bridge is religious, but the soundness of an impulse is no warrant that it will create a sound
art form. The form depends on too many factors beyond the
control of the poet. The age is scientific and pseudo-scientific,
and our philosophy is Dewey's instrumentalism. And it is
possibly this circumstance that has driven the religious attitude into a corner where it lacks the right instruments for
its defense and growth, and where it is in a vast muddle
about just what these instruments are. Perhaps this disunity
of the intellect is responsible for Crane's unphilosophical belief that the poet, unaided and isolated from the people, can
create a myth.

If anthropology has helped to destroy the credibility of
myths, it has shown us how they rise: their growth is mysterious from the people as a whole. It is probable that no
one man ever put myth into history. It is still a nice problem
among higher critics, whether the authors of the Gospels
were deliberate myth-makers, or whether their minds were
simply constructed that way; but the evidence favors the
latter. Crane was a myth-maker, and in an age favorable to
myths he would have written a mythical poem in the act
of writing an historical one.

It is difficult to agree with those critics who find his epic
a single poem and as such an artistic success. It is a collection
of lyrics, the best of which are not surpassed by anything in
American literature. The writing is most distinguished when
Crane is least philosophical, when he writes from sensation.
"The River" has some blemishes towards the end, but by

and large it is a masterpiece of order and style; it alone is enough to place Crane in the first rank of American poets, living or dead. Equally good but less ambitious are the "Proem: To Brooklyn Bridge," and "Harbor Dawn," and "The Dance" from the section called "Powhatan's Daughter."

These poems bear only the loosest relation to the symbolic demands of the theme; they contain allusions to the historical pattern or extend the slender structure of analogy running through the poem. They are primarily lyrical, and each has its complete form. The poem "Indiana," written presumably to complete the pattern of "Powhatan's Daughter," does not stand alone, and it is one of the most astonishing failures ever made by a poet of Crane's genius. "The Dance" gives us the American background for the coming white man, and "Indiana" carries the stream of history to the pioneer West. It is a nightmare of sentimentality. Crane is at his most "philosophical" in a theme in which he feels no poetic interest whatever.

The structural defect of *The Bridge* is due to this fundamental contradiction of purpose. In one of his best earlier poems, "The Wine Menagerie," he exclaims: "New thresholds, new anatomies!"—new sensation, but he could not subdue the new sensation to a symbolic form.

His pantheism is necessarily a philosophy of sensation without point of view. An epic is a judgment of human action, an implied evaluation of a civilization, a way of life. In *The Bridge* the civilization that contains the subway hell of the section called "The Tunnel" is the same civilization of the aëroplane that the poet apostrophizes in "Cape Hatteras": there is no reason why the subway should be a fitter symbol of damnation than the aëroplane: both were produced by the same mentality on the same moral plane. There is a concealed, meaningless analogy between, on the one hand, the height of the plane and the depth of the subway, and, on the other, "higher" and "lower" in the religious sense. At one moment Crane faces his predicament of blindness to any rational order of value, and knows that he is damned; but he cannot face it long, and he tries to rest secure upon the intensity of sensation.

To the vision of the abyss in "The Tunnel," a vision that Dante passed through midway of this mortal life, Crane had no alternative: when it became too harrowing he cried to his Pocahontas, a typically romantic and sentimental symbol:

> Lie to us—dance us back our tribal morn!

It is probably the perfect word of romanticism in this century. When Crane saw that his leading symbol, the bridge, would not hold all the material of his poem, he could not sustain it ironically, in the classical manner, by probing its defects; nor in the personal sections, like "Quaker Hill," does he include himself in his Leopardian denunciation of life. He is the blameless victim of a world whose impurity violates the moment of intensity, which would otherwise be enduring and perfect. He is betrayed, not by a defect of his own nature, but by the external world; he asks of nature, perfection—requiring only of himself, intensity. The persistent, and persistently defeated, pursuit of a natural absolute places Crane at the center of his age.

Alternately he asserts the symbol of the bridge and abandons it, because fundamentally he does not understand it. The idea of bridgeship is an elaborate blur leaving the inner structure of the poem confused.

Yet some of the best poetry of our generation is in *The Bridge*. Its inner confusion is a phase of the inner cross-purposes of the time. Crane was one of those men whom every age seems to select as the spokesmen of its spiritual life; they give the age away. The accidental features of their lives, their place in life, their very heredity, seem to fit them for their rôle; even their vices contribute to their preparation. Crane's biographer will have to study the early influences that confirmed him in narcissism, and thus made him typical of the rootless spiritual life of our time. The character formed by those influences represents an immense concentration, and becomes almost a symbol, of American life in this age.

Crane's poetry has incalculable moral value: it reveals our defects in their extremity. I have said that he knew little of the history of his country. It was not merely a defect of education, but a defect, in the spiritual sense of the modern mind. Crane lacked the sort of indispensable understanding of his country that a New England farmer has who has never been out of his township. *The Bridge* attempts to include all American life, but it covers the ground with seven-league boots and, like a sightseer, sees nothing. With reference to its leading symbol, it has no subject-matter. The poem is the effort of a solipsistic sensibility to locate itself in the external world, to establish points of reference.

It seems to me that by testing out his capacity to construct a great objective piece of work, in which his definition of himself should have been articulated, he brought his work to an end. I think he knew that the structure of *The Bridge* was finally incoherent, and for that reason—as I have said— he could no longer believe even in his lyrical powers; he could not return to the early work and take it up where he had left off. Far from "refuting" Eliot, his whole career is a vindication of Eliot's major premise—that the integrity of the individual consciousness has broken down. Crane had, in his later work, no individual consciousness: the hard firm style of "Praise for an Urn," which is based upon a clear-cut perception of moral relations, and upon their ultimate inviolability, begins to disappear when the poet goes out into the world and finds that the simplicity of a child's world has no universal sanction. From then on, instead of the effort to define himself in the midst of almost overwhelming complications—a situation that might have produced a tragic poet —he falls back upon the intensity of consciousness, rather than the clarity, for his center of vision. And that is romanticism.

His world had no center, and the thrust into sensation is responsible for the fragmentary quality of his most ambitious work. This thrust took two directions—the blind assertion of the will, and the blind desire for self-destruction. The

poet did not face his first problem, which is to define the
limits of his personality and to objectify its moral implications in an appropriate symbolism. Crane could only assert
a quality of will against the world, and at each successive failure of the will he turned upon himself. In the failure of
understanding—and understanding, for Dante, was a way of
love—the romantic modern poet of the age of science attempts to impose his will upon experience and to possess the
world.

It is this impulse of the modern period that has given us
the greatest romantic poetry: Crane instinctively continued
the conception of the will that was the deliberate discovery
of Rimbaud. A poetry of the will is a poetry of sensation,
for the poet surrenders to his sensations of the object in his
effort to identify himself with it, and to own it. Some of
Crane's finest lyrics—those written in the period of *The
Bridge*—carry the modern impulse as far as you will find
it anywhere in the French romantics. "Lachrymae Christi"
and "Passage," though on the surface made up of pure
images without philosophical meaning of the explicit sort
in *The Bridge*, are the lyrical equivalents of the epic: the
same kind of sensibility is at work. The implicit grasp of his
material that we find in "Praise for an Urn," the poet has
exchanged for an external, random symbol of which there
is no possibility of realization. *The Bridge* is an irrational
symbol of the will, of conquest, of blind achievement in
space; its obverse is "Passage," whose lack of external symbolism exhibits the poetry of the will on the plane of sensation; and this is the self-destructive return of the will upon
itself.

Criticism may well set about isolating the principle upon
which Crane's poetry is organized. Powerful verse over-
whelms its admirers, and betrays them into more than technical imitation. That is one of the arguments of Platonism
against literature; it is the immediate quality of an art rather
than its whole significance that sets up schools and traditions.
Crane not only ends the romantic era in his own person; he

ends it logically and morally. Beyond Crane no future poet
can go. (This does not mean that the romantic impulse may
not rise and flourish again.) The finest passages in his work
are single moments in the stream of sensation; beyond the
moment he goes at his peril; for beyond it lies the discrepancy between the sensuous fact, the perception, and its
organizing symbol—a discrepancy that plunges him into sentimentality and chaos. But the "bridge" is empty and static,
it has no inherent content, and the poet's attribution to it of
the qualities of his own moral predicament is arbitrary.
That explains the fragmentary and often unintelligible framework of the poem. There was neither complete action nor
ordered symbolism in terms of which the distinct moments
of perception could be clarified.

This was partly the problem of Rimbaud. But Crane's
problem was nearer to the problem of Keats, and *The Bridge*
is a failure in the sense that "Hyperion" is a failure, and
with comparable magnificence. Crane's problem, being farther removed from the epic tradition, was actually more
difficult than Keats's, and his treatment of it was doubtless
the most satisfactory possible in our time. Beyond the quest
of pure sensation and its ordering symbolism lies the total
destruction of art. By attempting an extreme solution of the
romantic problem Crane proved that it cannot be solved.

# JOHN PEALE BISHOP

## *1935*

OF THE American poets whose first books were published between 1918 and 1929 not more than six or seven are likely to keep their reputations until the end of the present decade. Eliot and Pound are pre-war. Crane, Marianne Moore, Stevens, MacLeish, and Ransom are among the slightly more than half a dozen. The two or three other places may be disputed; but I take it that since 1929 there has been no new name unless it be that of a young man, James Agee, whose first volume appeared in 1934. John Peale Bishop, whose first poetry goes back to the war period but whose first book, *Now with His Love*,[1] came out in 1932, will, I believe, rank among the best poets of the last decade.

His position has been anomalous. His contemporaries made their reputations in a congenial critical atmosphere, and they have been able to carry over a certain prestige into virtually a new age. (Ages crowd upon one another in a country that has never been young.) But Bishop has lacked that advantage. The first criticism accorded him was largely of the Marxist school. Mr. Horace Gregory, shrewdly discerning the poet's

---

[1] Bishop's first book, *Green Fruit*, a collection of undergraduate verse, appeared in 1917. See *The Collected Poems of John Peale Bishop* (New York, 1948). Bishop was born in 1892 and died in 1944.

technical skill, became quickly concerned about the sincerity of a man who ignored the "class struggle." Bishop was not, in fact, asked whether he was a poet but whether he expected to survive capitalism: whether given his roots in the war-generation and the prejudices of the "ruling class," he could hope to achieve the portage over to the "main stream" of American letters recently discovered by Mr. Granville Hicks.

The problems of poetry must necessarily be the same in all ages, but no two ages come to the same solutions. Happiest is that age which, like the age of Sidney and Spenser, felt no need to reduce the problems to ultimate philosophical terms: our critical apparatus is immeasurably more thorough than theirs, our poetic performance appreciably looser. But our problems are inevitably theirs. They are the problem of language and the problem of form. The Elizabethan solution was practical, not speculative. The simple didacticism of the neo-classical Renaissance was as far as the sixteenth century got philosophically. The poets wrote better than they knew. Our knowledge is better than our performance.

In ages weak in form, such as our own age, theory will concentrate upon form, but practice upon the ultimate possibilities of language. Ages that create great varieties of forms, as the Elizabethans did in every branch of poetry, talk about language but actually take it for granted, and score their greatest triumphs with form. The powers of the language were not in the long run determined by theory, but instinctively by poets whose dominating passion was form: the language was determined by the demands of the subject. The more comprehensive the subject, the broader the symbolism, and the more profoundly relevant the scheme of reference to the whole human experience, the richer the language became. The experiment with language as such is *The Shepherd's Calendar*, and it is a failure; but even there the poet attempts only to enlarge his vocabulary with archaic words for "poetical" effect. There is no trace of that forcing of language beyond its natural limits that we find in modern verse. Propriety of diction was the problem, and it was ably discussed by Puttenham in his long *Arte of English Poesie*, a work in some respects comparable to *The Principles of Literary Criticism* by Mr. I. A. Richards, who talks not about the propriety of language but about its ultimate meaning. He thus leaves behind him language as an instrument and, by going into the *kinds* of meaning, converts the discussion into the peculiarly modern problem of form. For form is meaning and nothing but meaning: scheme of reference, supporting symbolism that ceases to support as soon as it is recognized as merely that.

Metrics as a phase of the problem of form needs attention from modern critics. It is a subject poorly understood. It is usually treated as an air-tight compartment of technical speculation. Yet surely a metrical pattern is usable only so long as it is attached to some usable form. It is a curious fact that modern metrics reflects the uncertainty of modern poets in the realm of forms. So the modern poet, struggling to get hold of some kind of meaning, breaks his head against the *impasse* of form, and when he finds no usable form he finds that he has available no metrical system either. For those fixed and, to us, external properties of poetry, rhyme and metrical pattern, are, in the ages of their invention, indeed fixed but not external. It is probable that there is an intimate relation between a generally accepted "picture of the world" and the general acceptance of a metrical system and its differentiations into patterns.

This is to say that the separate arts achieve their special formalisms out of a common center of experience. And from this center of experience, this reference of meaning, any single art will make differentiations within itself: epic, lyric, tragedy, comedy, each with its appropriate pattern of development. When the center of life disappears, the arts of poetry become the art of poetry. And in an advanced stage of the evil, in the nineteenth century and today, we get the *mélange des genres*, one art living off another, which the late Irving Babbitt so valiantly combated without having understood the influences that had brought it about. Painting tries to be music; poetry leans upon painting; all the arts "strive toward the condition of music"; till at last seeing the mathematical structure of music, the arts become geometrical and abstract, and destroy themselves.

The specialization of scientific techniques supplanting a central view of life has, as Mr. John Crowe Ransom showed in a recent essay,[2] tended to destroy the formal arts: poetry has in turn become a specialization of aesthetic effects without formal limitations. And, as Mr. Edmund Wilson has argued,[3] the novel now does the work formerly done by epic and tragedy, forms too "limited" and "artificial" for modern minds. The novel is the least formal of the literary arts; it rose, in fact, upon the débris of the *genres;* and it has been able to drive the formal literary arts from the public interest because, appealing to the ordinary sense of reality fostered by information, science, and journalism, the novelist neither sets forth symbolic fictions nor asks the reader to observe formal limitations.

The poet then at this time must ask, not what limitations he will be pleased, after the manner of the young Milton, to accept, but whether there are any that he can get. I assume that a poet is a man eager to come under the bondage of limitations if he can find them. As I understand John Peale Bishop's poetry, he is that eager man. It is a moral problem, but that phase I cannot touch here. Bishop has no settled metrics; but that too is an aspect of the formal problem that cannot be discussed in the limited space of a note.

It has been said that Bishop has imitated all the chief modern poets. He has virtually conducted his poetical education in public. But the observation is double-edged. In our age of personal expression the poet gets credit for what is "his own": the art is not the thing, but rather the informa-

---

[2] "Poets Without Laurels," first published in 1935; reprinted in *The World's Body* (1938), pp. 55-75.
[3] "*Is Verse a Dying Technique?*" *The Triple Thinkers* (1938), pp. 20-41. For discussion of this essay see pp. 53-54 of the present work.

tion conveyed about a unique personality. Applauding a poet only for what is uniquely his own, we lose thereby much that is good. If a poem in Yeats's manner appears in Bishop's book, and is as good as Yeats's, it is as good there as it is anywhere else.

More than most living poets Bishop has felt the lack of a central source of form. He is not the poet of personal moods and idle sensation. He constantly strives for formal structure. He has studied closely the poets of his time who, like Yeats, seem to have achieved, out of a revived or invented mythology or by means of a consciously restricted point of view, a working substitute for the supernatural myth and the concentration that myth makes possible. It is, I think, interesting to observe that in Bishop two contemporary influences, Yeats and Eliot, meet strongly, and meet only in him of all the contemporary poets whom I know anything about: Yeats for form, Eliot for the experiment in language. Only the best Yeats is better than this:

> And Mooch of the bull-red
> Hair who had so many dears
> Enjoyed to the core
> And Newlin who hadn't one
> To answer his shy desire
> Are blanketed in the mould
> Dead in the long war.
> And I who have most reason
> Remember them only when the sun
> Is at his dullest season.

It is not necessary to illustrate the early influence of Eliot, for it appears everywhere in *Now with His Love.* I will quote two poems that are harder to "place." To critics interested in poetry as private property it may be said that they are evidently his own. The poems—they must be read as carefully climaxed wholes—seem to me to be among the most successful in modern verse:

## THE RETURN

Night and we heard heavy and cadenced hoofbeats
Of troops departing: the last cohorts left
By the North Gate. That night some listened late
Leaning their eyelids toward Septentrion.

Morning flared and the young tore down the trophies
And warring ornaments: arches were strong
And in the sun but stone; no longer conquests
Circled our columns; all our state was down

In fragments. In the dust, old men with tufted
Eyebrows whiter than sunbaked faces, gulped
As it fell. But they no more than we remembered
The old sea-fights, the soldiers' names and sculptors'

We did not know the end was coming: nor why
It came; only that long before the end
Were many wanted to die. Then vultures starved
And sailed more slowly in the sky.

We still had taxes. Salt was high. The soldiers
Gone. Now there was much drinking and lewd
Houses all night loud with riot. But only
For a time. Soon the taverns had no roofs.

Strangely it was the young the almost boys
Who first abandoned hope; the old still lived
A little, at last a little lived in eyes.
It was the young whose child did not survive.

Some slept beneath the simulacra, until
The gods' faces froze. Then was fear.
Some had response in dreams, but morning restored
Interrogation. Then O then, O ruins!

Temples of Neptune invaded by the sea
And dolphins streaked like streams sportive
As sunlight rode and over the rushing floors
The sea unfurled and what was blue raced silver.

The poem avoids the difficulty of form by leaning upon a certain violence of language. The form of "The Return" is a very general idea about the fall of Rome. The implications of the form are not wide; and it is a typical modern form in that it offers a rough parallelism with the real subject— which in this poem is modern civilization—and not a direct approach to the subject. Where shall the poet get a form that will permit him to make direct, comprehensive statements about modern civilization? Doubtless nowhere. As a feat of historical insight the "form" of "The Return" is commonplace; yet the poem is distinguished. The poet has manipulated language into painting. The line "Temples of Neptune invaded by the sea" is by no means the same as its prose paraphrase: civilizations die of an excess of the quality that made them great; we, too, shall perish when we no longer have the temple of Neptune, the form, to preserve us from the limitless energy of the sea, which the form held in check. But "Rome" is here not a symbol of anything; our inferences about modern civilization are obvious, but they are not authorized by the poem. "The poem," writes Bishop, "is a simile in which one term of the comparison is omitted." It is rather that by means of a new grasp of language, very different from the "word-painting" of eighteenth-century nature poetry, the poet achieves a plastic objectivity that to some degree liberates him from the problem of finding a structural background of idea.

What I have said about "The Return" applies with even greater force to "Perspectives Are Precipices":

> *Sister Anne, Sister Anne,*
> *Do you see anybody coming?*

> I see a distance of black yews
> Long as the history of the Jews

> I see a road sunned with white sand
> Wide plains surrounding silence. And

Far off, a broken colonnade
That overthrows the sun in shade.

*Sister Anne, Sister Anne,*
*Do you see nobody coming?*

A man
Upon that road a man who goes
Dragging a shadow by its toes.

Diminishing he goes, head bare
Of any covering even hair.

A pitcher depending from one hand
Goes mouth down. And dry is sand

*Sister Anne, Sister Anne,*
*What do you see?*

His dwindling stride. And he seems blind
Or worse to the prone man behind.

*Sister Anne! Sister Anne!*

I see a road. Beyond nowhere
Defined by cirrus and blue air.

I saw a man but he is gone
His shadow gone into the sun.

This poem I would cite as the perfect example of certain effects of painting achieved in poetry. Criticism of this kind of poetry must necessarily be tentative. Yet I think it is plain that this particular poem has not only the immediate effect of a modern abstract painting; it gives the illusion of perspective, of objects-in-the-round. Take the "road sunned with white sand"—instead of "sunlight on a sandy road," the normal word-structure for this image. Even more striking is "Wide plains surrounding silence." I leave it to the schoolmen, wherever they are, to decide whether "silence" is commonly abstract or concrete; yet it is certain that in Bishop's

phrase it acquires a spatial, indeed almost sensory, value that
would have been sacrificed had he written: "silence over the
surrounding plains."

It is worth remarking here that the line, "Long as the history of the Jews," is the only clear example of "metaphysical
wit" that I have been able to find in Bishop's verse. It is
possibly a direct adaptation of a passage from Marvel:

> And you should if you please refuse
> Till the conversion of the Jews.

Bishop's line is the more striking for its isolation in his work,
but I think it is clearly a violation of the plastic technique
of the poem, and a minor blemish. The influence of Eliot,
which could lead two ways, to the metaphysicals and to the
symbolists, led Bishop almost exclusively to the latter. And
he has perfected this kind of poetry in English perhaps more
than any other writer.

It is an obscure subject: the Horatian formula *ut pictura
poesis* bore fruit long before Hérédia and Gautier—as early,
in English verse, as Milton. But the mixtures of the *genres*
acquired a new significance after the late nineteenth-century
French poets began to push the borders of one sense over
into another. It was not merely that the poet should be allowed to paint pictures with words—that much the Horatian phrase allowed. It was rather that the new "correspondences" among the five senses multiplied the senses and
extended the medium of one art into the medium of another.
Rimbaud's absurd sonnet on the colors of the vowels was
the extreme statement of an experiment that achieved, in
other poets and in Rimbaud's own "Bateau Ivre," brilliant
results. But the process cannot go on beyond our generation
unless we are willing to accept the eventual destruction of
the arts. There is no satisfactory substitute in poetry for the
form-symbol.

It is on this dilemma of symbolic form or plastic form that
Bishop is intelligent and instructive. He has recently written:
"I am trying to make more and more *statements*, without giv-

ing up all that we have gained since Rimbaud." The difficulty could not be more neatly put. Two recent poems, "The
Saints" and "Holy Nativity," are the result of this effort. The
statement is form, the fixed point of reference; "all that we
have gained since Rimbaud" is the enrichment of language
that we have gained to offset our weakness in form.

The new experiment of Bishop's is not complete. In "Holy
Nativity" the attempt to use the Christian myth collapses
with a final glance at anthropology:

> Eagle, swan or dove
> White bull or cloud . . .

His treatment of the supernatural, the attempt to replace
our secular philosophy, in which he does not believe, with
a vision of the divine, in which he tries to believe, is an instance of our modern unbelieving belief. We are so constituted as to see our experience in two ways. We are not so
constituted as to see it two ways indefinitely without peril.
Until we can see it in one way we shall not see it as a whole,
and until we see it as a whole we shall not see it as poets.
Every road is long, and all roads lead to the problem of
form.

# NARCISSUS AS NARCISSUS

## 1938

ON THIS first occasion, which will probably be the last, of my writing about my own verse, I could plead in excuse the example of Edgar Allan Poe, who wrote about himself in an essay called "The Philosophy of Composition." But in our age the appeal to authority is weak, and I am of my age. What I happen to know about the poem that I shall discuss is limited. I remember merely my intention in writing it; I do not know whether the poem is good; and I do not know its obscure origins.

How does one happen to write a poem: where does it come from? That is the question asked by the psychologists or the geneticists of poetry. Of late I have not read any of the genetic theories very attentively: years ago I read one by Mr. Conrad Aiken; another, I think, by Mr. Robert Graves; but I have forgotten them. I am not ridiculing verbal mechanisms, dreams, or repressions as origins of poetry; all three of them and more besides may have a great deal to do with it. Other psychological theories say a good deal about compensation. A poem is an indirect effort of a shaky man to justify himself to happier men, or to present a superior account of his relation to a world that allows him but little certainty, and would allow equally little to the happier men if they did not wear blinders—according to the poet. For example, a poet might be a man who could not get enough self-justification out of being an automobile sales-man (whose certainty is a fixed quota of cars every month) to rest comfortably upon it. So the poet, who wants to be something that he cannot be, and is a failure in plain life, makes up fictitious versions of his predicament that are interesting even to other persons because nobody is a per-fect automobile salesman. Everybody, alas, suffers a little . . . I constantly read this kind of criticism of my own verse. According to its doctors, my one intransigent desire is to have been a Confederate general, and because I could not or would not become anything else, I set up for poet and began to invent fictions about the personal ambitions that my society has no use for.

Although a theory may not be "true," it may make certain insights available for a while; and I have deemed it proper to notice theories of the genetic variety because a poet talk-ing about himself is often expected, as the best authority, to explain the origins of his poems. But persons interested in origins are seldom quick to use them. Poets, in their way, are practical men; they are interested in results. What is the poem, after it is written? That is the question. Not where it came from, or why. The Why and Where can never get beyond the guessing stage because, in the language of those who think it can, poetry cannot be brought to "laboratory conditions." The only real evidence that any critic may bring before his gaze is the finished poem. For some reason most critics have a hard time fixing their minds directly under their noses, and before they see the object that is there they use a telescope upon the horizon to see where it came from. They are wood-cutters who do their job by finding out where the ore came from in the iron of the steel of the blade of the ax that Jack built. I do not say that this procedure is without its own contributory insights; but the insights are merely con-tributory and should not replace the poem, which is the object upon which they must be focused. A poem may be an instance of morality, of social conditions, of psychological history; it may instance all its qualities, but never one of them alone, nor any two or three; never less than all.

Genetic theories, I gather, have been cherished academically with detachment. Among "critics" they have been useless and not quite disinterested: I have myself found them applicable to the work of poets whom I do not like. That is the easiest way.

I say all this because it seems to me that my verse or anybody else's is merely a way of knowing something: if the poem is a real creation, it is a kind of knowledge that we did not possess before. It is not knowledge "about" something else; the poem is the fullness of that knowledge. We know the particular poem, not what it says that we can restate. In a manner of speaking, the poem is its own knower, neither poet nor reader knowing anything that the poem says apart from the words of the poem. I have expressed this view elsewhere in other terms, and it has been accused of aestheticism or art for art's sake. But let the reader recall the historic position of Catholicism: *nulla salus extra ecclesiam.* That must be religion*ism.* There is probably nothing wrong with art for art's sake if we take the phrase seriously, and not take it to mean the kind of poetry written in England forty years ago. Religion always ought to transcend any of its particular uses; and likewise the true art for art's sake view can be held only by persons who are always looking for things that they can respect apart from use (though they may be useful), like poems, fly-rods, and formal gardens. . . . These are negative postulates, and I am going to illustrate them with some commentary on a poem called "Ode to the Confederate Dead."

## I I

THAT poem is "about" solipsism, a philosophical doctrine which says that we create the world in the act of perceiving it; or about Narcissism, or any other *ism* that denotes the failure of the human personality to function objectively in nature and society. Society (and "nature" as modern society constructs it) appears to offer limited fields for the exercise of the whole man, who wastes his energy piecemeal over separate functions that ought to come under a unity of being. (Until the last generation, only certain women were whores, having been set aside as special instances of sex amid a social scheme that held the general belief that sex must be part of a whole; now the general belief is that sex must be special.) Without unity we get the remarkable self-consciousness of our age. Everybody is talking about this evil, and a great many persons know what ought to be done to correct it. As a citizen I have my own prescription, but as a poet I am concerned with the experience of "solipsism." And an experience *of* it is not quite the same thing as a philosophical statement *about* it.

I should have trouble connecting solipsism and the Confederate dead in a rational argument; I should make a fool of myself in the discussion, because I know no more of the Confederate dead or of solipsism than hundreds of other people. (Possibly less: the dead Confederates may be presumed to have a certain privacy; and as for solipsism, I blush in the presence of philosophers, who know all about Bishop Berkeley; I use the term here in its strict etymology.) And if I call this interest in one's ego Narcissism, I make myself a logical ignoramus, and I take liberties with mythology. I use Narcissism to mean only preoccupation with self; it may be either love or hate. But a good psychiatrist knows that it means self-love only, and otherwise he can talk about it more coherently, knows more about it than I shall ever hope or desire to know. He would look at me professionally if I uttered the remark that the modern squirrel cage of our sensibility, the extreme introspection of our time, has anything whatever to do with the Confederate dead.

But when the doctor looks at literature it is a question whether he sees it: the sea boils and pigs have wings because in poetry all things are possible—if you are man enough. They are possible because in poetry the disparate elements are not combined in logic, which can join things only under certain categories and under the law of contradiction; they are combined in poetry rather as experience, and experience has decided to ignore logic, except perhaps as another field of experience. Experience means conflict, our natures being what they are, and conflict means drama. Dramatic experience is not logical; it may be subdued to the kind of coherence that we indicate when we speak, in criticism, of form. Indeed, as experience, this conflict is always a logical contradiction, or philosophically an antinomy. Serious poetry deals with the fundamental conflicts that cannot be logically resolved: we can state the conflicts rationally, but reason does not relieve us of them. Their only final coherence is the formal re-creation of art, which "freezes" the experience as permanently as a logical formula, but without, like the formula, leaving all but the logic out.

Narcissism and the Confederate dead cannot be connected logically, or even historically; even were the connection an historical fact, they would not stand connected as art, for no one experiences raw history. The proof of the connection must lie, if anywhere, in the experienced conflict which is the poem itself. Since one set of references for the conflict is the historic Confederates, the poem, if it is successful, is a certain section of history made into experience, but only on this occasion, and on these terms: even the author of the poem has no experience of its history apart from the occasion and the terms.

It will be understood that I do not claim even a partial success in the junction of the two "ideas" in the poem that I am about to discuss. I am describing an intention, and the labor of revising the poem—a labor spread over ten years— fairly exposes the lack of confidence that I have felt and still feel in it. All the tests of its success in style and versification would come in the end to a single test, an answer, yes or no, to the question: Assuming that the Confederates and Narcissus are not yoked together by mere violence, has the poet convinced the reader that, on the specific occasion of this poem, there is a necessary yet hitherto undetected relation between them? By necessary I mean dramatically relevant, a relation "discovered" in terms of the particular occasion, not historically argued or philosophically deduced. Should the question that I have just asked be answered yes, then this poem or any other with its specific problem could be said to have form: what was previously a merely felt quality of life has been raised to the level of experience—it has become specific, local, dramatic, "formal"—that is to say, *in*-formed.

## III

THE structure of the Ode is simple. Figure to yourself a man stopping at the gate of a Confederate graveyard on a late autumn afternoon. The leaves are falling; his first impressions bring him the "rumor of mortality"; and the desolation barely allows him, at the beginning of the second stanza, the conventionally heroic surmise that the dead will enrich the earth, "where these memories grow." From those quoted words to the end of that passage he pauses for a baroque meditation on the ravages of time, concluding with the figure of the "blind crab." This creature has mobility but no direction, energy but from the human point of view, no purposeful world to use it in: in the entire poem there are only two explicit symbols for the looked-in ego; the crab is the first and less explicit symbol, a mere hint, a planting of the idea that will become overt in its second instance—the jaguar towards the end. The crab is the first intimation of the nature of the moral conflict upon which the drama of the poem develops: the cut-off-ness of the modern "intellectual man" from the world.

The next long passage or "strophe," beginning "You know who have waited by the wall," states the other term of the conflict. It is the theme of heroism, not merely moral heroism, but heroism in the grand style, elevating even death from mere physical dissolution into a formal ritual: this heroism is a formal ebullience of the human spirit in an entire society, not private, romantic illusion—something better than moral heroism, great as that may be, for moral heroism, being personal and individual, may be achieved by certain men in all ages, even ages of decadence. But the late Hart Crane's commentary, in a letter, is better than any I can make; he described the theme as the "theme of chivalry, a tradition of excess (not literally excess, rather active faith) which cannot be perpetuated in the fragmentary cosmos of today—'those desires which should be yours tomorrow,' but which, you know, will not persist nor find any way into action."

The structure then is the objective frame for the tension between the two themes, "active faith" which has decayed, and the "fragmentary cosmos" which surrounds us. (I must repeat here that this is not a philosophical thesis; it is an analytical statement of a conflict that is concrete within the poem.) In contemplating the heroic theme the man at the gate never quite commits himself to the illusion of its availability to him. The most that he can allow himself is the fancy that the blowing leaves are charging soldiers, but he rigorously returns to the refrain: "Only the wind"—or the "leaves flying." I suppose it is a commentary on our age that the man at the gate never quite achieves the illusion that the leaves are heroic men, so that he may identify himself with them, as Keats and Shelley too easily and too beautifully did with nightingales and west winds. More than this, he cautions himself, reminds himself repeatedly of his subjective prison, his solipsism, by breaking off the half-illusion and coming back to the refrain of wind and leaves—a refrain that, as Hart Crane said, is necessary to the "subjective continuity."

These two themes struggle for mastery up to the passage,

> We shall say only the leaves whispering
> In the improbable mist of nightfall—

which is near the end. It will be observed that the passage begins with a phrase taken from the wind-leaves refrain—

the signal that it has won. The refrain has been fused with the main stream of the man's reflections, dominating them; and he cannot return even to an ironic vision of the heroes. There is nothing but death, the mere naturalism of death at that—spiritual extinction in the decay of the body. Autumn and the leaves are death; the men who exemplified in a grand style an "active faith" are dead; there are only the leaves.

Shall we then worship death . . .

> . . . set up the gráve
> In the house? The ravenous grave . . .

that will take us before our time? The question is not answered, although as a kind of morbid romanticism it might, if answered affirmatively, provide the man with an illusory escape from his solipsism; but he cannot accept it. Nor has he been able to live in his immediate world, the fragmentary cosmos. There is no practical solution, no solution offered for the edification of moralists. (To those who may identify the man at the gate with the author of the poem I would say: He differs from the author in not accepting a "practical solution," for the author's personal dilemma is perhaps not quite so exclusive as that of the meditating man.) The main intention of the poem has been to make dramatically visible the conflict, to concentrate it, to present it, in Mr. R. P. Blackmur's phrase, as "experienced form"—not as a logical dilemma.

The closing image, that of the serpent, is the ancient symbol of time, and I tried to give it the credibility of the commonplace by placing it in a mulberry bush—with the faint hope that the silkworm would somehow be implicit. But time is also death. If that is so, then space, or the Becoming, is life; and I believe there is not a single spatial symbol in the poem. "Sea-space" is allowed the "blind crab"; but the sea, as appears plainly in the passage beginning, "Now that the salt of their blood . . ." is life only in so far as it is the source of the lowest forms of life, the source perhaps of all life, but life undifferentiated, halfway between life and death. This passage is a contrasting inversion of the conventional

> . . . inexhaustible bodies that are not
> Dead, but feed the grass . . .

the reduction of the earlier, literary conceit to a more naturalistic figure derived from modern biological speculation. These "buried Caesars" will not bloom in the hyacinth but will only make saltier the sea.

The wind-leaves refrain was added to the poem in 1930, nearly five years after the first draft was written. I felt that the danger of adding it was small because, implicit in the long strophes of meditation, the ironic commentary on the vanished heroes was already there, giving the poem such dramatic tension as it had in the earlier version. The refrain makes the commentary more explicit, more visibly dramatic, and renders quite plain, as Hart Crane intimated, the subjective character of the imagery throughout. But there was another reason for it, besides the increased visualization that it imparts to the dramatic conflict. It "times" the poem better, offers the reader frequent pauses in the development of the two themes, allows him occasions of assimilation; and on the whole—this was my hope and intention—the refrain makes the poem seem longer than it is and thus eases the concentration of imagery—without, I hope, sacrificing a possible effect of concentration.

### I V

I HAVE been asked why I called the poem an ode. I first called it an elegy. It is an ode only in the sense in which Cowley in the seventeenth century misunderstood the real structure of the Pindaric ode. Not only are the meter and rhyme without fixed pattern, but in another feature the poem is even further removed from Pindar than Abraham Cowley was: a purely subjective meditation would not even in Cowley's age have been called an ode. I suppose in so calling it

I intended an irony: the scene of the poem is not a public celebration, it is a lone man by a gate.

The dominant rhythm is "mounting," the dominant meter iambic pentameter varied with six-, four-, and three-stressed lines; but this was not planned in advance for variety. I adapted the meter to the effect desired at the moment. The model for the irregular rhyming was "Lycidas," but other models could have served. The rhymes in a given strophe I tried to adjust to the rhythm and the texture of feeling and image. For example, take this passage in the second strophe:

> Autumn is desolation in the plot
> Of a thousand acres where these memories grow
> From the inexhaustible bodies that are not
> Dead, but feed the grass row after rich row.
> Think of the autumns that have come and gone!—
> Ambitious November with the humors of the year,
> With a particular zeal for every slab,
> Staining the uncomfortable angels that rot
> On the slabs, a wing chipped here, an arm there:
> The brute curiosity of an angel's stare
> Turns you, like them, to stone,
> Transforms the heaving air
> Till plunged to a heavier world below
> You shift your sea-space blindly
> Heaving, turning like the blind crab.

*There* is rhymed with *year* (to many persons, perhaps, only a half-rhyme), and I hoped the reader would unconsciously assume that he need not expect further use of that sound for some time. So when the line, "The brute curiosity of an angel's stare," comes a moment later, rhyming with *year-there*, I hoped that the violence of image would be further reinforced by the repetition of a sound that was no longer expected. I wanted the shock to be heavy; so I felt that I could not afford to hurry the reader away from it until he had received it in full. The next two lines carry on the image at a lower intensity: the rhyme, "Transforms the heaving *air*," prolongs the moment of attention upon that passage, while at the same time it ought to begin dissipating the shock, both by the introduction of a new image and by reduction of the "meaning" to a pattern of sound, the ere-rhymes. I calculated that the third use of that sound (stare) would be a surprise, the fourth (air) a monotony. I purposely made the end words of the third from last and last lines—*below* and *crab*—delayed rhymes for *row* and *slab*, the last being an internal and half-dissonant rhyme for the sake of bewilderment and incompleteness, qualities by which the man at the gate is at the moment possessed.

This is elementary but I cannot vouch for its success. As the dramatic situation of the poem is the tension that I have already described, so the rhythm is an attempt at a series of "modulations" back and forth between a formal regularity, for the heroic emotion, and a broken rhythm, with scattering imagery, for the failure of that emotion. This is "imitative form," which Yvor Winters deems a vice worth castigation. I have pointed out that the passage, "You know who have waited by the wall," presents the heroic theme of "active faith"; it will be observed that the rhythm, increasingly after "You who have waited for the angry resolution," is almost perfectly regular iambic, with only a few initial substitutions and weak endings. The passage is meant to convey a plenary vision, the actual presence, of the exemplars of active faith: the man at the gate at that moment is nearer to realizing them than at any other in the poem; hence the formal rhythm. But the vision breaks down; the wind-leaves refrain supervenes; and the next passage, "Turn your eyes to the immoderate past," is the irony of the preceding realization. With the self-conscious historical sense he turns his eyes into the past. The next passage after this, beginning, "You hear the shout . . ." is the failure of the vision in both phases, the pure realization and the merely historical. He cannot "see" the heroic virtues; there is wind, rain, leaves. But there is sound; for a moment he deceives himself with it. It is the noise of the battles that he has evoked. Then comes the figure of the rising sun of those battles; he is "lost in that orient of the thick and fast," and he curses his own moment, "the setting sun." The "setting sun" I tried to use as a triple image, for the decline of the heroic age and for the actual scene of late afternoon, the latter being not only natural desolation but spiritual desolation as well. Again for a moment he thinks he hears the battle shout, but only for a moment; then the silence reaches him.

Corresponding to the disintegration of the vision just described, there has been a breaking down of the formal rhythm. The complete breakdown comes with the images of the "mummy" and the "hound bitch." (*Hound* bitch because the hound is a hunter, participant of a formal ritual.) The failure of the vision throws the man back upon himself, but upon himself he cannot bring to bear the force of sustained imagination. He sees himself in random images (random to him, deliberate with the author) of something lower than he ought to be: the human image is only that of preserved death; but if he is alive he is an old hunter, dying. The passages about the mummy and the bitch are deliberately brief —slight rhythmic stretches. (These are the only verses I have written for which I thought of the movement first, then cast about for the symbols.)

I believe the term modulation denotes in music the uninterrupted shift from one key to another: I do not know the term for change of rhythm without change of measure. I wish to describe a similar change in verse rhythm; it may be convenient to think of it as modulation of a certain kind. At the end of the passage that I have been discussing the final words are "Hears the wind only." The phrase closes the first main division of the poem. I have loosely called the longer passages strophes, and if I were hardy enough to impose the classical organization of the lyric ode upon a baroque poem, I should say that these words bring to an end the Strophe, after which must come the next main division, or Antistrophe, which was often employed to answer the matter set forth in the Strophe or to present it from another point of view. And that is precisely the significance of the next main division, beginning: "Now that the salt of their blood . . ." But I wanted this second division of the poem to arise out of the collapse of the first. It is plain that it would not have suited my purpose to round off the first section with some sort of formal rhythm; so I ended it with an unfinished line. The next division must therefore begin by finishing that line, not merely in meter but with an integral rhythm. I will quote the passage:

> The hound bitch
> Toothless and dying, in a musty cellar
> *Hears the wind only.*
>
>             *Now that the salt of their blood*
> Stiffens the saltier oblivion of the sea,
> Seals the malignant purity of the flood. . . .

The caesura, after *only,* is thus at the middle of the third foot. (I do not give a full stress to *wind,* but attribute a "hovering stress" to *wind* and the first syllable of *only.*) The reader expects the foot to be completed by the stress on the next word, *Now,* as in a sense it is; but the phrase, "Now that the salt of their blood," is also the beginning of a new movement; it is two "dactyls" continuing more broadly the falling rhythm that has prevailed. But with the finishing off of the line with *blood,* the mounting rhythm is restored; the whole line from *Hears* to *blood* is actually an iambic pentameter with liberal inversions and substitutions that were expected to create a counter-rhythm within the line. From the caesura on, the rhythm is new; but it has—or was expected to have—an organic relation to the preceding rhythm; and it signals the rise of a new statement of the theme.

I have gone into this passage in detail—I might have chosen another—not because I think it is successful, but because I labored with it; if it is a failure, or even an uninteresting success, it ought to offer as much technical instruction to other persons as it would were it both successful and

interesting. But a word more: the broader movement introduced by the new rhythm was meant to correspond, as a
sort of Antistrophe, to the earlier formal movement beginning, "You know who have waited by the wall." It is a new
formal movement with new feeling and new imagery. The
heroic but precarious illusion of the earlier movement has
broken down into the personal symbols of the mummy and
the hound; the pathetic fallacy of the leaves as charging
soldiers and the conventional "buried Caesar" theme have
become rotten leaves and dead bodies wasting in the earth,
to return after long erosion to the sea. In the midst of this
naturalism, what shall the man say? What shall all humanity
say in the presence of decay? The two themes, then, have
been struggling for mastery; the structure of the poem thus
exhibits the development of two formal passages that contrast the two themes. The two formal passages break down,
the first shading into the second ("Now that the salt of their
blood . . ."), the second one concluding with the figure of
the jaguar, which is presented in a distracted rhythm left
suspended from a weak ending—the word *victim*. This figure of the jaguar is the only explicit rendering of the Narcissus motif in the poem, but instead of a youth gazing into
a pool, a predatory beast stares at a jungle stream, and leaps
to devour himself.

The next passage begins:

> What shall we say who have knowledge
> Carried to the heart?

This is Pascal's war between heart and head, between *finesse*
and *géométrie*. Should the reader care to think of these lines
as the gathering up of the two themes, now fused, into a
final statement, I should see no objection to calling it the
Epode. But upon the meaning of the lines from here to the
end there is no need for further commentary. I have talked
about the structure of the poem, not its quality. One can no
more find the quality of one's own verse than one can find

its value, and to try to find either is like looking into a glass for the effect that one's face has upon other persons.

If anybody ever wished to know anything about this poem that he could not interpret for himself, I suspect that he is still in the dark. I cannot believe that I have illuminated the difficulties that some readers have found in the style. But then I cannot, have never been able to, see any difficulties of that order. The poem has been much revised. I still think there is much to be said for the original *barter* instead of *yield* in the second line, and for *Novembers* instead of *November* in line fifteen. The revisions were not undertaken for the convenience of the reader but for the poem's own clarity, so that, word, phrase, line, passage, the poem might at worst come near its best expression.

# THE PROFESSION OF LETTERS IN THE SOUTH

## 1935

THE profession of letters in France dates, I believe, from the famous manifesto of Du Bellay and the Pléiade in 1549. It is a French habit to assume that France has supported a profession of letters ever since. There is no other country where the writer is so much honored as in France, no other people in western culture who understand so well as the French the value of literature to the state. The national respect for letters begins far down in society. In a French village where I was unknown I was able to use a letter-of-credit without identification upon my word that I was a man of letters. The French have no illusions; we are not asked to believe that all French writers are respectable. The generation of Rimbaud and Verlaine was notoriously dissolute. French letters are a profession, as law, medicine, and the army are professions. Good writers starve and lead sordid lives in France as elsewhere; yet the audience for high literature is larger in France than in any other country; and a sufficient number of the best writers find a public large enough to sustain them as a class.

It goes somewhat differently with us. The American public sees the writer as a business man because it cannot see any other kind of man, and respects him according to his income. And, alas, most writers themselves respect chiefly and fear only their competitors' sales. A big sale is a "success." How could it be otherwise? Our books are sold on a competitive market; it is a book market, but it is a luxury market; and luxury markets must be fiercely competitive. It is not that the natural depravity of the writer as fallen man betrays him into imitating the tone and standards of his market; actually he cannot find a public at all, even for the most lost of lost causes, the *succès d'estime*, unless he is willing to enter the competitive racket of publishing. This racket, our society being what it is, is a purely economic process, and literary opinion is necessarily manufactured for its needs. Its prime need is shoddy goods, because it must have a big, quick turnover. The overhead in the system is so high that the author gets only 10 to 15 per cent of the gross. It is the smallest return that any producer gets in our whole economic system. To live even frugally, a novelist, if he does not do odd jobs on the side, must have a sale of about 30,000 copies every two years. Not only the publisher's but his turnover, too, must be quick. He has his own self-sweat shop. One must agree with Mr. Herbert Read, in the February, 1935, London *Mercury*, that authors under modern capitalism are a sweated class.

We have heard for years, we began hearing it as early as Jeffrey's review of the first "Hyperion," that science is driving poetry to cover. I suppose it is; and we have the weight of Mr. I. A. Richards' arguments to prove it, and Mr. Max Eastman's weight, which is fairly light. Nineteenth-century science produced a race of "problem" critics and novelists. The new "social" point of view has multiplied the race. Literature needs no depth of background or experience to deal with problems; it needs chiefly the statistical survey and the conviction that society lives by formula, if not by bread alone. The nineteenth century began this *genre*, which has become the standard mode. I confess that I cannot decide whether "science" or the mass production of books, or the Spirit that made them both, has given us shoddy in literature.

We were given, for example, Bennett and Wells; Millay and Masefield. And I surmise that not pure science but shoddy has driven the poets into exile, where, according to Eastman, they are "talking to themselves."

I shall not multiply instances. The trouble ultimately goes back to the beginnings of finance-capitalism and its creature, machine-production. Under feudalism the artist was a member of an organic society. The writer's loss of professional standing, however, set in before the machine, by which I mean the machine-age as we know it, appeared. It began with the rise of mercantile aristocracy in the eighteenth century. The total loss of professionalism in letters may be seen in our age—an age that remembers the extinction of aristocracy and witnesses the triumph of a more inimical plutocratic society.

If my history is not wholly incorrect, it must follow that our unlimited pioneering, the pretext of the newness of the country, and our low standards of education, do not explain the decline of the professional author. Pioneering became our way of industrial expansion, a method of production not special to us; we are a new country in so far as our industrialism gave to the latent vices of the European mind a new opportunity; and our standards of education get lower with the increasing amount of money spent upon them. For my purposes, then, it is sufficient that we should look at the history of professionalism in letters in terms of the kinds of rule that European society, which includes American society, has had.

The South once had aristocratic rule; the planter class was about one fifth of the population; but the majority followed its lead. And so, by glancing at the South, we shall see in American history an important phase of the decline of the literary profession. There was, perhaps, in and around Boston, for a brief period, a group of professional writers. But not all of them, not even most of them, made their livings by writing. Even if they had, we should still have to explain why they were second-rate, and why the greatest of the

Easterners, Hawthorne, Melville, Dickinson, had nothing to do with them or with the rising plutocracy of the East. But it is a sadder story still in the South. We had no Hawthorne, no Melville, no Emily Dickinson. We had William Gilmore Simms. We made it impossible for Poe to live south of the Potomac. Aristocracy drove him out. Plutocracy, in the East, starved him to death. I prefer the procedure of the South; it knew its own mind, knew what kind of society it wanted. The East, bent upon making money, could tolerate, as it still tolerates, any kind of disorder on the fringe of society as long as the disorder does not interfere with money-making. It did not know its own social mind; it was, and still is, plutocracy.

But let us look a little at the backgrounds of Southern literature. I say backgrounds, for the South is an immensely complicated region. It begins in the Northeast with southern Maryland; it ends with eastern Texas; it includes to the north a little of Missouri. But that the people in this vast expanse of country have enough in common to bind them in a single culture cannot be denied. They often deny it themselves—writers who want to have something to jabber about, or other writers who want to offset the commercial handicap of being Southern; or newly rich persons in cities that would rather be like Pittsburgh than like New Orleans. It must be confessed that the Southern tradition has left no cultural landmark so conspicuous that the people may be reminded by it constantly of what they are. We lack a tradition in the arts; more to the point, we lack a literary tradition. We lack even a literature. We have just enough literary remains from the old régime to prove to us that, had a great literature risen, it would have been unique in modern times.

The South was settled by the same European strains as originally settled the North. Yet, in spite of war, reconstruction, and industrialism, the South to this day finds its most perfect contrast in the North. In religious and social feeling I should stake everything on the greater resemblance to France. The South clings blindly to forms of European feeling and conduct that were crushed by the French Revolution and that, in England at any rate, are barely memories. How many Englishmen have told us that we still have the eighteenth-century amiability and consideration of manners, supplanted in their country by middle-class reticence and suspicion? And where, outside the South, is there a society that believes even covertly in the Code of Honor? This is not idle talk; we are assured of it by Professor H. C. Brearley, who, I believe, is one of the most detached students of Southern life. Where else in the modern world is the patriarchal family still innocent of the rise and power of other forms of society? Possibly in France; probably in the peasant countries of the Balkans and of Central Europe. Yet the "orientation"—let us concede the word to the University of North Carolina—the rise of new Southern points of view, even now in the towns, is tied still to the image of the family on the land. Where else does so much of the reality of the ancient land-society endure, along with the infatuated avowal of beliefs that are hostile to it? Where in the world today is there a more supine enthusiasm for being amiable to forces undermining the life that supports the amiability? The anomalous structure of the South is, I think, finally witnessed by its religion. Doctor Poteat of South Carolina deplores a fact which he does not question, that only in the South does one find a convinced supernaturalism: it is nearer to Aquinas than to Calvin, Wesley, or Knox. Nor do we doubt that the conflict between modernism and fundamentalism is chiefly the impact of the new middle-class civilization upon the rural society; nor, moreover, should we allow ourselves to forget that philosophers of the State, from Sir Thomas More to John C. Calhoun, were political defenders of the older religious community.

The key to unlock the Southern mind is, fortunately, like Bluebeard's, bloody and perilous; there is not the easy sesamé to the cavern of gaping success. The South has had reverses that permit her people to imagine what they might have been. (And only thus can people discover what they *are*.) Given the one great fact of the expanding plantation system at the dawn of the last century, which voice should the South have listened to? Jefferson, or Marshall, or Calhoun? I mean, which voice had the deepest moral and spiritual implications for the permanence of Southern civilization?

There was not time to listen to any voice very long. The great Southern ideas were strangled in the cradle, either by the South herself (for example, by too much quick cotton money in the Southwest) or by the Union armies. It is plain to modern historians of culture that peoples do not make, much less buy, a culture overnight; it takes time. Which view would have given the South a unified sense of its own destiny? Our modern "standard of living" is not a point of view, and it is necessary that a people should gather its experience round some seasoned point of view before it may boast a high culture. It must be able to illuminate from a fixed position all its experience; it must bring to full realization the high forms as well as the contradictions and miseries inherent in human society.

The miseries and contradictions bemuse and alarm us now. I hope I shall not be called flint-hearted if I dare to believe that the humanitarian spirit can never remove them. So long as society is committed to a class-system—and it will probably never be committed to a classless system—the hard-hearted will keep on believing that the high forms are as necessary to the whole of society as bread to the major fraction to whom it is now denied. If man does not live by bread alone, he lives thinly upon bread and sentiment; for sentiment and bread will nourish him but little unless they partake of the peculiarly elevating virtues of form. I might even quote Shelley, whom it is becoming fashionable again to quote: "Our calculations have outrun conception; we have eaten more than we can digest." I am willing to take the sentence in full literalness, if I may read form for conception, and produced for eaten. For the concrete forms of the social and religious life are the assimilating structure of society. Where, as in the Old South, there were high forms, but no deep realization of the spirit was achieved, we must ask questions. (The right questions: not why the South refused to believe in Progress, or why it did not experiment with "ideas.") Was the structure of society favorable to a great literature? Suppose it to have been favorable: Was there something wrong with the intellectual life for which the social order cannot be blamed?

The answer is both yes and no to the first question. It is emphatically yes and no to the second. So our answers are confused. At a glance one would expect the rich leisured class, well-educated as the Southern aristocracy was—for the South of the fifties had proportionately a larger educated minority than Massachusetts—to devote a great part of its vitality to the arts, the high and conscious arts. As for the arts otherwise, even peasant societies achieve the less conscious variety—manners, ritual, charming domestic architecture.

Assuming, as I do not think I am allowed to assume very confidently, that this society was a good soil for the high arts, there was yet a grave fault in the intellectual life. It was hag-ridden with politics. We like to think that Archimago sent the nightmare down from the North. He did. But it was partly rooted in the kind of rule that the South had, which was aristocratic rule. All aristocracies are obsessed politically. (Witness *Henry IV*, Parts One and Two; *Henry V*.) The best intellectual energy goes into politics and goes of necessity; aristocracy is class-rule; and the class must fight for interest and power. Under the special conditions of the nineteenth century, the South had less excess of vitality for the disinterested arts of literature than it might have had ordinarily. There are no simple answers to the questions that I have asked. The South was a fairly good place for the arts, as good possibly as any other aristocratic country, only its inherent passion for politics was inflamed by the furious contentions that threatened its life. Every gifted person went into politics, not merely the majority.

The furious contentions themselves provided later answers to the problem of the arts in the South. At the end of the century one of the popular answers was that of the distinguished William Peterfield Trent, who laid bare all the Southern defects with the black magic talisman, Slavery. The defects could be whisked away, he argued in his life of Simms, with "essential faith in American democracy." The Northern people, at that time, may be forgiven this faith; it was the stuffed shirt of plutocracy and it was making them money; they had a right to believe in it. I cannot decide between credulity and venality as the reason for its being believed in the South. I am certain that in Trent's case it was credulity. If slavery was the cause of war, then slavery explained the political mania of the Old South; and the political mania stunted the arts. Partly true; partly false. Such an answer is more dangerous than an answer wholly false. In this instance it led the people to believe that their sole obstacle to perfection, slavery, had been removed. There was no need to be critical of anything else, least of all of the society that had come down and removed the blight: a society that by some syllogistic process unknown to me was accepted as perfect by the new Southern Liberals.

But the abolition of slavery did not make for a distinctively Southern literature. We must seek the cause of our limitations elsewhere. It is worth remarking, for the sake of argument, that chattel slavery is not demonstrably a worse form of slavery than any other upon which an aristocracy may base its power and wealth. That *African* chattel slavery was the worst groundwork conceivable for the growth of a great culture of European pattern, is scarcely at this day arguable. Still, as a favorable "cultural situation" it was probably worse than white-chattel, agricultural slavery only in degree. The distance between white master and black slave was unalterably greater than that between white master and white serf after the destruction of feudalism. The peasant *is* the soil. The Negro slave was a barrier between the ruling class and the soil. If we look at aristocracies in Europe, say in eighteenth-century England, we find at least genuine social classes, each carrying on a different level of the common culture. But in the Old South, and under the worse form of slavery that afflicts both races today, genuine social classes could not exist. The enormous "difference" of the Negro doomed him from the beginning to an economic status purely: he has had much the same thinning influence upon the class above him as the anonymous city proletariat has had upon the culture of industrial capitalism.

All great cultures have been rooted in peasantries, in free peasantries, I believe, such as the English yeomanry before the fourteenth century: they have been the growth of the soil. What the Southern system might have accomplished we do not know: it would have been, as I have said, something new. Of course, the absence of genuine cultural capitals in the South has been cited as a cause of lassitude in the arts; perhaps it was a cause, as it is today. But it does not wholly explain the vague and feeble literature that was produced. The white man got nothing from the Negro, no profound image of himself in terms of the soil.

I suspect that, in the age of social science, the term image is not clear, and this, I suppose, is due to the disappearance, in such an age, of the deep relation between man and a local habitation. An environment is an abstraction, not a place; Natchez is a place but not an environment. The difference will be clear to those who are morally able to see that it exists. The citizen of Natchez lived in a place but he could not deepen his sense of its life through the long series of gradations represented by his dependents, who stood between him and the earth. He instructed his factor to buy good furniture of the Second Empire, and remained a Colonial. But the Negro, who has long been described as a responsibility, got everything from the white man. The history of French culture, I suppose, has been quite different. The high arts have been grafted upon the peasant stock. We could graft no new life upon the Negro; he was too different, too alien.

Doubtless the confirmed if genteel romanticism of the old

Southern imaginative literature (I make exception for the political writers of South Carolina—Hammond, Harper, Calhoun: they are classical and realistic) was in the general stream of romanticism; yet the special qualities that it produced, the unreal union of formless revery and correct sentiment, the inflated oratory—even in private correspondence you see it witness a feeble hold upon place and time. The roots were not deep enough in the soil. Professor Trent was right; but he was right for the wrong reason. It was not that slavery was corrupt "morally." Societies can bear an amazing amount of corruption and still produce high cultures. Black slavery could not nurture the white man in his own image.

Although the Southern system, in spite of the Negro, was closer to the soil than the mercantile-manufacturing system of the Middle and New England states, its deficiencies in spiritual soil were more serious even than those of the debased feudal society of eighteenth-century rural England. With this society the ante-bellum South had much in common.

The South came from eighteenth-century England, its agricultural half; there were not enough large towns in the South to complete the picture of an England reproduced. The Virginian and the Carolinian, however, imitated the English squire. They held their land, like their British compeer, in absolute, that is to say unfeudal, ownership, as a result of the destruction, first under Henry VIII and then under Cromwell, of the feudal system of land tenure. The landlord might be humane, but he owed no legal obligation to his land (he could wear it out) or to his labor (he could turn it off: called "enclosure" in England, "selling" under Negro slavery). A pure aristocracy, or the benevolent rule of a landed class in the interest of its own wealth and power, had superseded royalty which, in theory at any rate, and often in practice, had tried to balance class interests under protection of the Crown.

It should be borne in mind, against modern egalitarian and

Marxian superstition, that royalty and aristocracy are fundamentally opposed systems of rule; that plutocracy, the offspring of democracy, and that Marxism, the child of plutocracy, are essentially of the aristocratic political mode: they all mean class rule. Virginia took the lead in the American Revolution, not to set up democracy, as Jefferson tried to believe, but to increase the power of the tobacco-exporting aristocracy. The planters wished to throw off the yoke of the British merchant and to get access to the free world market.

But the Southern man of letters cannot permit himself to look upon the old system from a purely social point of view, or from the economic view: to him it must seem better than the system that destroyed it, better, too, than any system with which the modern planners, Marxian or other color, wish to replace the present order. Yet the very merits of the Old South tend to confuse the issue: its comparative stability, its realistic limitation of the acquisitive impulse, its preference for human relations compared to relations economic, tempt the historian to defend the poor literature simply because he feels that the old society was a better place to live in than the new. It is a great temptation—if you do not read the literature.

There is, I believe, a nice object-lesson to be drawn from the changed relation of the English writer to society in the eighteenth century; it is a lesson that bears directly upon the attitude of the Old South towards the profession of letters. In the seventeenth century, in the year 1634, a young, finical man, then in seclusion at Horton after taking his degrees at Cambridge, and still unknown, was invited by the Earl of Bridgewater to write a masque for certain revels to be celebrated at Ludlow Castle. The masque was *Comus*, and the revels were in the feudal tradition. The whole celebration was "at home"; it was a part of the community life, the common people were present, and the poet was a spiritual member of the society gathered there. He might not be a gentleman: had Milton become a member of Egerton's "household" he would have been a sort of upper servant.

But he would have been a member of the social and spiritual community.

Now examine the affair of Johnson and the Earl of Chesterfield: it is the eighteenth century. It was conducted in the new "aristocratic" style. For the flattery of a dedication the nobleman was loftily willing to give his patronage, a certain amount of money, to an author who had already completed the work, an author who had faced starvation in isolation from society. There is no great publishing system in question here; there were only booksellers. But there was already the cash nexus between the writer and society. The Earl of Chesterfield was a capitalist, not a feudal noble as Egerton to some extent still was: Chesterfield had lost the community; he required of the arts a compliment to the power of his class.

He was the forerunner of the modern plutocrat who thinks that the arts are thriving so long as he can buy Italian paintings, or so long as he creates "foundations" for the arts, or the sales sheets of the publishers show a large volume of "business." But the plutocrat no less than the artist participates in his society through the cash nexus. I hope I do not convince the reader that this wicked fellow has undertaken a deliberate conspiracy against the artist. The artist as man invariably has the same relation to the society of his time as everybody else has: his misfortune and his great value is his superior awareness of that relation. The "message" of modern art at present is that social man is living, without religion, morality, or art (without the high form that concentrates all three in an organic whole) in a mere system of money references through which neither artist nor plutocrat can perform as an entire person.

Is there anything in common between the Earl of Chesterfield and a dour Scots merchant building a fortune and a place in the society of Richmond, Virginia, in the first third of the nineteenth century? I think that they have something in common. It was not John Allan who drove Poe out of Virginia. The foreigner, trying to better himself, always knows the practical instincts of a society more shrewdly than the society knows them. Allan was, for once, the spokesman of Virginia, of the plantation South. There was no place for Poe in the spiritual community of Virginia; there was no class of professional writers that Poe could join in dedicating their works to the aristocracy under the system of the cash nexus. The promising young men were all in politics bent upon more desperate emergencies. It was obvious, even to John Allan, I suppose, that here was no dabbler who would write pleasant, genteel poems and stories for magazines where other dabbling gentlemen printed their pleasant, genteel stories and poems. Anybody could have looked at Poe and known that he meant business.

And until the desperate men today who mean business can become an independent class, there will be no profession of letters anywhere in America. It remains only to add to the brief history adumbrated in this essay some comment on the present situation of the desperate men of the South in particular. There are too many ladies and gentlemen, too many Congreves whose coxcombry a visit from Voltaire would do a great deal of good. I trust that I do not argue the case too well. Congreve frivolously gave up the honor of his profession when Voltaire asked to see the great dramatist and got the answer that Mr. Congreve was no scribbler but a man of fashion. They were more explicit about those things in those days. I should barely hope that the Southern writer, or the Northern or Western, for that matter, may decide that his gentility, being a quality over which he has no control, may get along as it can. For the genteel tradition has never done anything for letters in the South; yet the Southern writers who are too fastidious to become conscious of their profession have not refused to write best-sellers when they could, and to profit by a cash nexus with New York. I would fain believe that matters are otherwise than so: but facts are facts. If there is such a person as a Southern writer, if there could be such a profession as letters in the South, the profession would require the speaking of unpleasant words and the violation of good literary manners.

I wish this were the whole story: only cranks and talents of the quiet, first order maintain themselves against fashion and prosperity. But even these desperate persons must live, and they cannot live in the South without an "independent income." We must respect the source of our income, that is, we ought to; and if we cannot respect it we are likely to fear it. This kind of writer is not luckier than his penniless fellow. (The only man I know who devotes a large income to changing the system that produced it is a New Yorker.) Because there is no city in the South where writers may gather, write, and live, and no Southern publisher to print their books, the Southern writer, of my generation at least, went to New York. There he was influenced not only by the necessity to live but by theories and movements drifting over from Europe.

It was, possibly, a dangerous situation. Mr. John Crowe Ransom has pointed out its implications:

> If modernism is regarded as nothing but a new technique, what was wrong with the old technique? Principally, perhaps, the fact that it was old; for modernism is apt to assume that tradition is not so much a prop which may be leant upon as a dead burden which must be borne. The substance of modernism is not a technique but an attitude. And a dangerous attitude . . .
>
> The Southern artists in going modern offer us their impression of a general decay, and that is not a pleasant thing to think about.[1]

The Southern writer was perilously near to losing his identity, becoming merely a "modern" writer. He lost the Southern feeling which, in the case of Mr. Young, informs the Southern style: he might retain a Southern subject and write about it as an outsider, with some novelty of technique and

[1] *Modern with a Southern Accent.* By John Crowe Ransom. *The Virginia Quarterly Review,* April, 1935.

in smart, superior detachment. These bad features of the last decade may be deplored, I hope, without asking the Southerner to stay at home and starve. That, it seems to me, is what Mr. Ransom asks the Southern writer to do. It was not an uprooted modern, but the classical Milton who remarked, "Wherever we do well is home": wherever we are allowed best to realize our natures—a realization that, for an artist, presupposes permission to follow his craft—is the proper place to live. The Southern writer should if possible be a Southerner in the South. The sole condition that would make that possible is a profession of letters.

But the arts everywhere spring from a mysterious union of indigenous materials and foreign influences: there is no great art or literature that does not bear the marks of this fusion. So I cannot assume, as Mr. Ransom seems to do, that exposure to the world of modernism (Petrarchism was modernism in the England of 1540) was of itself a demoralizing experience. Isn't it rather that the Southerner before he left home had grown weak in his native allegiance? That his political and social history, and his domestic life, had been severely adulterated no less by his fellow Southerners than by the people in the North to whom he fled? Apart from this menace abroad, who cannot bring himself to wish that Miss Glasgow had studied James and Flaubert in her apprenticeship, and spared herself and us her first three or four novels? Could Mr. Young have written his fiction, to say nothing of his plays and criticism, had he read only Cable and Page? And, lastly, what shall we say of Mr. Ransom's own distinguished and very modern poetry?

Is not Mr. Ransom really deploring the absence, as I deplore it, of a professional spirit and professional opportunities in Southern literature? There is no reason why the Southern writer should not address a large public, but if he does he will learn sooner or later that—but for happy accidents—the market, with what the market implies, dictates the style. To create a profession of literature in the South we should require first an independent machinery of publication. I fall into the mechanical terms. A Southern publishing system would not, I imagine, publish Southern books alone; nor should Southern magazines print only Southern authors. The point of the argument leads to no such comforting simplicity. The literary artist is seldom successful as a colonial; he should be able to enjoy the normal belief that he is at the center of the world. One aid to that feeling would be a congenial medium of communication with his public. Let the world in this fashion sit at his feet; let him not have to seek the world.

The exact degree of immediate satisfaction that Southern publication would bring to its authors I cannot predict. It, too, would be the system of the cash nexus; and the Southern publisher would be a capitalist plutocrat not noticeably different from his colleague in the North. Like his Northern friend he would, for a few years at least, sell the Southern article mostly north of the border. Until he could be backed by a powerful Southern press he would need the support of the New York journals for his authors, if he expected them to be read at home. I suppose the benefits of a Southern system would lie chiefly in this: that the Southern writer would not have to run the New York gauntlet, from which he emerges with a good understanding of what he can and cannot do.

We have exchanged the reasoned indifference of aristocracy for the piratical commercialism of plutocracy. Repudiating the later master, the new profession in the South would have to tell New York, where it had hitherto hawked its wares, that no more wares of the prescribed kind would be produced. For the prescribed ware is the ware that the Southerner also must produce, and it is not heartening to observe that his own Southern public waits for the New York journals to prescribe the kind, before he can get a hearing at home. Can there be a profession of letters in the South? Our best critical writing—and we have critical writing of distinction—can never constitute a Southern criticism so long as it must be trimmed and scattered in Northern magazines, or published in books that will be read as curiously as travel literature, by Northern people alone.

The considerable achievement of Southerners in modern American letters must not beguile us into too much hope for the future. The Southern novelist has left his mark upon the age; but it is of the age. From the peculiarly historical consciousness of the Southern writer has come good work of a special order; but the focus of this consciousness is quite temporary. It has made possible the curious burst of intelligence that we get at a crossing of the ways, not unlike, on an infinitesimal scale, the outburst of poetic genius at the end of the sixteenth century when commercial England had already begun to crush feudal England. The Histories and Tragedies of Shakespeare record the death of the old régime, and Doctor Faustus gives up feudal order for world power.

The prevailing economic passion of the age once more tempts, even commands, the Southern writer to go into politics. Our neo-communism is the new form in which the writer from all sections is to be dominated by capitalism, or "economic society." It is the new political mania. And there is no escape from it. The political mind always finds itself in an emergency. And the emergency, this time real enough, becomes a pretext for ignoring the arts. We live in the sort of age that Abraham Cowley complained of —a good age to write about but a hard age to write in.

# THE NEW PROVINCIALISM

*With an Epilogue on the Southern Novel*

## 1945

A NOTE written around a subject needs a formidable title to remind the writer where he is going and to make the elusive subject a little clearer to the reader. I confess to feelings of peculiar inadequacy on this occasion;[1] it reminds me of a similar occasion ten years ago, when I was writing an essay for the tenth anniversary number of *The Virginia Quarterly Review*. That essay (as I recall it: I have not been able to bring myself to reread it as I begin to write)—that essay was possibly a little stuffy and more certain of itself than these notes can be. It was written at the height of the Southern literary renascence. That renascence is over; or at any rate that period is over; and I write, we all write, in the time of the greatest war. Will the new literature of the South, or of the United States as a whole, be different from anything that we knew before the war? Will American literature be more alike all over the country? And more like the literature of the world?

An affirmative answer to the last question would make our literary nationalists—Mr. Van Wyck Brooks, Mr. Kazin, and Mr. De Voto—look a little old-fashioned, very much as they

[1] The present essay was written for the twentieth anniversary of *The Virginia Quarterly Review*, April, 1945.

have actually been all along as the intellectual contemporaries of Buckle and Taine. Their influence is no longer very much felt by anybody who seriously writes; and it is sufficient here merely to state the paradox that not even literary nationalism could abort a genuine national literature when it is ready to appear; when, in fact, we become a nation. But it is more likely that we may become an internation first. These reflections are set down to prepare for something that I have long wanted the occasion to say: that mere regionalism, as we have heard it talked about in recent years, is not enough. For this picturesque regionalism of local color is a by-product of nationalism. And it is not informed enough to support a mature literature. But neither is nationalism.

Yet no literature can be mature without the regional consciousness; it can only be senile, with the renewed immaturity of senility. For without regionalism, without locality in the sense of local continuity in tradition and belief, we shall get a whole literature which Mr. John Dos Passos might have written: perhaps a whole literature which, in spite of my admiration for Mr. Dos Passos's novels, I shall not even be able to read. This new literature will probably be personal, sentimentally objective, tough, and "unsocial," and will doubtless achieve its best effects in a new version of the old travel story (like most of Mr. Dos Passos's books, which are travel stories) both abroad and at home: the account of voyages to the South and West, and to the ends of the world. New Crusoes, new Captain Singletons, new Gullivers will appear, but Gullivers who see *with*, not *through* the eye. It will not be a "national" literature, or even an "international"; it may be a provincial literature with world horizons, the horizons of the geographical world, which need not be spiritually larger than Bourbon County, Kentucky: provincialism without regionalism.

## I I

IF REGIONALISM is not enough, is a world provincialism enough? It has béen generally supposed in our time that the limitations of the mere regional interest, which are serious, could be corrected by giving them up for·a "universal" point of view, a political or social doctrine which would "relate" or "integrate" the local community with the world in the advance of a higher culture. What this higher culture is or might be nobody was ever quite clear about. It looked political, or at any rate "social," and it ranged in imaginative emphasis all the way from the Stalinist party line, upon whose front, in this country, was written the slogan, Defense of Culture (*whose culture?*), to Mr. Wallace's Common Man, whom Mr. Wallace seemed willing to let remain common.

What it never occurred to anybody to ask was this simple question: What happens if you make the entire world into one vast region? This, it seems to me, is the trouble with our world schemes today: they contemplate a large extension of the political and philosophical limitations of the regional principle. "Let's get closer to the Chinese." "Know your fellow men, and you will like them better, and cease to fight them." Are these propositions true? I doubt it. Europeans are fighting one another today not because they didn't "know" one another. It does not, of course, follow that they are fighting because they did know one another; but that proposition makes as good sense as its contrary. For the real end is not physical communication, or parochial neighborliness on a world scale. The real end, as I see it, is *what* you are communicating after you get the physical means of communication. It is possible for men to face one another and not have anything to say. In that case it may occur to them, since they cannot establish a common understanding, to try to take something away from one another; and they may temporarily establish, as they did a generation ago, certain rules of mutual plunder that look for a time like "international co-operation."

All this has a bearing on literature today, the literature of the United States, and of the South, in the recent past and in the near future. For the logical opposite, or the historic complement, of the isolated community or region is not the world community or world region. In our time we have been the victims of a geographical metaphor, or a figure of space: we have tried to compensate for the limitations of the little community by envisaging the big community, which is not necessarily bigger spiritually or culturally than the little community. The complement of the regional principle, the only force which in the past has kept the region (of whatever size) from being provincial, from being committed to the immediate interest, is a non-political or supra-political culture such as held Europe together for six hundred years and kept war to the "limited objective." That is to say, there was sufficient unity, somewhere at the top, to check the drive of mere interest, and to limit war to a few massacres prompted by religious zeal or by the desire of rulers to keep their neighbors from getting out of hand. The small professional army at the top never tried to use and thus to menace the vast, stable energy of the masses, until the age of Louis XIV; and it was not until Napoleon that it was thought possible to make a whole nation fight.

The kind of unity prevailing in the West until the nineteenth century has been well described by Christopher Dawson as a peculiar balance of Greek culture and Christian other-worldliness, both imposed by Rome upon the northern barbarians. It was this special combination that made European civilization, and it was this that men communicated in the act of living together. It was this force which reduced the regional heterogeneity to a manageable unity, or even sublimated it into universal forms. Is not this civilization just about gone? Only men who are committed to perverse illusion or to public oratory believe that we have a Christian civilization today: we still have Christians in every real sense, but in neither politics nor education, by and large, do Christian motives or standards, or even references, have an effective part. We do not ask: Is this right? We ask: Will this work? It is the typical question for men who represent the decadent humanism of the Greek half of our tradition. For that humanism has ended up as the half of a half: it stands for only half of the Greek spirit, the empirical or scientific half which gives us our technology. Technology without Christianity is, I think, barbarism quite simply; but barbarism refined, violent, and decadent, not the vigorous barbarism of the forest and the soil. I do not believe that we could say of our culture what Burke said of the English in 1790, that we have not "subtilized ourselves into savagery."

This is the catastrophic view. I did not originate it. And I suppose it cannot be wholly true. A few men will still somehow evade total efficiency, and live much as they did in the past; many will be bored by machines or, like the retired banker in my community, refuse to use their products by making by hand the articles of daily utility. The individual human being will probably have in the future as in the past a natural economy to which he can occasionally return, if he is not meddled with too much by power at a distance.

This natural economy cannot be an effective check upon the standardizing forces of the outside world without the protection of the regional consciousness. For regionalism is that consciousness or that habit of men in a given locality which influences them to certain patterns of thought and conduct handed to them by their ancestors. Regionalism is thus limited in space but not in time.

The provincial attitude is limited in time but not in space. When the regional man, in his ignorance, often an intensive and creative ignorance, of the world, extends his own immediate necessities into the world, and assumes that the present moment is unique, he becomes the provincial man. He cuts himself off from the past, and without benefit of the fund of traditional wisdom approaches the simplest problems of life as if nobody had ever heard of them before.

A society without arts, said Plato, lives by chance. The provincial man, locked in the present, lives by chance.

## III

IT MUST be plain from this train of ideas whither I am leading this discussion. For the world today is perhaps more provincial in outlook than it has been at any time since the ninth century, and even that era had, in its primitive agrarian economy, a strong regional basis for individual independence. Industrial capitalism has given us provincialism without regionalism: we are committed to chance solutions of "problems" that seem unique because we have forgotten the nature of man. And having destroyed our regional societies in the West, we are fanatically trying to draw other peoples into our provincial orbit, for the purpose of "saving" them.

Our Utopian politics is provincial. It is all very well to meet at Dumbarton Oaks or on the Black Sea to arrange the world, but unless the protagonists of these dramas of journalism have secret powers the presence of which we have hitherto had no reason to suspect, the results for the world must almost necessarily be power politics, or mere *rules of plunder which look like co-operation.* The desired co-operation is for the physical welfare of man. But it is a curious fact (I have not been able to find any history which denies the fact) that the physical welfare of man, pursued as an end in itself, has seldom prospered. The nineteenth century dream of a secular Utopia produced Marxian socialism, National Socialism, and the two greatest wars of history; and it is perhaps only another sign of our provincialism that we ignore the causation between the dream and the wars, and urge more of the same dream to prevent other wars which the dream will doubtless have its part in causing. Nobody wants to see the Oriental peoples dominated by the Japanese and to go hungry and ill-clad; yet so far in the history of civilization it has been virtually impossible to feed and clothe people with food and clothing. It is my own impression that they get fed and clothed incidentally to some other impulse, a creative power which we sometimes identify with religion and the arts.

It is small game; yet are not the Four Freedoms a typical expression of our world provincialism? Here is a radio fantasy on the secular dream of the nineteenth century. We guarantee to the world freedom of thought—to think about what? (I had supposed we were opposed to freedom of thought for the Germans and the Japanese.) Is it freedom to think *our* thoughts? We guarantee to the world freedom of worship—to worship what? Unless you cut the worship off from everything else that the Javanese, the Hottentots, the Russians, and the Americans may be doing (in our own case we have almost succeeded in this), what is to keep the Javanese, the Hottentots, the Russians, and ourselves from worshiping a war-god and putting this religion to the test of action? We guarantee to the world freedom from want. We had better—or somebody had better guarantee it, even if the guarantee is no good; for nineteenth-century industrial capitalism and our own more advanced technology have made it very difficult for "backward peoples" (to say nothing of ourselves in small units and groups) to make their living independently of somebody else nine thousand miles away. In other words we have destroyed the regional economies, and we offer a provincial remedy for the resulting evils; that is to say, a Utopian remedy which ignores our past experience. We guarantee to the world freedom from fear. On this freedom I confess that I have nothing to say. Provincial arrogance could not go further; and if my own religion had not been destroyed by the same forces that destroyed Mr. Roosevelt's and Mr. Churchill's (I do not deny them or myself feelings of common piety), I should expect the wrath of God to strike them. I infer from the hedging cynicism of their repudiation of the Four Freedoms as an "official document" the casual frivolity with which they must have written it in the first place. There was a radio on the ship. The ease of modern communication compelled these gentlemen to communicate with the world, when there was nothing to communicate.

## I V

I AM a little embarrassed at having used so many large conceptions, with so little specification. I ought to make plainer, before I go further, certain connections between regionalism and provincialism that I have only implied. The regional society is, with respect to high civilization, the neutral society: it can be primitive or highly cultivated, or any of the steps between. In the West our peculiar civilization was based upon regional autonomy, whose eccentricities were corrected and sublimated by the classical-Christian culture which provided a form for the highest development of man's potentialities *as man*. Man belonged to his village, valley, mountain, or sea-coast; but wherever he was he was a Christian whose Hebraic discipline had tempered his tribal savagery and whose classical humanism had moderated the literal imperative of his Christianity to suicidal other-worldliness.

If this peculiar culture of the West is weakening or is even gone as a creative force, we are left with our diverse regionalisms; or *were* left with them. For the myth of science which undermined this culture and created the modern economic man rooted out the regional economies, and is now creating a world regional economy. Regional economy means interdependence of the citizens of a region, whether the region be an Alpine village or the world. And the world, like the Alpine village, can be neutral with respect to high civilization. Regionalism without civilization—which means, with us, regionalism without the classical-Christian culture—becomes provincialism; and world regionalism becomes world provincialism. For provincialism is that state of mind in which regional men lose their origins in the past and its continuity into the present, and begin every day as if there had been no yesterday.

We are committed to this state of mind. We are so deeply involved in it (I make no exception of myself) that we must participate in its better purposes, however incomplete they may be; for good-will, even towards the Four Freedoms, is better than ill-will; and I am convinced that even the die-hard traditionalist would deny his own shrinking tradition if he refused to act for the remnant of it left because he can't have it all. For this remnant may be useful; there will be a minority with a memory which has not been dimmed by what Christian Gauss has called the Reversal of the Time Sense. We shall not all derive our standards of human nature and of the good society from an unexperienced future imagined by the late H. G. Wells or Mr. Henry Wallace.

# V

THE brilliant and unexpected renascence of Southern writing between the two wars is perhaps not of the first importance in the literature of the modern world; yet for the first time the South had a literature of considerable maturity which was distinctive enough to call for a special criticism which it failed to get. The provincial ideas of the critics of the North and East (there was no Southern criticism: merely a few Southern critics)—the provincial views of Southern writing of the recent renascence followed a direction somewhat as follows: The South, backward and illiberal, and controlled by white men who cherish a unique moral perversity, does not offer in itself a worthy subject to the novelist or the poet; it follows that the only acceptable literature that the South can produce must be a literature of social agitation, through which the need of reform may be publicized.

There were dozens of Southern novels written to this prescription. (I can think of only one Southern novelist of the period who ignored it and who was continuously popular: the late Elizabeth Madox Roberts.) The formula generally imposed two limitations upon the Southern writer: first, he must ignore the historical background of his subject; and second, he must judge the subject strictly in terms of the

material welfare of his characters and of the "injustice" which
keeps them from getting enough of it. My testimony is perhaps not wholly disinterested, yet I am convinced that not
one distinguished novel was produced in or about the South
from this point of view. The novel that came nearest to real
distinction was probably Miss Glasgow's *Barren Ground;*
but even this excellent novel is written outside the subject,
with the result that the frustration of her Virginia farmers
is not examined as an instance of the decay of rural culture
everywhere, but rather as a simple object-lesson in the lack
of standard American "advantages." (Miss Glasgow's other
and later books pose other problems, chiefly the problem of
the consciously "liberal" writer who draws his knowledge of
human nature from a source richer than that of his ideas,
and who thus writes somewhat below the level of his historical tradition.) But this is not a roster of all the sociological
novels about the South from 1918 to the present. If these
notes were a parlor game, I should challenge the "critics"
who hailed them in the twenties and thirties to exhibit just
one novel of this school which they would be willing to let
compete with the best European writing of the period.

  ˙ There has been some confusion in the South as well as
elsewhere about the subjects accessible to Southern writers;
this confusion results from the appeal to history:-what *is* the
structure of Southern society? What *was* it in the eighteen-
forties and -fifties? It is not necessary, fortunately, to answer
those questions here. To bring these notes to a close I should
like to make a few elementary distinctions. If the Southern
subject is the destruction by war and the later degradation
of the South by carpetbaggers and scalawags, and a consequent lack of moral force and imagination in the cynical
materialism of the New South, then the sociologists of fiction
and the so-called traditionalists are trying to talk about the
same thing. But with this difference—and it is a difference
between two worlds: the provincial world of the present,
which sees in material welfare and legal justice the whole
solution to the human problem; and the classical-Christian

world, based upon the regional consciousness, which held that honor, truth, imagination, human dignity, and limited acquisitiveness, could alone justify a social order however rich and efficient it may be; and could do much to redeem an order dilapidated and corrupt, like the South today, if a few people passionately hold those beliefs.

So, in the period of the Southern renascence, our writers, poets as well as novelists, may be put into the two broad groups which I have indicated. Among the traditionalists whose work I believe will last I should name Stark Young, Elizabeth Madox Roberts, Katherine Anne Porter, Robert Penn Warren, Caroline Gordon, Ellen Glasgow (especially in *The Sheltered Life*), and William Faulkner, who is the most powerful and original novelist in the United States and one of the best in the modern world. It ought to be plain that by traditionalist I do not mean a writer who either accepts or rejects the conventional picture of Southern life in the past. By the traditional as opposed to the provincial writer, I mean the writer who takes the South as he knows it today or can find out about it in the past, and who sees it as a region with some special characteristics, but otherwise offering as an imaginative subject the plight of human beings as it has been and will doubtless continue to be, here and in other parts of the world.

But if the provincial outlook, as I have glanced at it here, is to prevail, there is no reason to think that the South will remain immune to it. With the war of 1914-1918, the South re-entered the world—but gave a backward glance as it stepped over the border: that backward glance gave us the Southern renascence, a literature conscious of the past in the present. In the essay to which I referred in the first paragraph of these notes (I have now reread it) I said: "From the peculiarly historical consciousness of the Southern writer has come good work of a special order; but the focus of this consciousness is quite temporary. It has made possible the curious burst of intelligence that we get at a crossing of the ways, not unlike, on an infinitesimal scale, the outburst of poetic genius at the end of the sixteenth century when commercial England had already begun to crush feudal England." I see no reason to change that view.

From now on we are committed to seeing *with*, not *through* the eye: we, as provincials who do not live anywhere.

# WHAT IS
# A TRADITIONAL SOCIETY?[1]

## *1936*


NOT long ago, I hope with no sinister purpose, I used the word tradition before a group of Southern men who had met to discuss the problems of the South. A gentleman from North Carolina rose; he said that tradition was meaningless, and he moved that we drop the word. I have a certain sympathy with that view. Many features of our lives that we call traditions are meaningless; we confuse with tradition external qualities which are now, in the rich American middle class, mere stage properties of a way of life that can no longer be lived. For the stage-set differs from the natural scene, I take it, in offering us a conventional surface without depth, and the additional facility of allowing us to stand before it on Saturday and Sunday and to resume, on Monday, the real business of life. Tradition as we see it today has little to do with the real business of life; at best it can make that grim reality two-sevenths less grim—if indeed the pretense of our week-end traditionalists is not actually grimmer than the reality they apologetically prefer but from which they desire, part of the time, to escape.

I do not understand this romanticism, and I bring it to

[1] The Phi Beta Kappa Address at the University of Virginia, June, 1936.

your attention because, here within the walls of Mr. Jefferson's University, there is a special tradition of realism in thinking about the nature of tradition. The presiding spirit of that tradition was clear in his belief that the way of life and the livelihood of men must be the same; that the way we make our living must strongly affect the way of life; that our way of getting a living is not good enough if we are driven by it to pretend that it is something else; that we cannot pretend to be landed gentlemen two days of the week if we are middle-class capitalists the five others. You will remember Ruskin's objection to the Gothic factory-architecture of his age—the ornamentation he suggested for the cornices of a kind of building that was new in that time. Ruskin's stylized money-bags set at the right rhythmic intervals around the cornices of the Bethlehem Steel Corporation might be symbolic of something going on inside, but I think the Chairman of the Board would rightly object that Ruskin was not a good satirist, but merely a sentimentalist; and the Chairman would leave his cornices bare. Yet, while the Chairman of the Board might be committed on the one hand to an economic realism, he might on the other indulge himself in softer materials in another direction; he might buy or build a Georgian mansion somewhere near Middleburg, Virginia, and add to it—if they were not already there—the correct row of columns that Mr. Jefferson adapted to Virginia after a visit to the Maison Carré at Nîmes.

Mr. Jefferson could not know Ruskin, but he knew about medieval Europe, and he disliked it. He never visited Mr. Walpole at Strawberry Hill, but I wish he had. He would have rejoiced that Walpole's week-end Gothic—if you will allow the anachronism for the sake of the moral—meant the final destruction, in England, of the Middle Ages. He would have known that to revive something is to hasten its destruction—if it is only picturesquely and not sufficiently revived. For the moment the past becomes picturesque it is dead. I do not agree with Mr. Jefferson about the Middle Ages, but I surmise that he would have considered a revival of the past very much in this light. He himself was trying to revive the small freeholder who had been dispossessed by the rising capitalist of the eighteenth century.

Now one of the curious features of our mentality since the Renaissance is the historical imagination. No other civilization, I believe, has had this gift. I use the term not in a strict sense, but in a very general sense, and perhaps in a somewhat pejorative sense. I mean that with the revival of Greek studies men in Europe began to pose as Greeks. After a couple of centuries, when the pose, too heroic to last, grew tired, they posed as Romans of the Republic. There we have a nice historical dramatization of the common sense of the eighteenth century. We on this side of the Atlantic were not unaffected by it. There is evidence that our Revolutionary fathers were the noblest Romans of them all. There is certainly not a Virginian, nor a Southerner of Virginian ancestry, whose great-great-grandfather did not write letters to his son in the style of Addison, a vehicle nicely fitted to convey the matter of Cicero. *Libidinosa enim et intemperans adulescentia effetum corpus tradit senectuti*—it is not from the orations, but the rhythm and sentiment here were the model of the *ore orotundo* style that dominated society in the South and other parts of America for three generations. Those generations, if our records of their more elegant representatives do not lie, were not much impressed with the ravages of youthful license upon the body, which, as Cicero has just told us, passes wearily into old age. The young blade of Albemarle of 1770, sitting over a punch-bowl in the tavern after a day of Cicero with the learned Parson Douglas, was not, at that moment, an examplar of Cicero's morals, but I suspect that his conversation, even after the bottom of the bowl began to be visible, retained a few qualities of the Ciceronian style.

The style is the point of a digression that I hope you will not think frivolous. I hold no brief for Cicero—he is a dull mind in any language—but I do hold that the men of the early American Republic had a profound instinct for high style, a genius for dramatizing themselves at their own particular moment of history. They were so situated economically and politically that they were able to form a definite conception of their human rôle: they were not ants in an economic ant-hill, nor were they investigating statistically the behavior of other ants. They knew what they wanted because they knew what they, themselves, were. They lived in a social and economic system that permitted them to develop a human character that functioned in every level of life, from the economic process to the county horse-race.

The Virginian of the 1790's might have found a better part in the play than that of the Roman in *toga virilis*—as Mr. Custis, the first Southern dilettante, liked to paint him—but it was the easiest rôle to lay hold upon at that time, and it was distinctly better than no imaginative version of himself at all. A few years ago Mr. T. S. Eliot told an audience at this University that there are two kinds of mythology, a higher and a lower. The Roman *toga* of our early Republic was doubtless of a sort of lower mythology, inferior to the higher mythology of the Christian thirteenth century, and I suppose Mr. Eliot would prefer the higher vision, as I myself should were I allowed a preference. But we must remember that the rationalism of the eighteenth century had made myths of all ranks exceedingly scarce, as the romantic poets were beginning to testify; yet the Virginian did remarkably well with the minor myth that his age permitted him to cultivate. Mr. Custis's paintings may seem to us to be afflicted with a sort of aesthetic giantism, and his blank-verse dramas, in which every hero is an alabaster Washington named Marcus Tullius Scipio Americanus, are unreadable today. They must have been a kind of inexquisite torture even when they were written. But Mr. Custis built Arlington, and Arlington is something to have built. He could not have built it, of course, if Mr. Jefferson had not first built a house upon a place that I believe is locally called the Little Mountain; but then Mr. Jefferson could not have built Monticello had he not been dominated by the lower myth of the *toga virilis*.

Perhaps this lower myth, from whatever source it may
come—Rome, Greece, the age of Cellini, the naturalism of
the South Seas, or even the Old South—this little myth is
a figment of the historical imagination, that curious faculty
of Western men that I have already mentioned. The men of
our early Republic were powerfully endowed in this faculty.
It is not the same as a religion, if by religion we mean Christianity in the Middle Ages; nor is it the same as the religious
imagination under any conceivable culture, for the religious
imagination is timeless and unhistoric. The minor myth is
based upon ascertainable history.

There is a chart that we might look at for a moment, but
only for a moment; I offer it not as history, but as a device
to ease the strain of the idea of traditional society that I am
trying to give in so short a space. First, there is the religious
imagination, which can mythologize indiscriminately history,
legend, trees, the sea, animals, all being humanly dramatized,
somehow converted to the nature of man. Secondly, there is
the historical imagination, which is the religious imagination
*manqué*—an exercise of the myth-making propensity of man
within the restricted realm of historical event. Men see themselves in the stern light of the character of Cato, but they
can no longer see themselves under the control of a tutelary
deity. Cato actually lived; Apollo was merely far-darting.

The third stage is the complete triumph of positivism. And
with the complete triumph of positivism, in our own time,
we get, in place of so workable a makeshift as the historical
imagination, merely a truncation of that phrase in which the
adjective has declared its independence. It has set up for a
noun. Under positivism we get just plain, everyday history.
If this is an obscure conception, I must hasten to say that
although history cannot write itself, although it must be
written by men whose minds are as little immune to prejudice as to the law of contradiction, it is true that any sort
of creative imagination is, on principle, eliminated. Yet in
recognition of history's impotence to bring itself into being,

the historians give us a new word: method. We live in the age of the historical method. Method brings history into being.

I shall not labor the point here, but I do think it is fair to say that *history*, although it has become attached to *method*, is still a noun of agency, as the grammarians call it, trying to do its own work. I think this is true simply because on principle scientific *method* is itself not attached to anything. It is just abstract method—from which plain, abstract, inhuman history differs not by a hair. Of course, I am talking about the historian's ideal of physical law—his belief that history must conform to the ideal of a normative science, whether or not it can mean anything written that way. The historical method then may be briefly described—by one who does not believe in its use—as the way of discovering historical "truths" that are true in some other world than that inhabited by the historian and his fellow men: truths, in a word, that are true for the historical method.

Most of you have read *The Waste Land*, but I shall ask you to hear a passage from it again for the sake of those who have not read it:

> The Chair she sat in, like a burnished throne
> Glowed on the marble, where the glass
> Held up by standards wrought with fruited vines
> From which a golden Cupidon peeped out
> (Another hid his eyes behind his wing)
> Doubled the flames of seven-branched candelabra
> Reflecting light upon the table as
> The glitter of her jewels rose to meet it
> From satin cases poured in rich profusion;
> In vials of ivory and colored glass
> Unstoppered, lurked her strange synthetic perfumes.

In this handsome *décor* the lady, I imagine, is about to dress for dinner. On the walls and ceilings are scenes from an heroic past:

> Huge sea-wood fed with copper
> Burned green and orange, framed by the colored stone,
> In which sad light a carvèd dolphin swam.
> Above the antique mantel was displayed
> As though a window gave upon the sylvan scene
> The change of Philomel, by the barbarous king
> So rudely forced; yet there the nightingale
> Filled all the desert with inviolable voice. . . .

People living in such favorable influences, partaking of the best of our history and of the arts of the great tradition, command our most interested attention: they will at least exhibit the benefits of a good lower mythology. We may expect them to show us, if not the innocence of the religious imagination, a high style that expresses, or is the expression of, the walls that we have just looked at. But no; the poet warns us as follows:

> And other withered stumps of time
> Were told upon the walls; staring forms
> Leaned out, leaning, hushing the room enclosed.
> Footsteps shuffled on the stair.

I hope you will forgive me if I venture to think that the shuffling feet are about to bring into the room the historical method. For, after some desperately aimless conversation, in which both the woman and the man seem to feel little but a bored exhaustion and vacuity of purpose, the woman suddenly says:

> "What shall I do now? What shall I do?
> "I shall rush out as I am, and walk the street
> "With my hair down, so. What shall we do tomorrow?
> "What shall we ever do?"

Her companion replies—and I ask you to place what he says against the heroic background of Renaissance art on the ceiling and walls: what he says does reduce it, I think, to withered stumps of time:

The hot water at ten.
And if it rains, a closed car at four.
And we shall play a game of chess,
Pressing lidless eyes, and waiting for a knock upon
the door.

Now fortunately upon this occasion I am neither poet nor
literary critic. Here I am a moralist, and if I find more to
my use in Mr. Eliot's poem than he would willingly allow,
you will remember that moralists these days are desperate
persons, and must in their weaker moments squeeze a moral
even out of modern poetry. If the chess game seems trivial
as a symbol of aimless intellectuality, its intention is nevertheless just. The rich experience from the great tradition de-
picted in the room receives a violent shock in contrast
with a game that symbolizes the inhuman abstraction of the
modern mind. In proposing the game of chess the man is
proposing an exercise in a kind of truth that has no meaning for either of them. The woman in this remarkable scene
has just said that she can think of nothing to do—the moralist
would gloss that as lack of purpose—and she intends to rush
out into the street with her hair down.

What does this mean? It means that in ages which suffer
the decay of manners, religion, morals, codes, our inde-
structible vitality demands expression in violence and chaos;
it means that men who have lost both the higher myth of
religion and the lower myth of historical dramatization have
lost the forms of human action; it means that they are no
longer capable of defining a human objective, of forming a
dramatic conception of human nature; it means that they
capitulate from their human rôle to a series of pragmatic
conquests which, taken alone, are true only in some other
world than that inhabited by men.

The woman in Mr. Eliot's poem is, I believe, the symbol
of man at the present time. He is surrounded by the gran-
deurs of the past, but he does not participate in them;
they do not sustain him. To complete the allegory, the man

represents a kind of truth that I have described in very
general terms as the historical method: he offers us the
exercise of intellect to no purpose, a game that we cannot
relate to our conduct, an instrument of power over both past
and present which we can neither control nor properly use.

Man in this plight lives in an untraditional society. For
an untraditional society does not permit its members to pass
to the next generation what it received from its immediate
past. Why is this so? I have tried to describe in moral terms
some of the defects of life in an untraditional society—and
I expect merely to ask, and not to answer, whether there
is not some kind of analysis that we may subject our situation
to, that will show us one way of understanding the fundamental difference between tradition and non-tradition?

I shall return to a question that I asked in the beginning.
Why do many modern people live one kind of life five days a
week and another the two other days? Why is it that a middle-
class capitalist from Pittsburgh or Birmingham desires an
ante-bellum Georgian house near Lexington, Kentucky, or
Middleburg, Virginia? And why was it that the men who
built those houses desired only those houses, and made
serious objections in the eighteen-sixties to being forcibly
removed from them? There are many answers to these questions, but I have space for only one. The middle-class capitalist does not believe in the dignity of the material basis of
his life; his human nature demands a homogeneous pattern
of behavior that his economic life will not give him. He
doubtless sees in the remains of the Old South a symbol of
the homogeneous life. But the ante-bellum man saw no difference between the Georgian house and the economic
basis that supported it. It was all of one piece.

I am exaggerating, but permit me the exaggeration so that I
may make this matter as clear as I can. Man has never achieved
a perfect unity of his moral nature and his economics; yet
he has never failed quite so dismally in that greatest of all
human tasks as he is failing now. Ante-bellum man, in so
far as he achieved a unity between his moral nature and his

livelihood, was a traditional man. He dominated the means of life; he was not dominated by it. I think that the distinguishing feature of a traditional society is simply that. In order to make a livelihood men do not have to put aside their moral natures. Traditional men are never quite making their living, and they never quite cease to make it. Or put otherwise: they are making their living all the time, and affirming their humanity all the time. The whole economic basis of life is closely bound up with moral behavior, and it is possible to behave morally all the time. It is this principle that is the center of the philosophy of Jefferson.

Yet what is there traditional about this? The answer is that if such a society could come into being now, and had no past whatever, it would be traditional because it could hand something on. That something would be a moral conception of man in relation to the material of life. The material basis of life, in such a society, is not hostile to the perpetuation of a moral code, as our finance-capitalist economics unquestionably is. It is an old story by this time that our modern economic system can be operated efficiently regardless of the moral stature of the men who operate it.

The kind of property that sustains the traditional society is not only *not* hostile to a unified moral code; it is positively the basis of it. Moreover it is the medium, just as canvas is the medium of the painter, through which that code is passed to the next generation. For traditional property in land was the primary medium through which man expressed his moral nature; and our task is to restore it or to get its equivalent today. Finance-capitalism, a system that has removed men from the responsible control of the means of a livelihood, is necessarily hostile to the development of a moral nature. Morality is responsibility to a given set of conditions. The further the modern system develops in the direction that it has taken for two generations, the more anti-traditional our society will become, and the more difficult it will be to pass on the fragments of the traditions that we inherit.

The higher myth of religion, the lower myth of history,

even ordinary codes of conduct, cannot preserve themselves; indeed they do not exist apart from our experience. Since the most significant feature of our experience is the way we make our living, the economic basis of life is the soil out of which all the forms, good or bad, of our experience must come.

# RELIGION AND THE OLD SOUTH

## 1930

AT a time not inconceivably long ago the ordinary layman, or even the extraordinary one who took up the mysteries as a gentlemanly pursuit, had an impressive respect for the professional man of religion, who for some reason not clear to us had authority to speak of the Higher Things. We have none of that respect now. The present writer, who is a layman of the more ordinary kind, is deficient in it. There are priests here and there, a Protestant clergyman or two, who as individuals seem to speak from the tripod. But they scarcely represent their class; they are only laymen of the more extraordinary kind. So I begin an essay on religion with almost no humility at all; that is to say, I begin it in a spirit of irreligion. One must think for oneself—a responsibility intolerable to the religious mind, whose proper business is to prepare the mysteries for others.

Religion is not properly a discussion of anything. A discussion of religion is an act of violence, a betrayal of the religious essence undertaken for its own good, or for the good of those who live by it. This is the sole justification of an amateur treatment of religion; my betrayal of religion betrays only my own, and instead of a public scandal it is an instance of personal indecorum that can injure no one but myself.

But there is also a certain pretension in this incivility. It is to the effect that my private fable was once more public, and that men have fallen away from it into evil days. I must therefore proceed at once to dress my fable in First Principles—which are indeed the only dress it will receive in this essay. I can hardly make a fiction convincing by leaving it in the simple condition that it enjoys in my own mind—that is, the condition of fairy story and myth. For a myth should be in conviction immediate, direct, overwhelming, and I take it that the appreciation of this kind of imagery is an art lost to the modern mind.

The reader must be entreated to follow a few pages of abstraction about religion that partakes of religion not at all. For abstraction is the death of religion no less than the death of everything else.

Religion, when it directs its attention to the horse cropping the blue-grass on the lawn, is concerned with the whole horse, and not with that part of him which he has in common with other horses, or that more general part which he shares with other quadrupeds or with the more general vertebrates; and not with the abstract horse in his capacity of horse-power in general, power that he shares with other machines of making objects move. Religion admits the existence of this horse, but says that he is only half of the horse. Religion undertakes to place before us the whole horse as he is in himself:

Since this essay is not religion, but a discussion of it, it does not pretend to put before you the complete horse. It does hope to do the following: to show that the complete horse may be there in spite of the impotence of this discussion to produce him. In other words, there is a complete and self-contained horse despite the now prevailing faith that there is none simply because the abstract and scientific mind cannot see him.

This modern mind sees only half of the horse—that half which may become a dynamo, or an automobile, or any other horsepowered machine. If this mind had had much respect for the full-bodied, grass-eating horse, it would never have invented the engine which represents only half of him. The religious mind, on the other hand, has this respect; it wants the whole horse; and it will be satisfied with nothing less.

It wants the whole horse if it is a religious mind that requires more than a half-religion. A religion of the half-horse is pre-eminently a religion concerning how things work, and this is a modern religion. By leaving half of the horse out of account, it can easily show that abstract horsepower, ideally, everywhere, infallibly, under other abstract and *half* conditions, works. Now the half of the animal that this religion leaves out won't work at all; it isn't workable; it is a vast body of concrete qualities constantly conflicting with the workable half; today the horse saddled admirably, but yesterday he ran away—he would not work.

From this it is clear that there is another possible half-religion. It is very common at present. It asserts that nothing works—a poor if desperate refutation of the other half-religion. It says that no horse is workable; the horse is just a locus of unpredictable and immeasurable qualities, and the more you contemplate him the more you see how futile it is to pretend that there is anything regular about him. He is unique beyond cure, and you can't predict the performance of Man-o'-War tomorrow from the performance of Man-o'-War yesterday. This is as bad as saying that you can predict everything. It is another half-religion: it is the religion of the symbolist poets and of M. Henri Bergson.

But how do we know that the religion of the completely workable is a religion? It has no altars—that is, no altars that befit it entirely, for it has only usurped the altars traditionally surviving; it has no formal ritual, and no priesthood wearing anything like a cassock or telling anything like beads. We know that the cult of infallible working is a kind of religion because it sets up an irrational value: the value is irrational (a false absolute) because the whole nature of man is not to be subsumed under a concept of logical necessity; the value would still be irrational even if "reason," or science, could reach absolute natural truth. T. E. Hulme would have said that it is contrary to the full content of our experience to assume that man is continuous with nature. It is, then, irrational to believe in omnipotent human rationality. Nothing, in short, infallibly works. The new half-religionists are simply worshiping a principle, and with true half-religious fanaticism they ignore what they do not want to see—which is the breakdown of the principle in numerous instances of practice. It is a bad religion, for that very reason; it can predict only success.

The religion, then, of the whole horse predicts both success and failure. It says that the horse will work within limits, but that it is folly to tempt the horse-providence too far. It takes account of the failures—that is, it is realistic, for it calls to witness the traditional experience of evil which is the common lot of the race. It is a mature religion, and it is not likely to suffer disillusion and collapse. Here it is very unlike the half-religion of work which has a short memory of failure; the half-religion can ignore its failures to a certain saturation point, beyond which they will be overwhelming, and the society living under it is riding for a crushing fall. It will be totally unprepared for collapse; it will have gone too far. It will have forgotten the symbol of itself in the career of the vaunting Oedipus, who, blind at last, cautioned us not to pronounce a man happy till we saw the end of his life. The half-religion of work has accomplished the murder of Laius and married Jocasta; it has applied its pragmatism of values with astonishing success *up to now;* but the end is yet to come. Tiresias is yet to come.

It is apparent that the image of the horse will "work" only in a limited number of illustrations; so I propose to try another image.

## I I

TAKE the far more complex image of history, if it may be called an image at all. For as an image its content is mixed and incoherent, and reduces to a vast clutter of particular images. We are able each of us to take our choice; we may reconstruct this scene or that period. We have those people who prefer the Renaissance, and those who like better the Periclean age, or perhaps they concentrate their loyalty to a special kind of life in a particular document of an age or a people: there are Platonists and Aristotelians, Stoics, and Hedonists, and there are the Christians, or at least there were the Christians who stood by the two Testaments, both of which we are now convinced are of ancient and obscure origin and of muddled contents.

These sad, more concrete minds may be said to look at their history in a definite and now quite unfashionable way. They look at it as a concrete series that has taken place in a very real time—by which I mean, without too much definition, a time as sensible, as full of sensation, and as replete with accident and uncertainty as the time they themselves are living in, moment by moment.

But if you do not take history as an image or many images, you have got to take it as idea, abstraction, concept. You need not feel any great interest in the rival merits of the Greek and Roman cultures; they were both "ideas" comprehensible after some study under a single concept which their chief business is now to illustrate. Consider Hegel: it is thesis-antithesis-synthesis—a process that includes not only Greece, Iraq, and Rome, but (as the author warns us about his rights of translation) the Scandinavian as well. It is not that the scientific historian refuses to see that Pericles dressed, ate, and loved differently from Cincinnatus; it is rather that the particular instance fades away into a realm of phenomena related as cause and effect. The historical ideal is the physicist's concept of natural law. There is then ideally no accident or contingency; for accident and contingency are names for our insufficient information. The illusion of contingency that harassed the past (when it was still the present) is dissolved by the Long View—which means that the ancient versions of nature and society were so limited that the ancients were not able to see their pluralism in the true light of all-embracing principle. For this Long View history becomes an abstract series, opposed to the concrete series of the Short View.

There are several questions here that need to be asked of the Long View: Is it not the religion of the half-horse? Does the law of cause and effect which joins up the Greek and Roman cultures make them identical in any other respect than law? Is it, in short, the Greek and Roman cultures themselves? Is it these cultures in any other sense than that the merely working horse is the actual horse?

I have said that this view makes the past an abstract series; let it be called a logical series, and there is nothing to do but to resort to the customary A, B, C of the textbooks. These letters may follow one another at all places at all times, without sensation, accident, or contingency. But did Greek culture live and have its being without sensation? The Short View maintains that it did not, for the Short View holds that the proper series for history to be placed in is the temporal or concrete series.

At this point I must do some violence to the reaches of the argument, and say briefly: for the Short View, history is the specific account of the doings of specific men who acted their parts in a rich and contemporaneous setting which bewildered them. In their bewilderment they invented, or preserved even older, simple stories with a moral. In the times of natural bewilderment—when contingency was called religious awe—men like Hesiod and Cynewulf pondered what they did not understand and gave us simple stories and charms with a moral that we find obvious. But, for the moment, I must leave the moral in a very general state, and close this part of the argument with another difference between the Long and the Short View.

It is apparent that a solvent which reduces the Greek and the Roman cultures to identity of natural law gives to us the privilege of choosing between them; for assuming even that we are the offshoot of one of them, there is yet no reason why we cannot take up the other. The Long View becomes, in brief, the cosmopolitan destroyer of tradition. Or, put otherwise, since the Christian myth is a vegetation rite, varying only in some details from countless other vegetation myths, there is no reason to prefer Christ to Adonis. Varying only in some details: this assumes that there is nothing but a quantitative difference between a horse and a dog, both being vertebrates, mammals, quadrupeds. But the Short View holds that the whole Christ and the whole Adonis are sufficiently differentiated in their respective qualities (details), and that our tradition compels us to choose more than that half of Christ which is Adonis and to take the whole, separate, and unique Christ.

There is a nice and somewhat slippery paradox here: Why should our tradition compel us to choose anything? Particularly in view of the all but accomplished fact that tradition is destroyed? If the agency is shut up, the business cannot be transacted. And we have to confess that merely living in a certain stream of civilized influence does not compel us to be loyal to it. Indeed, the act of loyalty, even the fact of loyalty, must be spontaneous to count at all. Tradition must, in other words, be automatically operative before it can be called tradition. For in its true function it is powerfully selective, and the moment it admits that Adonis is able to compete with Christ, though it regret the rivalry, it has gone over to the Long View; its faith has weakened; and we are on the verge of committing ourselves to the half religions that are no religions at all, but quite simply decisions passed on the utility, the workableness, of the religious objects with respect to the practical aims of society. The utility of the religious object is not impressive.

So this is the paradox: Is it tradition or the Long View itself which prompts the present defense of the religious attitude? It is probably a little of both; though this conception is wholly irrational. It is irrational to defend religion with the weapon that invariably discredits it, and yet this is what seems to be happening. I am trying to discover the place that religion holds, with abstract instruments, which of course tend to put religion into some logical system or series, where it vanishes.

### III

BUT this is due to our nature, which is a very different nature from that of the Russian or eastern European mind, whose religion is quite simply supernaturalism or the naïve religion of the entire horse. It never suspects the existence of those halves that render our sanity so precarious and compel us to vacillate between a self-destroying naturalism and practicality, on the one hand, and a self-destroying mysticism, on the other. For it seems that we are not able to contemplate those qualities of the horse that are specifically religious without forgetting his merely spatial and practicable half: we cannot let the entire horse fill our minds all at once. And thus we have a special notion of tradition—a notion that tradition is not simply a fact, but a fact that must be constantly defended.

This defense is dogma. The strictly qualitative half of the horse, his special uniqueness as a sensible fact, in a word, his image, must be defended against pure practicality, or his abstraction. His defense with us is abstraction itself. For the only defense we know is rational and scientific, and it is thus evident that dogma is not a personal property of religion, but is a mere instrument. And it is an act of sheer generosity when this instrument sets about the defense of its natural enemy, the qualitative view of experience. But, in the Middle Ages, it was so enamored of this enemy that it could not be brought to destroy him, even if dogma as rationality is a half-religion and is on the way to becoming science or practicality.

It was both a great discovery and a great calamity when the Europeans found that reason could be used in another

way than the defense of something alien to it. It must always
seem to us a scandal that Scholasticism should have tried to
make rational all those unique qualities of the horse which
are spirits and myths and symbols. The men of the Renaissance effectively hushed the scandal up; they said: *Entia
non sunt multiplicanda praeter necessitatem.* This razor of
William of Occam's at first went only after the superfluous
entities of scholastic science. Don't, it says in effect, explain
reason in terms of faculties when sub-laryngeal agitation ac-
counts adequately for the phenomena of thought. But it was
only a step up from natural phenomena to supernatural
noumena, once the razor had become a standard feature of
the *Zeitgeist* of the Renaissance. Throw over the spirits and
symbols, which are mystical anyhow, not empirically necessary, and find those quantities in nature that will explain,
not *what* nature is, but *how* nature works, the quantities that
are barely necessary to the working.

This was always the peril of the European mind and
the medieval Church knew it. By making reason, science, or
nature, an instrument of defense for the protection of the
other than reasonable, the other than scientific, the other
than natural, it performed a tremendous feat of spiritual
unity. It was the only kind of unity that the Western mind
is capable of. Its special feature is the implied belief, which
of course became often explicit—I simply mean that the
belief, beginning unconsciously in experience, became later
necessary as a reasoned part of the system—its special feature
is an ineradicable belief in the fundamental evil of nature.
Western Reason has always played the ostrich by sticking
its head in the Supernatural. Woe betide when it took its
head out and got so used to the natural setting that it found
it good. And this is what happened. For the Church had
known that the only way to restrain the practical impulses
of her constituency was to put into the mouth of nature the
words *Noli me tangere.* The Eastern Church never had to do
this, nor did it ever have to construct a plausible rationality round the supernatural to make it acceptable; it has

never had a philosophy, nor a dogma in our sense; it never needed one.

The Western Church established a system of quantity for the protection of quality, but there was always the danger that quantity would revolt from servitude and suppress its master; the danger that it would apply its genius to a field more favorable to spectacular success. Once reason ceased to be the instrument through which the purely qualitative features of nature could be contemplated and enjoyed, without being corrupted by too much use, it began to see the natural setting as so many instances of quantity; that is, nature began to see the practical possibilities of knowing herself. For reason and nature are one, and that is the meaning of naturalism. The symbol and the myth meant that the external world was largely an inviolable whole; once the symbol and the myth were proved to be not natural facts, but unnatural fictions that fitted into no logical series tolerable to the rational mind, nature became simply a workable half. The votaries of this nature now think that it is a Whole of limitless practicability.

## I V

THIS being true, how can tradition, which is always embarrassing to practicality on a large scale, be defended? Has it not disappeared? And was it not always on the brink of compromise in the fact that it needed the support of its enemy? The answer doubtless is: It can always be defended, but a recovery and restoration is a more difficult performance.

Moreover, where can an American take hold of tradition? His country is supposed to have preserved none from Europe, and if we take the prototype of the European tradition to be medieval society, we must confess that America has performed wonders, considering her youth, in breaking it down.

Yet the very idea "America" must give us pause, for it is almost anything that a determined apologist may wish to make it. In a brief three hundred years she has recapitulated practically every form of European polity, if these separate polities may be seen as devoid of their religious background. She has repeated all the chief economic and political forms. But she has not repeated the religious forms. The religious history of America is perfectly continuous with that of Europe.

This anomaly gave us that remarkable society of the old South, which was a feudal society, without a feudal religion; hence only a semi-feudal society. The reason for this is by no means obscure. It is just possible to see the Jamestown project as the symbol of what later happened to America: it was a capitalistic enterprise undertaken by Europeans who were already convinced adherents of large-scale exploitation of nature, not to support a stable religious order, but to advance the interests of *trade as an end in itself*. They stood thus for a certain stage in the disintegration of the European religion, and their descendants stuck to their guns, which theoretically at least were Protestant, aggressive, and materialistic guns.

At the same time certain conditions of economy supported a society which was, again theoretically, Protestant, but which was not aggressive and materialistic. It was a throwback, a case of atavism. A distinguished Southern writer has argued that the Southern population was originally less rebellious against European stability than was the Northern. It is doubtful if history will support this, though I should personally like to do so, for the belief implies the mythmaking tendency of the mind in one of its most valuable forms. The enemy, abstraction, or the view of history as the logical series, gives us, alas, another story. It is that soil and climate made the agrarian life generally more attractive than a barrener soil and a colder climate could have ever done, and that the propitious soil and climate made it possible for a semi-feudal system of labor to take root and thrive. A people may, in short, return to an older economy, under certain local conditions; but international conditions, certainly since the sixteenth century, have made it impossible for any community of European origin to remain spiritually isolated and to develop its genius, unless that genius is in harmony with the religious and economic drift of the civilization at large.

The South could temporarily return to an older secular polity, but the world was too much with it, and it could not create its appropriate religion.

There were two results of this anomalous position that may be stated without too much historical argument. The South, as a political atmosphere charged with eighteenth-century ideas, did not realize her genius in time. She consistently defended herself with the political terms of eighteenth-century liberalism, a doctrine better suited to the middle-class economics of the North, into whose hands she neatly played. So, waiting too long, she let her more powerful rival gain the ascendancy. The South did not achieve that inward conviction of destiny that empowers societies no less than individuals to understand their position and to act from inner necessity: we do nothing without symbols and we cannot do the right thing with the wrong symbol. There was no unity of purpose between the Southern Protestant religion and the Southern Protestant semi-feudalism. The South's religious mind was inarticulate, dissenting, and schismatical. She had a non-agrarian and trading religion that had been invented in the sixteenth century by a young finance-capitalist economy: hardly a religion at all but rather a disguised secular ambition. The Southern politicians quoted scripture to defend slavery, yet they defended their society as a whole with the catchwords of eighteenth-century politics. And this is why the South separated from the North too late, and so lost her cause.

The second result of the anomalous structure of the Southern mind is a near and contemporary one. Because the South never created a fitting religion, the social structure of the South began grievously to break down two generations after the Civil War. For the social structure depends on the economic structure, and economic conviction is still, in spite of the beliefs of economists from Adam Smith to Marx, the secular image of religion. No nation is ever simply and unequivocally beaten in war; nor was the South. Is it possible that the South shows signs of defeat? If she does, it is due to her lack of a religion which would make her special way of life the inevitable and permanently valuable one. We have been inferior to the Irish in this virtue, though much less than the Irish have we ever been beaten in war.

It appears that the question put at the beginning of this section, How can the American, or the Southern man, take hold of tradition? is further from being answered than ever.

## V

LET us return to the two ways of looking at horses and history. Which are we permitted to say was the way of the Old South? The answer to this question is not necessarily disconcerting, even if we must admit both ways. And it is bound to be both because the South was a Western community, and a Western community is one that does not live in sackcloth and ashes and erect all its temples to the gods. The Southerners were capable of using their horses, as they did one day at Brandy Station, but they could also contemplate them as absolute and inviolable objects; they were virtually incapable of abstracting from the horse his horsepower, or from history its historicity. For the horse fact and the historical fact, by remaining concrete, retained a certain status as *images*, and images are only to be contemplated, and perhaps the act of contemplation after long exercise initiates a habit of restraint, and the setting up of absolute standards which are less formulas for action than an interior discipline of the mind. There is doubtless from the viewpoint of abstract history not much difference between a centaur, since we speak of horses, and a Christ, since we speak of historicity. Both are mythical figments reducible in one set of properties to the abstraction man-ness. But the Short View, as we have seen, is incorrigibly selective, and has been known to prefer Christ to the man horse.

After about 1820, in America, the Southern communities alone stood for that preference with anything like a single mind. The heresy of New England is beautifully recorded in the correspondence of John Adams and Thomas Jefferson, where the two sages discuss the possibility of morals. Jefferson calls his judgment "taste"—reliance on custom, breeding, ingrained moral decision. But Adams needs a "process of moral reasoning," which forces the individual to think out from abstract principle his rôle at a critical moment of action. The view of John Adams tells us how far New England had gone from Europe, how deeply she had broken with the past.

While the South in the nineteenth century trafficked with Europe in cotton, she took in exchange very little of manners, literature, or the arts. The Southerners were another community on the complete European plan, and they had no need, being independent, of importing foreign art and noblemen, commodities that New England became frantic about after 1830. For New England was one of those abstract-minded, sharp-witted, trading societies that must be parasites in two ways: they must live economically on some agrarian class or country, and they must live spiritually likewise. New England lived economically on the South, culturally on England. And this was doubtless a disguised and involved nostalgia for the land—the New England "land" being old England. The houses and the universities of New England became a European museum, stuffed with the dead symbols of what the New Englander could not create because provision for it had been left out of his original foundation.

In the nineteenth century New England confessed her loss of the past by being too much interested in Europe. If you take the Adams family at its best, you find a token of the whole New England mind: there is the tragedy of the *Education of Henry Adams,* who never quite understood what he was looking for. He spent much of his youth, like Henry James, learning the amenities of the English agrarians, without being by right of soil entitled to them, and never suspecting that the best he might hope to do was to learn them by rote. More significantly he passed his last days in Washington despising the "ignorant" and "simple" minds south of the Potomac, again never suspecting that his efforts in behalf of defeating this simplicity and ignorance in a recent war did something towards undermining the base of the civilized values that he coveted most.

If New England's break with Europe made her excessively interested in the European surface, the ignorance and the simplicity of the South's independence of Europe, in the cultural sense, witness a fact of great significance. The South could be ignorant of Europe because she *was* Europe; that is to say, the South was trying to take root in a native soil. And the South could remain simple-minded because she had no use for the intellectual agility required to define its position. Her position, alas, seemed to be self-sufficient and self-evident; it was European where the New England position was self-conscious and colonial. The Southern mind was simple, not top-heavy with learning it had no need of, un-intellectual, and composed; it was personal and dramatic, rather than abstract and metaphysical; and it was sensuous because it lived close to a natural scene of great variety and interest.

Because she lived by images not highly organized, it is true, as dogma, but rather more loosely gathered from the past, the South was a traditional European community. The Southerners were incurable in their preference for Cato over the social conditions in which he historically lived. They looked at history as the concrete and temporal series —a series at all only because they required a straight meta-phorical line back into the past, for the series, such as it was, was very capricious, and could hardly boast of a natural logic. They could add to the classics a lively medievalism from the novels of Sir Walter Scott. They saw themselves as human beings living by a human principle, from which they were unwilling to subtract the human so as to set the prin-ciple free to operate on an unlimited program of inhuman practicality. For that is what a principle is—the way things will work. But the Southerner, or more generally the die-hard agrarian, was not willing to let the principle proceed alone, uncontrolled; for what he valued most in the working of principle was the capacity that he retained of enjoying the fruits of the work. The old Southerners were highly critical of the kinds of work to be done. They planted no corn, they grew no cotton that did not directly contribute to the upkeep of a rich private life; and they knew little history for the sake of knowing it, but simply for the sake of contemplating it and seeing in it an image of themselves. It is probable that they liked Plutarch better than Suetonius, and both better than Thucydides. Like all unscientific societies they cared little for natural knowledge, and cared more for that unnaturalism which is morals. They liked very simple stories with a moral in which again they could see an image of themselves.

We have already considered some of the possible reasons why they broke down.

## V I

THEY had a religious life, but it was not enough organized with a right mythology. In fact, their rational life was not powerfully united to the religious experience, as it was in medieval society, and they are a fine specimen of the tragic pitfall upon which the Western mind has always hovered. Not having a rational system for the defense of their religious attitude and its base in a feudal society, they elaborated no rational system whatever, no full-grown philosophy; so that, when the post-bellum temptations of the devil, who, according to Milton and Aeschylus, is the exploiter of nature, confronted them, they had no defense. Since there is, in the Western mind, a radical division between the religious, the contemplative, the qualitative, on the one hand, and the scientific, the natural, the practical, on the other, the scientific mind always plays havoc with the spiritual life when it is not powerfully enlisted in its cause; it cannot be permitted to operate alone.

It operated separately (yet along with other ideas that ignored it and one another) in Thomas Jefferson, and the form that it took in his mind may be reduced to a formula: *The ends of man are sufficiently contained in his political destiny.* Now the political destiny of men is the way they work, toward ends they hope to achieve in community by the operation of secular laws. It is not necessary to labor the point, or to draw out the enormous varieties that such a theory may exhibit. It is sufficient to point out that the ante-bellum Southerners never profoundly believed it. It is highly illuminating to reflect that, as I have said, *they acted as if they did.* There was, of course, a good deal of dissent: the Virginia Constitutional Convention repudiated Jefferson in 1832. It was a first step; but the last step was so far off that it could not possibly have preceded 1861.

The modern Southerner inherits the Jeffersonian formula. This is only to say that he inherits a concrete and very unsatisfactory history. He can almost wish for his ease the Northern contempt for his kind of history; he would like to believe that history is not a vast body of concrete fact to which he must be loyal, but only a source of mechanical formulas; for then he might hope to do what the Northern industrialist has just about succeeded in doing—making a society out of abstractions. The Southerner would conjure up some magic abstraction to spirit back to him his very concrete way of life. He would, in short, in his plight, apply the formula, because he has no other, of his inheritance—that the ends of man may be fully achieved by political means.

The South would not have been defeated had she possessed a sufficient faith in her own kind of God. She would not have been defeated, in other words, had she been able to bring out a body of doctrine setting forth her true conviction that the ends of man require more for their realization than politics. The setback of the war was of itself a very trivial one.

We are very near an answer to our question—How may the Southerner take hold of his tradition? The answer is: by violence. For this answer, if we want an answer, is inevitable. He cannot fall back upon his religion, simply because it was never articulated and organized for him. If he could do this, he would constitute himself a "borer from within," and might hope to effect gradually a secular revolution in his favor. As we have said, economy is the secular image of religious conviction. His religious conviction is inchoate and unorganized; it never had the opportunity to be anything else.

Since he cannot bore from within, he has left the sole alternative of boring from without. This method is political, active, and, in the nature of the case, violent and revolutionary. Reaction is the most radical of programs; it aims at cutting away the overgrowth and getting back to the roots. A forward-looking radicalism is a contradiction; it aims at rearranging the foliage.

The Southerner is faced with this paradox: He must use an instrument, which is political, and so unrealistic and pretentious that he cannot believe in it, to re-establish a private, self-contained, and essentially spiritual life. I say that he must do this; but that remains to be seen.

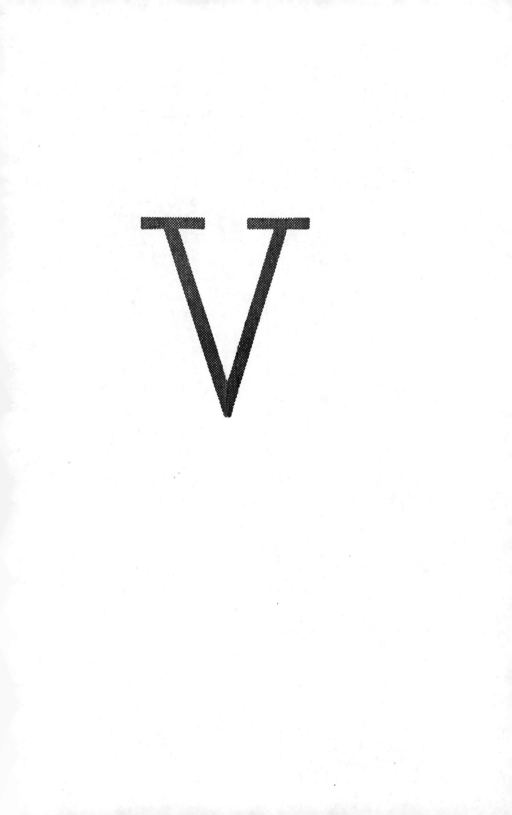

# A NOTE ON DONNE

## 1932

DONNE'S modern reputation has risen so suddenly that writers born since 1900 may look back to the time when he was a name in *The Oxford Book of English Verse* at the head of seven poems, two of which we now know that he did not write. *A Garland for John Donne*,[1] the collection of essays edited by Mr. Theodore Spencer for the tercentenary of the poet's death, attempts to revalue the poetry and to enquire into the causes of its present influence. The uncertainty of these critics about Donne's place is remarkable in the case of a poet three hundred years dead. The uncertainty comes of Donne's being still alive. He "ranks" possibly a little above Marvel, but Marvel's interest for us is not nearly so great. The reasons for his influence are at once more difficult to discover and more fruitful to pursue than his rank. The essayists in this volume are united in the belief that many of Donne's problems are our own.

Johnson blamed the vices of metaphysical style upon "a voluntary deviation from nature in pursuit of something new and strange." The eighteenth century on the whole regarded Donne as a prodigy of perverse learning. Although Donne's

[1] *A Garland for John Donne, 1631-1931*, edited by Theodore Spencer. Harvard University Press, 1932.

style, the bold images and learned conceits, had a distinct effect upon Cowley and Carew, and even Richard Crashaw; although the conversational tone influenced Dryden, it has remained for our own age to relate him to the main stream of English verse. It has been our task to understand the seriousness of the impulse and the integrity, which once seemed the perversity, of style; our task to see the whole intellectual structure of the poetry, along with the rough versification, in the light of the underlying problems of the age of Donne. For the first time he is being felt as a contemporary.

The eight essays are admirably distributed over the two kinds of problem that a great poet of the past inevitably creates—the historical and the critical problem. There are five historical essays. Mr. Spencer has written, in *Donne and His Age*, a study of the intellectual climate in which Donne lived: although he suggests more problems than he can solve in so brief a space, his discussion of the revolutionary effect of the sixteenth-century "picture of the physical world" on moral ideas is a valuable contribution to Elizabethan criticism. Mr. John Sparrow's *The Date of Donne's Travels* reviews difficult and perhaps insoluble problems of the poet's biography; incidentally Mr. Sparrow throws some light on the origin of Donne's geographical allusions—whether they were bookish or drawn from observation. *A Note on Donne the Preacher*, by Mr. John Hayward, presents a side of Donne that would have only a minor historical value had he never written his verse. Mrs. Evelyn M. Simpson's analysis of the *Paradoxes and Problems* brings out the early influence of Martial, an influence that Mr. Spencer finds general in the 1590's and not peculiar to Donne; Mrs. Simpson's paper is chiefly valuable for its emphasis on his early "interest in science."

But here, just as Mr. Eliot warns us that Donne's skepticism, being mainly an uncertainty about the right terms of faith, was not like ours, Mrs. Simpson might well have distinguished between science as we know it and Donne's "interest" in the new cosmologists, Copernicus and Kepler. This

was rather an anxiety about the physical limits of consciousness and the bearing of that question on the scholastic conception of body and soul, which Donne presents in the
terminology of St. Thomas. Donne knew nothing of a scientific age, or of the later, open conflict between the two world-
views, science and religion. Far from having a scientific
attitude towards the problem of body and soul, he grapples
with it, not to get any truth out of it apart from his own
personality, but to use it as the dramatic framework for
his individual emotion.

This is the center of Donne. Mr. Mario Praz, in *Donne's
Relation to the Poetry of His Time*, says: "Donne's technique stands in the same relation to the average technique
of Renaissance poetry as that of baroque to that of Renaissance painting. His sole preoccupation is with the whole
effect." And, involved in the whole effect, is the quality of
experience known to modern criticism as "emotional tone,"
an implicit form that is functional to the precise rendition of
the individual experience. "He was," writes Mr. Praz, "like
a lawyer choosing the fittest arguments for the case in hand;
not a searcher after a universally valid truth": the fittest
images and tropes by which to set forth, not a truth, but a
complete emotion. The terms are not the terms of objective
truth, to which the individual experience is trimmed down,
and all the implications rejected that the terms do not contain. They are rather occasional indications of an experience
that is no longer implicit in them, to be used only when they
serve the purpose. The scholastic terms in "The Extasie" are
quite as illustrative, and no more "philosophical," than the
merely denoted violet:

> But as all severall soules containe
>     Mixture of things, they know not what,
> Love, these mixt soules, doth mixe againe,
>     And makes both one, each this and that.
> A single violet transplant,
>     The strength, the colour, and the size . . .

Scholastic love occupies indifferent ground, with respect to truth, quite like that of the neutral conceit of the compasses in "A Valediction forbidding mourning":

> If they be two, they are two so
> As stiffe twin compasses are two,
> Thy soule the fixt foot, makes no show
> To move, but doth, if the other doe.

The conceits in both passages are "neutral" because they may be either true or false with respect to the inherent demands of the perceptions to be set forth in the poem.

This is the modernism of Donne: it is the modernism that re-establishes our own roots in the age of Donne. Mr. Praz's essay is the link between the two problems of Donne—his place in his own time and his value for us. Here Mr. T. S. Eliot, prophesying the speedy decline of Donne's new reputation, leaves its future ominously obscure. Mr. Eliot's belief that Donne's prose—the sermons, *Biathanatos*, the *Paradoxes and Problems*—is ready for oblivion, and quickly, is not to be questioned; the sermons have been mildly popular, among people who wish to be in the Donne fashion without taking the trouble to read the verse. But that the *Songs and Sonets*, the *Elegies*, most of the *Satires* and the *Divine Poems*, will not continue to be read for an indefinite time is an opinion harder to maintain.

"His learning," says Mr. Eliot, "is just information suffused with emotion . . . rather a humorous shuffling of the pieces; and we are inclined to read our own more conscious awareness of the apparent unrelatedness of things into the mind of Donne."

How much longer this "unrelatedness of things" will continue to be the background of poetry; whether it is not by now an emotional convention out of which minor poetic heresies, like Imagism or the more recent Objectivism,[2] will at intervals appear; whether the local excitement of sensation will indefinitely obscure the formal qualities of the

[2] Or the still more recent and more pretentious novelty, Existentialism.

Spenserian-Miltonic kind of verse—these are questions that Mr. Spencer's memorial volume asks, but wisely does not answer. The answers, perhaps, would contain the immediate future of poetry.

## I I

WHY we are concerned with the future of any art is a mystery that Donne and his contemporaries could not have understood. But the difference between Donne and our age is not, in this respect, a radical one, and there was a definite place in Mr. Spencer's book for an essay on the rise of the historical consciousness.

The position of Mr. George Williamson, in his excellent paper, *Donne and Today*, falls into two parts that tend to undermine each other. On the one hand, he suggests abstract analogies between Donne and some living poets, which would be interesting if true, but on the other hand, his quotations from Eliot, Read, Ransom, and the late Elinor Wylie offer as little evidence of the influence of Donne, as Mr. Williamson understands it, as one might derive from Tennyson. Mrs. Ramsay, in *Donne's Relation to Philosophy*, quotes stanzas from Donne and "In Memoriam" in order to distinguish two uses of "philosophy" in verse. But the lines of Tennyson come within Mr. Williamson's formula for Donne: "One may say that Donne's emotion is commonly given 'conceptual' form, but not that he is a philosophical poet."

Mr. Eliot remarks that Donne first made it possible to *think* in English lyrical verse; but it does not follow that his thinking in verse was our kind of thought. We are actually nearer to Tennyson. What thinking there is in modern verse has the general character of historical thinking—"And all the wars have dwindled since Troy fell." Tennyson confidently culled the scraps from the tables of "culture"; but our dietetics is more self-conscious. We use the past and we think about its meaning. Our framework of idea is the cultural cycle, or the awareness of the "pastness" of the past, as in the case of

Mr. Archibald MacLeish. The vulgarity of the present and the purity of the past make the framework of Mr. John Crowe Ransom's irony. Even Mr. Jeffers performs a fusion of literary psychology with a fictitious primitivism that places him in the historical consciousness. Although Mr. Ezra Pound's method is a cunning imitation of the pre-historical view that seized past and present naïvely as a whole, the *Cantos* is a monument to the historical mentality. There is none of this explicitly in Donne.

There is, so far as I know, only the slightest evidence, in seventeenth-century poetry, of a sense of historical rise-and-fall affecting the moral temper of individuals. Milton's Latin poem, *Naturam non pati senium,* argues that nature does not inwardly decay. Civilization apart from nature is not mentioned; and the poem ends with an allusion to the Christian myth: *Ingentique rogo flagrabit machina mundi.* The decay of nature was a frequent subject of controversy in the universities, and Milton must have felt its latent hostility to his own settled belief in the relation between a fixed human nature and a perfect divine order.

It is this perfect divine order that makes Milton's mythology possible. It is the threat to such an order from the direction of the "new philosophy" which "calls all in doubt," the new cosmology, that compelled Donne to ignore the popular pastoral convention of his time; nor could he rest secure upon the more comprehensive classical or Christian mythology. These imaginative structures (to describe them in the lowest terms) were by habit or in essence involved in the medieval system. Mr. Williamson remarks: "Although mythology is banished from his verse, medieval philosophy and Renaissance science take its place, in fact become his mythology." The distinction between abstract ideas and mythology is extremely important in the study of Donne, and I believe Mr. Williamson misses a capital point. Dante could afford to be philosophical; the terms were a system that he acknowledged as truth. But it is different with Donne; the vocabulary is merely vocabulary, and it lacks the ultimate, symbolic character of a myth. It is only a step from his lawyer-like use of ingenious terms to the intricacy of personal sensation as the center of consciousness. And from this it is but one more step, for the philosophical egoist, to the dramatization of oneself against the background of society or history. It is a step that Donne could not take, but doubtless would take were he alive today.

There was the mythological, pastoral school, begun by Wyat and Surrey, and Nicholas Grimald, improved by Sidney and Spenser, and perfected by Milton at a single stroke. There was the dramatic, introspective school which, whether in the lyric or on the stage, centered after Chapman in the individual sensibility. In the non-dramatic poets of this school, of whom Donne is the great figure before Dryden, the poet himself becomes the dramatic character: Mr. Spencer finds an analogy between Donne and Hamlet's philosophical egoism of inaction: the poet's ideas, now the framework of intense excitement, are pitted against one another like characters in a play.

Therein lies the nature of the "conceit." It is an idea not inherent in the subject, but exactly parallel to it, elaborated beyond the usual stretch of metaphor into a supporting structure for a long passage or even an entire poem. It may be torn away from its original meaning, like the Angels in Donne's "Elegie XI," and yet remain the vehicle of "poetic truth"; that is to say, of heightened emotion in the poet's dramatization of his own personality. The conceit in itself is neither true nor false. From this practice it is but a step to Dryden and the eighteenth century, to the rise of the historical consciousness, and to ourselves. It is the peculiar fascination of Donne that he presents the problem of personal poetry in its simplest terms. There is the simple awareness, complicated at the surface by his immense intellectual resources, of frustration and bewilderment—to which, for us, is added the frustration of historical relativity. Milton stood

ON THE LIMITS OF POETRY

for the historical absolute, which is the myth. And unless it will again be possible for men to give themselves up to a self-contained, objective system of truths, the principles of Donne, whether we know him or not, will continue to be our own.

# A NOTE ON ELIZABETHAN SATIRE

## 1 9 3 2

AS THE Oxford anthologies come off the press, the disadvantages of dividing English poetry into exact centuries become more and more conspicuous. Sir Edmund Chambers, in his preface to *The Oxford Book of Sixteenth Century Verse,* remarks that the year 1600 "still finds a continuous flood of literature in mid-career." He points out that "Drayton and Chapman, who hopelessly overlap the dividing line, must be cut asunder." Drayton, for example, suffers for the absence of his "ballads" of Agincourt and the Virginian Voyage. Donne is wholly omitted, for reasons that we shall see. Given the limited range, which, in the poetry of Donne, Sir Edmund seems to define with excessive narrowness, he has done his work well, even brilliantly.

There is a good reason for the success of this anthology. It is the editor's superior taste, a gift that historical scholars a generation ago feared to exercise. "In the present case," writes Sir Edmund, "an attempt has been made to apply a standard of absolute poetry, rather than one of merely historical interest. . . ." It is a difficult standard to uphold, and if it cannot be said that the editor applies it infallibly, one must remember that the power to perceive the best does not always carry with it the will to reject the second rate.

A debatable assumption underlies Sir Edmund's view of the whole period, and there are some minor disproportions in the representation of the poets. The disproportion between Raleigh and Sir John Davies is enormous. Raleigh wrote less than Davies but that less is immeasurably superior; yet Davies has fifty-one pages to Raleigh's thirty-seven. Here one feels that Sir Edmund in spite of himself is beguiled by the historical interest of Davies's *Orchestra,* perhaps by the interminable facility of its versification—although Davies at times is still as clumsy as the earlier Gascoigne or Grimald.

One mark of Davies's inferiority is the lack of tension in his style, a lack of concentrated purpose. This inferiority is at the center of the whole Spenserian school, in which, as Sir Edmund points out, "the slightness of invention is overhung with ornamental decoration, like some great composition of Paolo Veronese. . . ." This ornamental decoration of image in Spenser and Davies arose along with the historical improvement of English versification between 1557 and 1579—a springe to catch the woodcocks of the historical method. It was, actually, the resistance, in the first half of the century, of a fluid vocabulary to the poet's meaning, joined to his metrical uncertainty, that contributed to Wyat's success in "They flee from me that sometime did me seek." It is one of a half-dozen great meditative lyrics in English.

Nevertheless, Sir Edmund justly attacks, from his own point of view, one of the hoariest pedantries in English criticism: "A rather irritating kind of scholarship insists that Wyat was chiefly notable for the acclimatization of the Italian sonnet. . . . But in lyric, sung or based on the models of song, he is a master of the first order." . . . In spite of the perhaps too generous excerpts from Davies, Daniel and Constable, one sees everywhere the evidence of Sir Edmund's proccupation with the quality of the verse. He has given us all of Sackville's *Induction;* sixteen poems by Fulke Greville, including the fine long piece, "Who grace for zenith had"; thirty-one pages of Sidney, who is better represented here than in any other popular collection ever made; and the ample selections from Raleigh already noticed—although a few more of his sonnets would have furthered the rising reputation of this most neglected of Elizabethan poets. Raleigh's direct, conversational ease, his intelligence and subtlety, are qualities that deserve to be better understood: it has been the custom to see in Raleigh's verse only a sort of thin lagging after Sidney. His poetry is, on the contrary, distinct, and needs separate consideration.

## I I

IT IS ungrateful to impute to Sir Edmund Chambers any trace of wrong insight into the quality of the age. The century as a whole falls into three periods—that of Skelton, lasting until the appearance of Wyat in Tottel's *Songes and Sonets* in 1557; the period of Wyat, the most considerable figure until Sidney and Spenser, whose *Shepherd's Calendar* brought in a new era in 1579. It was by then the English Renaissance full-blown. *The Shepherd's Calendar,* a dull but original exercise in theory, offered to Spenser's successors an example of new possibilities of poetic English, and set up a pastoral convention that was to reach perfection as late as 1637. In singling out the leading impulse of the Elizabethan age one is constantly guided by the genius and magnitude of Spenser. Yet it is Milton in the next age who puts the seal of perfection on the pastoral, mythological school, and who, to no little extent, permits us to rank as highly as we do merely competent poets like Davies and Constable.

Our comparatively low rating of Greville no less than of Raleigh—Saintsbury says that Greville is "sententious and difficult"—is due to the constant introspection, the difficult self-analysis, the cynical melancholy, that break through the courtly pastoral convention to a level of feeling deeper, and historically purer, than the facile despair of the Sidneian sonneteers. Doubtless both Greville and Raleigh, as minor masters, were too much impressed with the glittering style of Sidney, and, later, of Spenser, to understand that their own sensibilities deserved a more perfectly matured style. Their work has the diffuseness of divided purpose.

There has never been enough made of Elizabethan satire. While Raleigh and Fulke Greville cannot be called pure satirists, they were not comfortable in the courtly, pastoral abstractions. In this negative feature of their verse they resemble certain of the satirists, Hall, Marston, Tourneur. If we put Raleigh and Greville together against the background of the widespread influence of Martial,[1] they, too, form a background not only for the *Satires* of Donne (1593) but for much of that great poet's most characteristic later writing.

Yet Sir Edmund says: "Only for chronology, indeed, can Donne be an Elizabethan"—an opinion that obscures the still powerful strain of medieval thought at the end of the sixteenth century. By another kind of reasoning Donne cannot be a Jacobean. For we find in Donne, significantly enough, not only the influence of Martial, but a resurgence of scholasticism—a union of classical satire and medievalism. And it is significant that "Go, soul, the body's guest" was written by the same Raleigh who wrote "The Passionate Man's Pilgrimage," a poem that is, I believe, occasionally described as charming. I cannot believe that, in order to write it, Raleigh invoked a muse different from the muse of a poem that is sophisticated, consciously erudite, and subtle. "The Passionate Man's Pilgrimage" is medieval allegory furbished up with a new awareness of the sensuous world; "Go, soul, the body's guest" is satire; and the two strains are not quite the disharmony that we are accustomed to believe them.

Possibly the last use of extended medieval allegory in verse of great distinction is Sackville's *Induction*. There are the familiar personifications—Remorse, Dread, Revenge, Misery, Death. Spenser's task was to revive allegory with a new

---

[1] See T. K. Whipple, *Martial and the English Epigram from Sir Thomas Wyat to Ben Jonson.* University of California Press, 1929; and Evelyn M. Simpson, *Paradoxes and Problems,* in *A Garland for John Donne.* Harvard University Press, 1931.

spirit alien to the medieval mind. Although Spenser's puritanism is manifest, his allegory has a voluptuous glitter that Sackville's more medieval spareness lacked; or if you go back to Gower's treatment of the seven deadly sins it is plain that as a medieval man he was too serious about them to dress them up.

The medieval minds left over at the end of the sixteenth century tended to see the world not in terms of a fixed moral system, but with an ingrained moral prejudice about the nature of man. I allude here to the decline of Catholic theology in England, and to the rise, conspicuously in the dramatic poets, of an unmoral and anti-doctrinal point of view. Marlowe is an example. But the moral temper of a less expansive, more melancholy age, a kind of interregnum between feudalism and Tudorism when the evil of life was expressed in ideas of all-pervasive mortality—this moral temper, having lost its theological framework, remained as an almost instinctive approach to the nature of man. And the nature of man, far from enjoying the easy conquest of evil that Spenser set forth in six books that might have been twelve, was on the whole unpleasant and depraved. This depravity is the theme of Elizabethan tragedy, I think, as early as *The Jew of Malta*. There is no need to cite Webster and Ford.

It is the prevailing attitude of the satirists and of most of those non-dramatic poets who stand apart from the Spenserian school. In such poets we find a quality that we have shortsightedly ascribed uniquely to modern verse—the analysis of emotion and an eye chiefly to the aesthetic effect. There is here the use of symbols that are too complex to retain, throughout a long work, or from one work to another, a fixed meaning. The allegorical symbol is constant and homogeneous, like the Red Cross Knight; the richer, poetic symbol, like Prospero, does not invite the oversimplification of certain of its qualities, but asks to be taken in all its manifold richness.

It is this stream of Elizabethan poetry that has never

been properly evaluated. We tend to forget, in fixing the relation of the Shakespearean drama to its sources, and of its text to the texts of contemporaries, that Shakespeare stands outside the allegorical school. It is thus difficult for us to take a further step and to see that he was closely connected with a much less conspicuous type of poetry that had been only superficially affected by the Renaissance. This was the dormant medieval which, even after the new language of Wyat, survived in Sackville's *Induction.*

In a later poet like Greene the new courtly conventions are too weak to sustain his restless sensibility. Although Greene never mastered a style, his great vitality of image and rhythm is largely due to a naïvely skeptical grasp of the conventions of Sidney and Spenser. He uses them without ever quite believing them: as in the verse of Raleigh the convention offers just enough resistance to expression to lend to the poetry tension and depth. Though Greene is imperfect, he has none of Daniel's complacently perfect dullness.

It is this resistance of the language to full expression, the strain between images and rhythm, opposites "yoked by violence together" in varying degrees of violence, that gives to English lyrical verse its true genius. It is a genius that permitted Milton to bring to the pastoral style a richness and subtlety of effect that Spenser never achieved. It is that quality of English style which is superior to age and school. It was perfectly mastered as early as Wyat:

> It was no dream; I lay broad waking:
>> But all is turned, thorough my gentleness
> Into a strange fashion of forsaking;
>> And I have leave to go of her goodness,
>> And she also to use newfangleness.
>> But since that I so kindly am served
>> I would fain know what she hath deserved.

It is in the lyrics, even in the political satires, of Dryden, but it begins to disappear in Pope, to reappear in the nineteenth century perhaps in Landor and Browning alone. It is a quality, not of system or of doctrine, but of immediate intelligence acting directly; a definite but unpremeditated limitation of. moral and metaphysical idea to the problem of the work to be done. It is unmoralistic and anti-allegorical. Out of that long and neglected stream of the English tradition comes a kind of poetry that we have named in our age symbolism—a curious misnomer borrowed from the French; for it has no elaborate symbolism at all in the Spenserian mode.

When Saintsbury thirty-five years ago issued the first edition of his *Short History of English Literature,* he announced that his chief interest throughout would be form—at that time a revolutionary point of view. But he gave to the Elizabethan satirists only a scant paragraph: they were both "coarse" and "insincere." This view will have to be changed before we shall be able to understand the early Donne—not only Donne, but a great deal of the finest work of our own time, poets like Eliot and Yeats. The satirists of the 1590's not only read Martial, they went back through Sackville to Lyndsay and Dunbar. The medieval sense of mortality, of the vanity of the world, survives in the satirists, who use it as a weapon of critical irony upon the vaunting romanticism of the Renaissance. And we, in this age, in so far as we maintain the traditions of English verse, are still criticizing the Renaissance.

### III

THE poetry of our own age that we find most moving and powerful, the poetry that is tough enough to reject the easy solutions of the human predicament that arise in every age, has a longer and more honorable lineage than we are accustomed to suppose. Yet Mr. Edmund Wilson, in *Axel's Castle,* would have us believe that modern symbolism is a method, invented by the poets, of evading the problems of modern economics: our belief in the inferiority of our own age to the past is due to the palsied irresponsibility of the Ivory

Tower. But this belief is the fundamental groundwork of all poetry at all times. It is the instinctive counter-attack of the intelligence against the dogma of future perfection for persons and societies. It is in this sense, perhaps, that poetry is most profoundly the criticism of life.

It must seem to readers who have preserved, in the midst of the "historical method," a vestige of the historical sense, that social and political writers wish to exempt the world of secular policy from the criticism with which the arts are constantly threatening the latest programs of social improvement. It has always been so with the proponents of "proletarian" art; it was so with Spenser. The poets are asked to oversimplify the human predicament with morality and allegory. The first great example of proletarian—that is, allegorical—poetry in English is Spenser's *Faerie Queen:* there is no real distinction possible between an art that oversimplifies our experience in favor of princes and an art that performs that callow office for the people. There has always been a small body of men—a saving remnant very different from the Victorian notion of such a minority—headed by William Shakespeare, who warn us to make haste slowly with the best-wrought schemes for the satisfaction of our desires. Let the plans be well-wrought indeed, but let the arts teach us—if we demand a moral—that the plans are not and can never be absolutes. Poetry perhaps more than any other art tests with experience the illusions that the human predicament tempts us in our weakness to believe.

# T. S. ELIOT

## *1931*

EVERY age, as it sees itself, is peculiarly distracted: its chroniclers notoriously make too much of the variety before their own eyes. We see the variety of the past as mere turbulence within a fixed unity, and our own uniformity of the surface as the sign of a profound disunity of impulse. We have discovered that the ideas that men lived by from about the twelfth to the seventeenth century were absolute and unquestioned. The social turmoil of European history, so this argument runs, was shortsighted disagreement as to the best ways of making these deep assumptions morally good.

Although writers were judged morally, poets purveyed ready-made moralities, and no critic expected the poet to give him a brand-new system. A poem was a piece of enjoyment for minds mature enough—that is, convinced enough of a satisfactory destiny—not to demand of every scribbler a way of life.

It is beyond the scope of this discussion, and of my own competence, to attempt an appraisal of any of the more common guides to salvation, including the uncommon one of the Thirty-nine Articles, lately subscribed to by Mr. T. S. Eliot, whose six poems published under the title *Ash Wednes-*

*day* [1] are the occasion of this review. For it is my belief that, in a discussion of Eliot's poetry, his religious doctrines in themselves have little that commands interest. Yet it appears that his poetry, notwithstanding the amount of space it gets in critical journals, receives less discussion each year. The moral and religious attitude implicit in it has been related to the Thirty-nine Articles, and to a general intellectual position that Eliot has defended in his essays. The poetry and the prose are taken together as evidence that the author has made an inefficient adaptation to the modern environment; or at least he doesn't say anything very helpful to the American critics in their struggles to adapt themselves. It is an astonishing fact that, near as we are to a decade obsessed by "aesthetic standards," there is less discussion of poetry in a typical modern essay on that fine art than there is in Johnson's essay on Denham. Johnson's judgment is frankly moralistic; he is revolted by unsound morals; but he seldom capitulates to a moral sentiment because it flatters his own moral sense. He requires the qualities of generality, copiousness, perspicuity. He hates Milton for a regicide; but his judgment of *Paradise Lost* is as disinterested as any judgment we should find today; certainly no more crippled by historical prejudice than Mr. Eliot's own views of Milton. Yet Eliot's critics are a little less able each year to see the poetry for Westminster Abbey; the wood is all trees.

I do not pretend to know how far our social and philosophical needs justify a prejudice which may be put somewhat summarily as follows: all forms of human action, economics, politics, even poetry, and certainly industry, are legitimate modes of salvation, but the historic religious mode is illegitimate. It is sufficient here to point out that the man who expects to find salvation in the latest lyric or a well-managed factory will not only not find it there; he is not likely to find it anywhere else. If a young mind is incapable of moral philosophy, a mind without moral philosophy is incapable of understanding poetry. For poetry, of all the arts,

---

[1] *Ash Wednesday.* By T. S. Eliot. New York: The Fountain Press, 1931.

demands a serenity of view and a settled temper of the mind, and most of all the power to detach one's own needs from the experience set forth in the poem. A moral sense so organized sets limits to human nature, and is content to observe them. But if the reader lack this moral sense, the poem will be only a body of abstractions either useful or irrelevant to that body of abstractions already forming, but of uncertain direction, in the reader's mind. This reader will see the poem chiefly as biography, and he will proceed to deduce from it a history of the poet's case, to which he will attach himself if his own case resembles it; if it doesn't, he will look for a more useful case. Either way, the poem as a specific object is ignored.

The reasoning that is being brought to bear upon Mr. Eliot's recent verse is as follows: Anglo-Catholicism would not at all satisfy me; therefore, his poetry declines under its influence. Moreover, the poetry is not "contemporary"; it doesn't solve any labor problems; it is special, personal; and it can do us no good. Now the poetry *is* special and personal in quality, which is one of its merits, but what the critics are really saying is this—that Eliot's case-history is not special at all, that it is a general scheme of possible conduct that will not do for them. To accept the poetry seems to amount to accepting an invitation to join the Anglican Church. For the assumption is that the poetry and the religious position are identical.

If this were so, why should not the excellence of the poetry induce writers to join the Church, in the hope of writing as well as Eliot, since the irrelevance of the Church to their own needs makes them reject the poetry? The answer is, of course, that both parts of this fallacy are common. There is an aesthetic Catholicism, and there is a communist-economic rejection of art because it is involved with the tabooed mode of salvation.

The belief is that Eliot's poetry—all other poetry—is a simple record of the responses of a personality to an environment. The belief witnesses the modern desire to judge an art scientifically, practically, industrially—according to how it works. The poetry is viewed first as a pragmatic instrument, then examined "critically" as a pragmatic result; neither stage of the approach gives us "useful" knowledge.

Now a different heredity-environment combination would give us, of mechanical necessity, a different result, a different quantity of power to do a different and perhaps better social work. Doubtless that is true. But there is something disconcerting in this simple solution to the problem when it is looked at more closely. Two vastly different records or case-histories might give us, qualitatively speaking, very similar results: Baudelaire and Eliot have in common many *qualities* but *no history*. Their "results" have at least the common features of irony, humility, introspection, reverence —qualities fit only for contemplation and not for judgment according to their utility in our own conduct.

It is in this, the qualitative sense, that Eliot's recent poetry has been misunderstood. In this sense, the poetry is special, personal, of no use, and highly distinguished. But it is held to be a general formula, not distinct from the general formula that Eliot repeated when he went into the Church.

The form of the poems in *Ash Wednesday* is lyrical and solitary, and there is almost none of the elaborate natural description and allusion that gave to *The Waste Land* a partly realistic and partly symbolic character. These six poems are a brief moment of religious experience in an age that believes religion to be a kind of defeatism and puts all its hope for man in finding the right secular order. The mixed realism and symbolism of *The Waste Land* issued in irony. The direct and lyrical method of the new poems is based upon the simpler quality of humility. The latter quality comes directly out of the former, and there is an even continuity in Eliot's work.

In *The Waste Land* the prestige of our secular faith gave to the style its special character. This faith was the hard, coherent medium through which the discredited forms of the historic cultures emerged only to be stifled; the poem is

at once their vindication and the recognition of their defeat. They are defeated in fact, as a politician may be
defeated by the popular vote, but their vindication consists
in the critical irony that their subordinate position casts upon
the modern world.

The typical scene is the seduction of the stenographer by
the clerk, in "The Fire Sermon." Perhaps Mr. J. W. Krutch has
not discussed this scene, but a whole generation of critics
has, and from a viewpoint that Mr. Krutch has recently made
popular: the seduction betrays the disillusion of the poet. The
mechanical, brutal scene shows what love really is—that is to
say, what it is scientifically, since "science" is truth: it is
only an act of practical necessity for procreation. The telling
of the story by the Greek seer Tiresias, who is chosen from a
past of illusion and ignorance, permits the scene to become
*a satire on the unscientific values of the past.* It was all pretense to think that love was anything but a biological necessity. The values of the past were pretty, absurd, and false;
the scientific truth is both true and bitter. This is the familiar
romantic dilemma, and the critics have read it into the scene
from their own romantic despair.

There is no despair in the scene itself. The critics, who
being in the state of mind I have described are necessarily
blind to an effect of irony, have mistaken the symbols of an
ironic contrast for the terms of a philosophic dilemma. It is
the kind of metaphorical "logic" typical of romantic criticism
since Walter Pater. Mr. Eliot knows too much about classical
irony to be overwhelmed by a popular dogma in literary
biology. For the seduction scene shows, not what man is, but
what *for a moment* he thinks he is. In other words, the clerk
stands for the secularization of the religious and qualitative
values in the modern world. And the meaning of the contrast between Tiresias and the clerk is not disillusion, but
irony. The scene is a masterpiece, perhaps the most profound vision that we have of modern man.

The importance of this scene as a key to the intention of
*Ash Wednesday* lies in the moral identity of humility and

irony and in an important difference between them aesthetically. Humility is subjective, a quality of the moral character: it is thus general, invisible, and can only be inferred, not seen. *Irony is the visible, particular, and objective instance of humility.* Irony is the objective quality of an event or situation which stimulates our capacity for humility. It is that arrangement of experience, either premeditated by art or accidentally appearing in the affairs of men, which permits to the spectator an insight superior to that of the actor; it shows him that the practical program, the special ambition, of the actor at that moment is bound to fail. The humility thus derived is the self-respect proceeding from a sense of the folly of men in their desire to dominate a natural force or a situation. The seduction scene is the picture of modern and dominating man. The arrogance and the pride of conquest of the "small house agent's clerk" are the badge of science, bumptious practicality, overweening secular faith. The very success of his conquest witnesses its aimless character; it succeeds as a wheel succeeds in turning: he can only conquer again.

His own failure to understand his position is irony, and the poet's insight into it is humility. But for the grace of God, says the poet in effect, there go I. This is essentially the poetic attitude, an attitude that Eliot has been approaching with increasing purity. It is not that his recent verse is better than that of the period ending with *The Waste Land.* Actually it is less spectacular and less complex in subject-matter; for Eliot less frequently objectifies his leading emotion, humility, into irony. His new form is simple, expressive, homogeneous, and direct, and without the early elements of violent contrast.

There is a single ironic passage in *Ash Wednesday,* and significantly enough it is the first stanza of the first poem. This passage presents objectively the poet *as he thinks himself for the moment to be.* It establishes that humility towards his own merit which fixes the tone of the poems that follow.

And the irony has been overlooked by the critics because they take the stanza as a literal exposition of the latest phase of the Eliot *case-history*—at a time when, in the words of Mr. Edmund Wilson, "his psychological plight seems most depressing." Thus, here is the vain pose of a Titan too young to be weary of strife, but weary of it nevertheless.

> Because I do not hope to turn again
> Because I do not hope
> Because I do not hope to turn
> Desiring this man's gift and that man's scope
> I no longer strive to strive towards such things
> (Why should the aged eagle stretch its wings?)
> Why should I mourn
> The vanished power of the usual reign?

If the six poems are taken together as the focus of a specific religious emotion, the opening stanza, instead of being a naïve personal "confession," appears in the less lurid light of a highly effective technical performance. This stanza has two features that are necessary to the development of the unique imagery which distinguishes the religious emotion of *Ash Wednesday* from any other religious poetry of our time. It is possibly the only kind of imagery that is valid for religious verse today.

The first feature is the regular yet halting rhythm, the smooth uncertainty of movement which may either proceed to greater regularity or fall away into improvisation. The second feature is the imagery itself. It is trite; it echoes two familiar passages from English poetry. But the quality to be observed is this: it is secular imagery. It sets forth a special ironic situation, but the emotion is not identified with any specific experience. The imagery is thus perfectly suited to the broken rhythm. The stanza is a device for getting the poem under way, starting from a known and general emotion, in a monotonous rhythm, for a direction which, to the reader, is unknown. The ease, the absence of surprise, with which

Eliot proceeds to bring out the subject of his meditation is
admirable. After some further and ironic deprecation of his
worldly powers, he goes on:

> And pray to God to have mercy upon us
> And pray that I may forget            ·
> These matters that with myself I too much discuss, ·
> Too much explain.

We are being told, of course, that there is to be some kind
of discourse on God, or a meditation; yet the emotion is still
general. The imagery is even flatter than before; it is "poetical"
at all only in that special context; for it is the diction of
prose. And yet, subtly and imperceptibly, the rhythm has
changed; it is irregular and labored. We are being prepared
for a new and sudden effect, and it comes in the first lines
of the second poem:

> Lady, three white leopards sat under a juniper-tree
> In the cool of the day, having fed to satiety
> On my legs my heart my liver and that which had been
>     contained
> In the hollow round of my skull. And God said
> Shall these bones live? shall these
> Bones live?

From here on, in all the poems, there is constant and sudden
change of rhythm, and there is a corresponding alternation
of two kinds of imagery—the visual and tactile imagery common to all poetry; without significance in itself for any kind
of experience, and the traditional religious symbols. The two
orders are inextricably fused.

It is evident that Eliot has hit upon the only method now
available of using the conventional religious image in poetry.
He has reduced it from symbol to image, from abstraction to
the plane of sensation. And corresponding to this process,
there are images of his own invention which he almost pushes
over the boundary of sensation into abstractions, where they

have the appearance of conventional symbols.[2] The passage
I have quoted above is an example of this: for the "Lady"
may be a nun, or even the Virgin, or again she may be a
beautiful woman; but she is presented, through the serious
tone of the invocation, with all the solemnity of a religious
figure. The fifth poem exhibits the reverse of the process; it
begins with a series of plays on the Logos, the most rarefied
of all the Christian abstractions; and it succeeds in creating
the effect of immediate experience by means of a broken
and distracted rhythm:

> If the lost word is lost, if the spent word is spent
> If the unheard, unspoken
> Word is unspoken, unheard;
> Still is the unspoken word, the word unheard,
> The word without a word, the Word within
> The world and for the world. . .

[2] Mr. Yvor Winters would doubtless call this feature of the poem "pseudo-reference."

# EZRA POUND

## 1931

> and as for text we have taken it
> from that of Messire Laurentius
> and from a codex once of the Lords Malatesta. . . .

ONE is not certain who Messire Laurentius was; one is not very certain that it makes no difference. Yet one takes comfort in the vast range of Mr. Pound's obscure learning, which no one man could be expected to know much about. In his great work one is continually uncertain, as to space, time, history. The codex of the Lords Malatesta is less disconcerting than Laurentius; for more than half of the first thirty cantos contain long paraphrases or garbled quotations from the correspondence, public and private, of the Renaissance Italians, chiefly Florentine and Venetian. About a third of the lines are versified documents. Another third are classical allusions, esoteric quotations from the ancients, fragments of the Greek poets with bits of the Romans thrown in; all magnificently written into Mr. Pound's own text. The rest is contemporary—anecdotes, satirical pictures of vulgar Americans, obscene stories, evenings in low Mediterranean dives, and gossip about intrigants behind the scenes of European power. The three kinds of material in the *Cantos* are antiquity, the Renaissance, and the modern world. They are combined on no principle that seems in the least consistent to a first glance. They appear to be mixed in an incoherent jumble, or to stand up in puzzling contrasts.

This is the poetry which, in early and incomplete editions, has had more influence on us than any other of our time; it has had an immense "underground" reputation. And deservedly. For even the early reader of Mr. Pound could not fail to detect the presence of a new poetic form in the individual cantos, though the full value and intention of this form appears for the first time in the complete work. It is not that there is any explicit feature of the whole design that is not contained in each canto; it is simply that Mr. Pound must be read in bulk; it is only then that the great variety of his style and the apparent incoherence turn into implicit order and form. There is no other poetry like the *Cantos* in English. And there is none quite so simple in form. The form is in fact so simple that almost no one has guessed it, and I suppose it will continue to puzzle, perhaps to enrage, our more academic critics for a generation to come. But this form by virtue of its simplicity remains inviolable to critical terms: even now it cannot be technically described.

I begin to talk like Mr. Pound, or rather in the way in which most readers think Mr. Pound writes. The secret of his form is this: conversation. The *Cantos* are talk, talk, talk; not by anyone in particular to anyone else in particular; they are just rambling talk. At least each canto is a cunningly devised imitation of a casual conversation in which no one presses any subject very far. The length of breath, the span of conversational energy, is the length of a canto. The conversationalist pauses; there is just enough unfinished business left hanging in the air to give him a new start; so that the transitions between the cantos are natural and easy.

Each canto has the broken flow and the somewhat elusive climax of a good monologue: because there is no single speaker, it is a many-voiced monologue. That is the method of the poems—though there is another quality of the form that I must postpone for a moment—*and that is what the poems are about.*

There are, as I have said, three subjects of conversation—ancient times, Renaissance Italy, and the present—but these are not what the *Cantos* are about. They are not about Italy, nor about Greece, nor are they about us. They are not about anything. But they are distinguished verse. Mr. Pound himself tells us:

> And they want to know what we talked about? *"de litteris*
>   *et de armis, praestantibus ingeniis,*
> Both of ancient times and our own; books, arms,
> And men of unusual genius
> Both of ancient times and our own, in short the usual
>   subjects
> Of conversation between intelligent men."

## I I

THERE is nothing in the *Cantos* more difficult than that. There is nothing inherently obscure; nothing too profound for any reader who has enough information to get to the background of the allusions in a learned conversation. But there is something that no reader, short of some years of hard textual study, will understand. This is the very heart of the *Cantos*, the secret of Mr. Pound's poetic character, which will only gradually emerge from a detailed analysis of every passage. And this is no more than our friends are constantly demanding of us; we hear them talk, and we return to hear them talk, we return to hear them again, but we never know what they talk about; we return for the mysterious quality of charm that has no rational meaning that we can define. It is only after a long time that the order, the direction, the rhythm of the talker's mind, the logic of his character as distinguished from anything logical he may say—it is a long time before this begins to take on form for us. So with Mr. Pound's *Cantos*. It is doubtless easier for us (who are trained in the more historic brands of poetry) when the poems are about God, Freedom, and Immortality, but there is no reason why poetry should not be so perplexingly simple as Mr. Pound's, and be about nothing at all.

The ostensible subjects of the *Cantos*—ancient, middle, and modern times—are only the materials round which Mr. Pound's mind plays constantly; they are the screen upon which he throws a flowing quality of poetic thought. Now in conversation the memorable quality is a sheer accident of character, and is not designed; but in the *Cantos* the effect is deliberate, and from the first canto to the thirtieth the set tone is maintained without a lapse.

It is this tone, it is this quality quite simply which is the meaning of the *Cantos*, and although, as I have said, it is simple and direct, it is just as hard to pin down, it is as hidden in its shifting details, as a running, ever-changing conversation. It cannot be taken out of the text; and yet the special way that Mr. Pound has of weaving his three materials together, of emphasizing them, of comparing and contrasting them, gives us a clue to the leading intention of the poems. I come to that quality of the form which I postponed.

The easiest interpretation of all poetry is the allegorical: there are few poems that cannot be paraphrased into a kind of symbolism, which is usually false, being by no means the chief intention of the poet. It is very probable, therefore, that I am about to falsify the true simplicity of the *Cantos* into a simplicity that is merely convenient and spurious. The reader must bear this in mind, and view the slender symbolism that I am going to read into the *Cantos* as a critical shorthand, useful perhaps, but which when used must be dropped.

One of the finest *Cantos* is properly the first. It describes a voyage:

> And then went down to the ship,
> Set keel to breakers, forth on the godly sea, and
> We set up mast and sail on that swart ship,
> Bore sheep aboard her, and our bodies also

> Heavy with weeping, and winds from sternward
> Bore us out onward with bellying canvas,
> Circe's this craft, the trim-coifed goddess.

They land, having come "to the place aforesaid by Circe"—whatever place it may be—and Tiresias appears, who says:

> "Odysseus
> Shall return through spiteful Neptune, over dark seas,
> Lose all companions." And then Anticlea came.
> Lie quiet Divus. I mean, that is, Andreas Divus,
> In officina Wecheli, 1538, out of Homer.
> And he sailed, by Sirens and thence outward and away
> And unto Circe.

Mr. Pound's world is the scene of a great Odyssey, and everywhere he lands it is the shore of Circe, where men "lose all companions" and are turned into swine. It would not do at all to push this hint too far, but I will risk one further point: Mr. Pound is a typically modern, rootless, and internationalized intelligence. In the place of the traditional supernaturalism of the older and local cultures, he has a cosmopolitan curiosity that seeks out marvels, which are all equally marvelous, whether it be a Greek myth or the antics in Europe of a lady from Kansas. He has the bright, cosmopolitan *savoir faire* which refuses to be "taken in": he will not believe, being a traditionalist at bottom, that the "perverts, who have set money-lust before the pleasures of the senses," are better than swine. And ironically, being modern and a hater of modernity, he sees all history as deformed by the trim-coifed goddess.

The *Cantos* are a book of marvels—marvels that he has read about, or heard of, or seen; there are Greek myths, tales of Italian feuds, meetings with strange people, rumors of intrigues of state, memories of remarkable dead friends like T. E. Hulme, comments on philosophical problems, harangues on abuses of the age; the "usual subjects of conversation between intelligent men."

It is all fragmentary. Now nearly every canto begins with a bit of heroic antiquity, some myth, or classical quotation, or a lovely piece of lyrical description in a grand style. It invariably breaks down. It trails off into a piece of contemporary satire, or a flat narrative of the rascality of some Italian prince. This is the special quality of Mr. Pound's form, the essence of his talk, the direction of these magnificent conversations.

For not once does Mr. Pound give himself up to any single story or myth. The thin symbolism from the Circe myth is hardly more than a leading tone, an unconscious prejudice about men which he is not willing to indicate beyond the barest outline. He cannot believe in myths, much less in his own power of imagining them out to a conclusion. None of his myths is compelling enough to draw out his total intellectual resources; none goes far enough to become a belief or even a momentary fiction. They remain marvels to be looked at, but they are meaningless, the wrecks of civilization. His powerful juxtapositions of the ancient, the Renaissance, and the modern worlds reduce all three elements to an unhistorical miscellany, timeless and without origin, and no longer a force in the lives of men.

### I I I

AND that is the peculiarly modern quality of Mr. Pound. There is a certain likeness in this to another book of marvels, stories of antiquity known to us as *The Golden Ass*. The *Cantos* are a sort of *Golden Ass*. There is a likeness, but there is no parallel beyond the mere historical one: both books are the productions of worlds without convictions and given over to a hard pragmatism. Here the similarity ends. For Mr. Pound is a powerful reactionary, a faithful mind devoted to those ages when the myths were not merely pretty, but true. And there is a cloud of melancholy irony hanging over the *Cantos*. He is persuaded that the myths are only beautiful, and he drops them after a glimpse, but he is not reconciled to this aestheticism: he ironically puts the myths against the ugly specimens of modern life that have defeated them. But neither are the specimens of modernity worthy of the dignity of belief:

> She held that a sonnet was a sonnet
> And ought never to be destroyed     .
> And had taken a number of courses
> And continued with hope of degrees and
> Ended in a Baptist learnery
> Somewhere near the Rio Grande.

I am not certain that Mr. Pound will agree with me that he is a traditionalist; nor am I convinced that Mr. Pound, for his part, is certain of anything but his genius for poetry. He is probably one of two or three living Americans who will be remembered as poets of the first order. Yet there is no reason to infer from that that Mr. Pound, outside his craft (or outside his written conversation) knows in the least what he is doing or saying. He is and always has been in a muddle of revolution; and for some appalling reason he identifies his crusade with liberty—liberty of speech, liberty of press, liberty of conduct—in short, liberty. I do not mean to say that either Mr. Pound or his critic knows what liberty is. Nevertheless, Mr. Pound identifies it with civilization and intelligence of the modern and scientific variety. And yet the ancient cultures, which he so much admires, were, from any modern viewpoint, hatched in barbarism and superstition. One is entitled to the suspicion that Mr. Pound prefers barbarism, and that by taking up the rôle of revolution against it he has bitten off his nose to spite his fa_e. He is the confirmed enemy of provincialism, never suspecting that his favorite, Lorenzo the Magnificent, for example, was provincial to the roots of his hair.

The confusion runs through the *Cantos*. It makes the irony that I have spoken of partly unconscious. For as the apostle of humane culture, he constantly discredits it by crying up a rationalistic enlightenment. It would appear from this that his philosophical tact is somewhat feminine, and that, as intelligence, it does not exist. His poetic intelligence is of the finest: and if he doesn't know what liberty is, he understands poetry, and how to write it. This is enough for one man to know. And the first thirty *Cantos* are enough to occupy a loving and ceaseless study—say a canto a year for thirty years, all thirty to be read every few weeks just for the tone.

# EDWIN ARLINGTON ROBINSON

## *1933*

EDWIN ARLINGTON ROBINSON, most famous of living American poets, was born at Head Tide, Maine, on December 22, 1869.[1] He attended Harvard from 1891 to 1893, but left college without taking a degree. In 1896 he printed privately his first book of verse, *The Torrent and the Night Before,* which was followed a year later by *The Children of the Night,* a volume little noticed at the time but one which marks the beginning of a new era in American poetry. In the next fourteen years he published two more books, *Captain Craig* (1902) and *The Town Down the River* (1910). But it was not until 1916 that he attracted wide attention and won a notable fame. For with *The Man Against the Sky* Mr. Robinson stepped quickly into the front rank of American poetry. In his early years he wrote some of the finest lyrics of modern times: these are likely to be his permanent claim to fame.

Able critics have thought otherwise. Not only, they say, are Mr. Robinson's long narrative poems his best work; they are the perfect realization of a "tragic vision." But hear Mr. Mark Van Doren, a distinguished critic whom I do not like to disagree with:

[1] Mr. Robinson died on April 5, 1935.

His vision is essentially tragic in that it stresses the degeneration of ideas, the dimming of the light, when these
become implicated in the rough action of the world.
(*Edward Arlington Robinson,* p. 34.)

Passion has its victories no less than reason. The tragic
picture would be incomplete without either of these. It
is because Mr. Robinson's picture is fairly complete that
he deserves the rare title of major American poet. (*Ibid.,*
p. 90.)

I should be the last person, I hope, to dispute Mr. Robinson's right to that title. Nor should I contend for a moment
that Mr. Robinson lacks the "tragic vision," but I am convinced that Mr. Van Doren's qualifying word, *essentially,*
is accurate. For Mr. Robinson writes, I believe, less from the
tragic vision than from the tragic sentiment; and the result
is the pathetic tale of obscure ambition or thwarted passion;
not tragedy.

It is true that he deals with the degeneration of ideas.
The question that Mr. Van Doren does not ask, it seems to
me, is this: What is the exact significance of the ideas? Is
their ultimate reference to a religious or philosophical background, a realm of ideas possessing at least for their time
and place the compulsion of absolute truth? Or are they
the private ideas of modern persons, the personal forms of
some egoistic thrust of the will? In other words, is Mr. Robinson a true tragic poet, or is he a modern poet like other
modern poets, whose distinguished gifts are not enough to
give him more than the romantic ego with which to work?

*Talifer* [2] is a psychological narrative of the order of *The
Man Against the Sky.* It is the eighth or ninth specimen of
this kind of poem that Mr. Robinson has given us. Because
the type has grown thinner with each example, the new
narrative being, I believe, the least satisfactory of them all,
it is the occasion of some inquiry into the causes of Mr. Rob-

[2] *Talifer.* By Edwin Arlington Robinson. New York: The Macmillan Co.,
1932.

inson's preference for this particular form. It is a form that includes the three Arthurian poems, *Merlin, Lancelot,* and *Tristram,* psychological stories that are in all respects similar to the New England tales of Nightingale, Cavender, Bartholow. All is the same but time and place; for the characters are the same.

In *Talifer* there are four characters, two men and two women. The woman Althea—the name is a dry piece of irony—is in love with Talifer; she is woman domestic, sensitive, but commonplace and child-bearing. Talifer himself is an ordinary person, but he talks of his "tradition," carries himself well, and expects of life more than his inner quality entitles him to: so he imagines that he is in love with the other woman, Karen, who is beautiful, treacherous, cold, and erudite, dividing her time between inscrutable moods and incredible reading in the ancients. But she is vaguely conceived by the poet, and the motivation of the hero's action remains obscure.

Talifer has been fatuous enough to say that with Karen he expects to find Peace. Life becomes, after a year or two with her, intolerable. Then, one day in his ancestral forest, he meets Althea, who still loves him, and he decides to leave Karen. Now all this time, the other man, Doctor Quick, could have been in love with either of the women; he is too skeptical to push his desires; and his place in the story is that of commentator. He explains the confusion to the other characters, and affords to the poet a device by which the real actors become articulate. The story ends with the reappearance, after a couple of years, of Quick: in the meantime Talifer has married Althea, who has by him a child. Although Quick himself has tried to participate in life by taking Karen off to a "cottage in Wales," his return witnesses his failure. But he is not much affected by it. He proceeds to analyze for Althea and Talifer the true basis of their love, which is thoroughly commonplace after a good deal of romantic pretense.

Mr. Robinson's style in the new poem is uniform with

the style of its predecessors, it is neither better nor worse than the style of *The Glory of the Nightingales* or of *Cavender's House*. It requires constant reviewing by Mr. Robinson's admirers to keep these poems distinct; at a distance they lose outline; blur into one another. They constitute a single complete poem that the poet has not succeeded in writing, a poem around which these indistinct narratives have been written.

We get, in them all, a character doomed to defeat, or a character who, when the tale opens, is a failure in the eyes of his town, but who wins a secret moral victory, as in *The Man Who Died Twice*. But Talifer, whose ego betrays him into an emotional life that he cannot understand, is not quite defeated. The tragic solution of his problem being thus rejected by Mr. Robinson, and replaced by a somewhat awkward bit of domestic irony, Talifer at first sight appears to be a new kind of Robinsonian character. Yet the novelty, I think, lies in the appearance. For Talifer is the standard Robinsonian character grown weary of the tragic sentiment, accepting at last the fact that his tilt at fate had less intensity than he supposed, and

> with grateful ears
> That were attuned again to pleasant music
> Heard nothing but the mellow bells of peace.

That is the Tennysonian end of the poem.

I have remarked that the character of Karen is vaguely conceived, with the result that Talifer's relation to her is incomprehensible. Those mellow bells of peace are therefore a little hollow in sound, for their ring is as inexplicable as the noisy chaos of the erudite Karen, upon whose prior significance they entirely depend. The plot, in brief, lacks internal necessity. And the domestic peace of the conclusion remains arbitrary, in spite of Mr. Robinson's efforts through his mouthpiece, Doctor Quick, to point it up with some sly irony at the end. The irony is external—as if Mr. Robinson had not been able to tell the story for what it was, and had to say: This is what life is really like, a simple wife and a child—while ring those bells of peace that would be romantically tiresome if one had tragic dignity.

Mr. Robinson's genius is primarily lyrical; that is to say, he seldom achieves a success in a poem where the idea exceeds the span of a single emotion. It is, I think, significant that in his magnificent "The Mill" the tragic reference sustains the emotion of the poem: his narrative verse yields but a few moments of drama that are swiftly dispersed by the dry casuistry of the commentary. The early "Richard Cory" is a perfect specimen of Mr. Robinson's dramatic powers—when those powers are lyrically expressed; similarly "Luke Havergal," a poem in which the hard images glow in a fierce intensity of light, is one of the great recent lyrics:

> No, there is not a dawn in eastern skies
> To rift the fiery night that's in your eyes;
> But there, where western glooms are gathering
> The dark will end the dark, if anything . . .

Mr. Van Doren is the first critic to appreciate this peculiarly Robinsonian legerdemain with figures of light.

It is probable that the explanation of the popular success of *Tristram,* and of most of Mr. Robinson's narratives, lies in our loss of the dramatic instinct. It is a loss increasingly great since the rise of middle-class comedy in the eighteenth century. Since then, in the serious play, instead of the tragic hero whose downfall is deeply involved with his suprahuman relations, we get the romantic, sentimental hero whose problem is chiefly one of adjustment to society, on the one hand, and, on the other, one of futile self-assertion in the realm of the personal ego. Mr. Robinson's Talifer exhibits both these phases of the modern sensibility: he plays with his ego in the irrational marriage with Karen, and he later sees his difficulty strictly in terms of a social institution, or of social adjustment, in the marriage with Althea, who, of course, represents "truth."

The dramatic treatment of the situation Mr. Robinson

permits himself to neglect; for the dramatic approach would have demanded the possession, by the hero, of a comprehensive moral scheme. He would have rigorously applied the scheme to his total conduct, with the result that it would have broken somewhere and thrown the hero into a tragic dilemma, from which it had been impossible for him to escape. The story as it is told is hardly more than anecdotal; Mr. Robinson turns his plot, at the end, into an easy joke about the deliquescent effects of marriage upon the pretensions of human nature.

It is one of the anomalies of contemporary literature that Mr. Robinson, who has given us a score of great lyrics, should continue to produce these long narrative poems, one after another, until the reader can scarcely tell them apart. We may only guess the reason for this. Our age provides for the poet no epos or myth, no pattern of well-understood behavior, which the poet may examine in the strong light of his own experience. For it is chiefly those times that prefer one kind of conduct to another, times that offer to the poet a seasoned code, which have produced the greatest dramatic literature. Drama depends for clarity and form upon the existence of such a code. It matters little whether it is a code for the realization of good, like Antigone's; or a code for evil like Macbeth's. The important thing is that it shall tell the poet how people try to behave, and that it shall be too perfect, whether in good or in evil, for human nature. The poet seizes one set of terms within the code—for example, feudal ambition in Macbeth—and shows that the hero's faulty application of the perfect code to his own conduct is doomed to failure. By adhering strictly to the code, the poet exhibits a typical action. The tension between the code and the hero makes the action specific, unique; the code is at once broken up and affirmed, the hero's resistance at once clarified and defined by the limits thus set to his conduct. Macbeth asserts his ego in terms of the code before him, not in terms of courtly love or of the idealism of the age of Werther: he has no choice of code. The modern character has the liberty of indefinite choice, but not the good fortune to be chosen, as Macbeth and Antigone were.

Mr. Robinson has no epos, myth, or code, no suprahuman truth, to tell him what the terminal points of human conduct are, in this age; so he goes over the same ground, again and again, writing a poem that will not be written.

It has been said by T. S. Eliot that the best lyric poetry of our time is dramatic, that it is good because it is dramatic. It is at least a tenable notion that the dramatic instinct, after the Restoration and down to our own time, survived best in the lyric poets. With the disappearance of general patterns of conduct, the power to depict action that is both single and complete also disappears. The dramatic genius of the poet is held to short flights, and the dramatic lyric is a fragment of a total action which the poet lacks the means to sustain.

It is to be hoped that Mr. Robinson will again exercise his dramatic genius where it has a chance for success: in lyrics. Meanwhile it would be no less disastrous to Mr. Robinson's later fame than to our critical standards, should we admire him too abjectly to examine him. Let him then escape the indignity of Hardy's later years when such a piece of bad verse as "Any Little Old Song" won egregious applause all over the British Isles. That Mr. Robinson is unable to write badly will not excuse us to posterity.

# Mac LEISH'S CONQUISTADOR [1]

## 1932

MR. MacLEISH has been up to this time a poet like most of his contemporaries, limited to the short flight. There is, in his earlier work, no premonitory sounding of the finely sustained tone of *Conquistador*. For modern poetry the poem is long. It is an epic in miniature of about two thousand lines. In versification and style, and with respect to the narrational "point of view," there is no other poem in English with which as a whole it may be compared. It is evident, of course, that MacLeish has studied Ezra Pound; but this is no disparagement of Pound's pupil. The *Cantos* are full of technical instruction for the poet who knows what he needs to learn. The followers of Eliot take his "philosophy" as well as his style, and give us work of "lower intensity" than the original. Pound's disciples are either less plausible or more independent. They exercise thinly with Mr. Dudley Fitts or practice the admirable craft of *Conquistador*.

The background of the poem is the conquest of Mexico. For a complete history of the conquest one will have to go to the historians. The poem is a reconstruction of the part played by one of the lesser heroes, Bernal Diaz del Castillo,

[1] *Conquistador.* By Archibald MacLeish. Boston: Houghton Mifflin Company, 1932.

who as an old man wrote his own story in resentment against
the official histories by Gomara and others—

> The quilled professors: the taught tongues of fame:
> What have they written of us: the poor soldiers . . .

> They call the towns for the kings that bear no scars:
> They keep the names of the great for time to stare at—
> The bishops rich men generals cocks-at-arms . . .

Bernal tells the story in flashes of recollection that have just
enough narrative progression to give to the narrator a constantly new field of imagery. But the historical pattern of
the conquest is never explicit, never obtrusive enough to take
the reader's attention from the personality of Bernal and the
quality of his character. For the personality of Bernal is the
subject of the poem.

Thus narrowing the action down to the focus of a single
mind and what it saw, MacLeish disposes of two enormous
difficulties of epic poetry: he eliminates the objective detail
of the total scene, at once the conventional privilege and the
burden of the classical poet; and he dispenses with the need
of cosmic machinery. There is no external "idea"; there is no
theme; there is no "typical action."

We get the peculiarly modern situation: the personality
of one man is dramatized against an historical setting. "What
have they written of us: the poor soldiers"—what can the
private sensibility get out of history to sustain it? What can
Bernal get out of his past? Nothing appears in the story that
Bernal did not see; it is all enriched by memory. Although
Bernal announces his subject as "That which I have myself
seen and the fighting," there is little fighting; there is little
action; for the dramatic tension of the poem grows out of
the narrator-hero's fear of death upon the gradual disappearance of sensation. The dramatic quality of the poem—a quality that has little to do with the story as such—lies thus in
the hero's anxiety to recover his sensuous early years, upon
which his identity as a person, and hence his life, depends.

This is the subject of the poem. The "meaning" of the poem is an implicit quality of Bernal's mind, but only a little logical violence will isolate it. It is the futility of individual action. For unless the hero, in his old age, can recapture the sensation of action, the action itself must fade into the obscure shuffle of abstract history. We have seen that Bernal cannot accept the public versions of the conquest. (Is Bernal, then, a soldier of the sixteenth century or of the first World War?) He cannot identify the moment of action with the ostensible common purpose for which the whole series of events took place He is confined to memories, to the mechanism of sensation.

I dwell upon this "meaning" of *Conquistador* for two reasons. It obviously, in the first place, explains the form in which MacLeish found it necessary to cast his narrative, a form that I have briefly described; the necessity of this form explains the presence, I believe, of those features of the style that MacLeish borrowed from Pound and perfected. And, secondly, the meaning of this distinguished poem, as I apprehend it, may lead some of the younger critics to reconsider, not their enthusiasm for the workmanship, which it richly deserves, but their hasty acceptance of its "philosophy." It is a mistake to suppose that MacLeish has offered a "way out" of the introspective indecision of the school of T. S. Eliot, affirming a faith in heroic action against the moral paralysis presumably suffered by the best minds of that older generation. Not only is there, in the poem, a lack of belief in any kind of action that we might imitate; the poet does not feel much interest in the action implied by the reminiscences that support the narrative.

There is not one moment of action rendered objectively in the entire poem. There is constantly and solely the pattern of sensation that surrounded the moment of action—the fringe of the physical shock and awareness that survive in memory. The technique of rendering this special quality of memory is MacLeish's contribution to poetic style:

> Gold there on that shore on the evening sand—
> "Colua" they said: pointing on toward the sunset:
> They made a sign on the air with their solemn hands . . .
>
> And that voyage it was we came to the Island:
> Well I remember the shore and the sound of that place
> And the smoke smell on the dunes and the wind dying.
>
> Well I remember the walls and the rusty taste of the
> New-spilled blood in the air: many among us
> Seeing the priests with their small arrogant faces . . .
>
> Ah how the throat of a girl and girl's arms are
> Bright in the riding sun and the young sky
> And the green year of our lives where the willows are!

This clarity of sensuous reminiscence that suffuses the poem
is a new quality in American verse. The images are not imbedded in metaphor; they exist spatially in the round. Pound
supplied the model:

> Eyes brown topaz,
> Brookwater over brown sand,
> The white hounds on the slope,
> Glide of water, lights on the prore,
> Silver beaks out of night,
> Stone, bough over bough, lamps fluid in water,
> Pine by the black trunk of its shadow
> The trees melted in air.

The images are impersonal, objective, and timeless, detached from Pound's moral position. The focus of MacLeish's
imagery is personal: the image exists in terms of Bernal's
recovery of memory, of his struggle for personal identity. Its
precision has been disciplined in the workshop of Ezra
Pound, whose quality of floating clarity is localized by Mac-
Leish in a Browningesque monologue, where the casuistry
gives way to a sophisticated version of the *chanson de geste*.

    Poets in this age cannot set forth with security a conscious
philosophical system. Reasons for this I have mentioned in

another place. When there is no systematic philosophy at hand, the poet is likely to slip into an unsystematic one of his own: this, perhaps, is better than an elaborate system that he cannot assimilate and understand. MacLeish's philosophy is personal and unarticulated. It may be stated in moral terms. We cannot linger over even the finest passages of *Conquistador* without becoming aware that we are in the presence of a sentimental view of experience. I have said that there is no objective design to uphold the sensibility of the narrator-hero. Perhaps, in this poem, MacLeish is no less able a poet than the young Milton of *Lycidas;* but Milton had an objective convention that absorbed every implication of his personal feeling. I use the term sentimental, then, in a strict, not a pejorative, sense. The melancholy of the hero's disgust with the "taught tongues of fame" is personal, sentimental; it is necessarily meaningless and obscure.

The disgust of Bernal does not rise to the level of rational criticism. It would serve as a rational evaluation of the "conquest" if there were a full stream of objective action in the light of which it could acquire significance. To have set off the private experience of the soldier against the grandiose avowals of purpose by the conquerors, might possibly have provided the poet with the situation of tragic irony. But there is no conflict of this order in the poem. The emotion is pathos. We get Bernal's sentimental regret; his anger rises at the failure of the official historians to re-create the sensuous correspondence to his own part in the campaign. He says in effect not *quorum pars magna fui* but rather *solus quorum omnis fui*—alone in his perceptions. The poem recovers the perceptions but it does not place them against a coherent stream of events. The hero is concerned with his personal survival. He is modern and sentimental; not tragic and ironic. The motivation of his story is the fear of death.

I am ungrateful to MacLeish; I have dwelt upon a philosophical limitation that is not peculiar to this poet, but is deeply rooted in the age. The technical perfection of *Conquistador* is, of course, not merely a technical feat. The poem is one of the examples of our modern sensibility at its best; it has the defect of its qualities.

The verse is *terza rima,* a metrical form enormously difficult in English. The paucity of English rhymes leaves it clumsy and monotonous in all but the hands of a master. Shelley tried it once with moderate success; Wyat adapted it to an epistolary style that doubtless should have been but never was a model for later poets. But MacLeish, foreseeing in a long poem the monotony of conventionally rhymed *terza rima,* varies rhyme with terminal assonance that is usually hidden and always cunningly placed. He achieves something of the fluent ease of the Italian, which is rich in rhyme-words, and gives us the first successful example of *terza rima* in a long English poem.

It is the only considerable metrical achievement by a poet of this generation. Yet the perfection of the experiment will make future use of *terza rima* dangerous. The technique of the verse is a quality of MacLeish's mind, and is inimitable. "Waller refined our numbers"—but this time Waller is a hard-pressed modern whose brilliance, once flashed, burns out before it can be passed to other hands. It is the present fate of poetry to be always beginning over again. The kind of "culture" in *Conquistador* is purely literary; the kind of experience in it is the sentimentality of moral isolation. The refinement of the craftsmanship hovers over a void.

# ACKNOWLEDGMENTS

FOR permission to reprint in this volume certain essays thanks are due the following publishers and periodicals:

TO Charles Scribner's Sons, for "Emily Dickinson," "Hart Crane," "John Peale Bishop," "The Profession of Letters in the South," "Religion and the Old South," "A Note on Donne," "A Note on Elizabethan Satire," "T. S. Eliot," "Ezra Pound," "Edwin Arlington Robinson," and "MacLeish's Conquistador," from *Reactionary Essays on Poetry and Ideas*, copyright, 1936, by Charles Scribner's Sons.

TO G. P. Putnam's Sons, for "The Present Function of Criticism," "Literature As Knowledge," "Miss Emily and the Bibliographer," "The Function of the Critical Quarterly," "Tension in Poetry," "Understanding Modern Poetry," "Hardy's Philosophic Metaphors," "Narcissus As Narcissus," and "What Is a Traditional Society?" from *Reason in Madness*, copyright, 1941, by Allen Tate.

TO the Cummington Press, for "Techniques of Fiction," "The Hovering Fly," "A Reading of Keats," "Yeats's Romanticism," and "The New Provincialism," from *The Hovering Fly*, copyright, 1948, by Allen Tate.

TO *The Southern Review*, for "The Present Function of Criticism," "Literature As Knowledge," "The Function of the Critical Quarterly," "Tension in Poetry," "Hardy's Philosophic Metaphors," "Yeats's Romanticism," and "John Peale Bishop."

TO *The American Scholar*, for "Miss Emily and the Bibliographer" and "A Reading of Keats."

TO *The English Journal*, for "Understanding Modern Poetry."

TO *The Outlook*, for a part of "Emily Dickinson."

TO *The Symposium*, for a part of "Emily Dickinson."

TO *The Sewanee Review*, for "Techniques of Fiction" and "The Hovering Fly."

TO *The Hound and Horn*, for a part of "Hart Crane" and for "T. S. Eliot."

TO *Poetry: A Magazine of Verse*, for a part of "Hart Crane."

TO *The Virginia Quarterly Review*, for "Narcissus As Narcissus," "The Profession of Letters in the South," and "The New Provincialism."

TO *The American Review*, for "What Is a Traditional Society?"

TO *The New Republic*, for "A Note on Donne," "A Note on Elizabethan Satire," "Edwin Arlington Robinson," and "MacLeish's Conquistador."

TO *The Nation*, for "Ezra Pound."

# INDEX

Titles of periodicals and works of book length are in italics; shorter works, in quotation marks.